Workbook

for

Writing

and

Reporting

News

A Coaching Method

Carole Rich

University of Kansas

Wadsworth Publishing Company
Belmont, California
A Division of Wadsworth, Inc.

International Thomson Publishing
The trademark ITP is used under license.

Printer: Malloy Lithographing, Inc.

Printed in the United States of America

2 3 4 5 6 7 8 9 10—98 97 96 95 94

0-534-19076-6

Contents

Write From the Start:
A Coaching Method

1

The following exercises are designed to help you start writing news stories. These exercises will help you identify the focus of a story and consider the importance of graphics. Use the tell-a-friend technique explained in Chapter 1 to write your story in a clear, conversational manner.

1-1. Crime story

Read the following information and write a focus sentence at the top of your story. Then jot down an order for your story. Assume that you are writing this story for the Monday morning newspaper.

Location: Riverview section of Tampa.

Facts: This information comes from Tampa sheriff's deputies: Two robbers burst into a home in Riverview at 11:30 p.m. Sunday. The home was owned by Grace Ford, 20. Ford was sitting in a front room with her baby, Brandi, 10 months old, who was in a playpen. Ford's sister, Cynthia, 16, also was in the room.

According to sheriff's reports: Both men were described as white, from 18 to 20 years old and of medium height and weight. One man was wearing a ski mask and jogging pants with the letters "UF" (for University of Florida) on the side. The other wore a white shirt and a baseball cap. Neighbors heard shots and called the sheriff's deputies. The men got away in a car that had been waiting in a nearby cemetery.

[This information comes from an interview with Grace Ford.]

She said the robbers pushed her, her baby and her sister from room to room. They took about $5,000 worth of jewelry. The dog, a Rottweiler named Elka, began barking. The robbers fired three shots at the dog. They missed. The baby began crying. Ford said she picked her up and found a bullet hole in Brandi's diaper. The bullet was not found. Direct quotes from Ford: "There was about an inch left to the diaper that it didn't pierce. They were extra thick."

Based on a story from the *St. Petersburg* (Fla.)*Times*. Used with permission.

1-2. Find the focus

Read the following information and ask yourself what is the most important or interesting fact. Write a focus sentence identifying that newsworthy angle:

a. The New England Journal of Medicine released a study today. The study says people who abruptly quit drinking coffee may suffer effects of caffeine withdrawal. Some of the symptoms include headaches, depression, anxiety and fatigue. The study says that even people who drink fewer than three cups of coffee a day may be affected.

b. A new law went into effect yesterday in Maine. The law affects all businesses that have more than 15 employees. The law requires employers to educate workers about sexual harassment. Under the law, employers must post notices explaining that sexual harassment is illegal and must notify workers about how they may file a complaint with the Maine Human Rights Commission.

c. A band is scheduled to perform on your campus this weekend. The band is named Elvis Hitler. The band was booked by John Musiclover, a senior who heads a group that promotes cultural diversity on campus. Musiclover says the band is not a racist group. But several students on campus claim the name of the band is offensive and they want the performance to be canceled.

d. Police suspected two men of drug dealing. Police witnessed the men exchanging money and what appeared to be heroin. But after they arrested the men, police couldn't find the heroin. Police called in their drug-sniffing dog. The dog headed directly to one man's sneakers. Inside the sneakers was a pound of heroin. The two men were charged with drug trafficking.

e. A man in your community received a postcard yesterday from his father, who lived in a nearby town and had just returned from a trip. "Please come over so your mother and I can show you pictures of our trip," the postcard said. "I guess my father wondered why I never came over," said the son, Jason Gott. His father and mother died several years ago. The postcard that arrived yesterday was sent 30 years ago.

1-3. Visual elements

a. Write a facts box for the following information:

The health center at your university has issued a press release about preventing frostbite in winter climates, especially for skiers. Mike Chapman, a physical therapist at the center, said students should not drink alcohol before they head outdoors. He said alcohol dehydrates the body and makes people more susceptible to frostbite. Some of the signs of frostbite include: extreme pain, numbness, white or whitish-blue or whitish-yellow areas, blisters and black coloration of the affected areas. If you suspect you have frostbite, follow these tips: Do not rub the affected areas. Re-warm the area with warm, not hot, water. If normal color does not return within 20 minutes, consult a physician.

b. Write an empowerment box for the following information:

The voter registration deadline for residents in your community is Oct. 19 for the Nov. 3 general election. The county clerk's office where people can register will be open from 8 a.m. to 9 p.m. starting Tuesday through Oct. 19. People who plan to be out of the county on Election Day can receive an absentee ballot. These voters must complete an affidavit at the clerk's office. They can cast the ballot there or take it with them. The absentee ballot must be received by noon Nov. 2 and must be returned by 7 p.m. Nov. 3. People who are physically sick or disabled also may apply for absentee ballots. Residents may register to vote at any one of these sites: the county' clerk's office at 11th and Main streets; the Democratic Party headquarters at 900 Main Street; the county public library at 300 Literary Drive.

c. Write a pull quote based on the following information:

The Women's Student Union sponsored a rally last night on your campus to celebrate Women's Equality Day. Connie Stauffer, president of the group, made the following comments: "I think we need to make sure that candidates for the upcoming election have a platform that includes women's rights. We need to make sure that government is held accountable. Our problems have not been addressed by our representatives in Congress. It makes me sick in my heart to think we are still fighting for things we were fighting for 20 years ago. It's time for a change."

Based on a story from *The University Daily Kansan.* Used with permission.

1-4. Style Quiz

The following sentences are based on information in the previous stories. Using The Associated Press style guide in the back of the textbook, correct the errors. The most common errors contained in these sentences involve age, numbers, money, time and percentages. Some of the sentences contain more than one error. Cross out the errors and write your corrections above them.

1. A diaper saved a 10 month old baby from a gunshot wound.

2. Grace Ford, a twenty year old mother, said the robbers stole 5000 dollars.

3. 10-month-old Brandi Ford was wearing an extra-thick diaper, which may have saved her life.

4. Only 7% of the responding men and nine % of the women believed they were at risk of acquiring a sexually transmitted disease.

5. 41 percent of the students said that they were sexually active.

6. More than seventy students participated in the survey.

7. The ten-month-old baby was not harmed.

8. Right-handed females tend to live 5 years longer than left-handed females. Right-handed males lived ten years longer than left-handed males.

9. Grace Ford was sitting in her living room at 11:30 P.M. Sunday night when robbers burst into her home.

10. The decision to limit alcohol at fraternity parties was made by seventeen campus fraternities.

Changing Concepts of News 2

Some of the basic qualities in news stories involve conflict, timeliness, proximity, unusual nature, human interest and news about celebrities or famous people. But other concepts of news are changing. A major goal at many newspapers is to write stories that interest readers in the newspaper's circulation area. These exercises are intended to help you understand some of the basic qualities of news and the changing values of news.

2-1. News 2000 exercise

This exercise is designed to teach you how to consider the interests of readers. The exercise is based on the concepts of the Gannett Company's News 2000 program. Assume that you are an editor at the *Battle Creek Enquirer*. It is an afternoon paper, which means that you will try to include any news that breaks in the morning. You are in a news meeting with the managing editor and other editors who decide what should go on the front page. Based on your knowledge of News 2000 goals to serve community interests, select five stories and two pictures that you think should be on the front page. Before you make your decision, read the following information that describes the Battle Creek community and the interests of readers. That information should be your guide to determining the stories and pictures you would select. Then read the story and picture budgets. In addition to stories and pictures for the front page, choose five items for a column of briefs to run on the left side of the page.

After you have selected your stories for the front page, justify your decision. What community needs did these stories meet? Why did you select the photos you did. There are many possible choices.

Market and readership Information.

The *Battle Creek Enquirer's* designated market includes Calhoun County as its primary market and small parts of Barry, Eaton, Kalamazoo and Branch counties for secondary markets. Battle creek is located in south central Michigan about halfway between Detroit and Chicago. Major employers are Kellogg Co., which has its world headquarters in Battle Creek and employs 4,000 people, and General Foods, which employs 1,800 people. The V.A. hospital employs 1,400 people.

Demographic information about the area:

Gender: Male – 48 percent; female – 52 percent.

Age: 18-34 – 37 percent

35-49 – 26 percent

50-64 – 20 percent

65 plus – 17 percent

Education:

High school degree or less – 55 percent

Some college or more – 45 percent

Income:

Under $15,000 – 15 percent

$12-25,000 – 23 percent

$25-35,000 – 26 percent

$35,000 plus – 36 percent

Median household income – $26,000

Home ownership:

80 percent of the people own their own home

Household sizes are shrinking as residents get older. Only one-third of the households in this market have children under 16 living at home.

Marital status:

Married or cohabitate – 63 percent; Single/divorced/widowed – 37 percent

Readership information:

Women and older adults are more likely to read the *Enquirer* exclusively and loyally, while men and younger adults are more likely to read a competitive paper exclusively. Readers said they were most interested in local news. Focus groups with readers narrowed that down to these eight topics of highest interests in the order in which they are listed: Stories about people, health and medicine news and tips, business news (with emphasis on the cereal industry), education, recreation and minor sports, crime news, government news and entertainment. The editors would like the newspaper to attract more women and younger people who are now reading the competition.

Here are the budgets (The numbers after the local budgets are the story lengths in inches; wire stories can be cut to any size. Stories are identified by slugs – one- or two-word titles):

Wire budget:

Airport trouble: A power failure closes New York's three major airports, snarling air traffic across the nation.

Cattle prices: Government warns packers to record all sales.

Cancer: Exercise continued through middle and late years of life seems to give protection against cancer.

Donors: Hispanics and other minorities have trouble finding bone-marrow donors.

Nielsens: CBS was the highest rated network during the last rating period.

Gas tax: A bid by House leaders to pay for transportation improvements through a 5-cent-a-gallon tax appears to be dead.

Cocaine: More than $500 million is spent each year to treat cocaine-addicted babies, according to a study published today.

Iraq: AP Bulletin (7:30 a.m.): The United States is sending military air support to Saudi Arabia to increase pressure on Saddam Hussein. The U.S. is prepared to renew an attack on Iraq if Saddam does not agree to a full inspection of weapons sites.

Jobless: The House approved a $6.3 billion expansion of jobless benefits by more than enough votes to override President Bush's threatened veto.

Lansing: The house mustered enough votes to make effective immediately a controversial tax-base sharing bill for schools.

Grand Rapids: A slumlord will spend the next month in the same unheated house he rented to a Grand Rapids woman where she and her four children had lived for three years.

Local budgets:

County: Political war erupts at county building as commissioners slash the clerk's department. 16 inches. Headshots and breakout of the vote.

Dead: An update on the death of Bedford Township businessman Robert M. Lockwood. He died in a double-shooting in which his ex-girlfriend was injured and he was killed. 9 inches.

Mark: This weekend marks the kickoff of local Hispanic Heritage Month at the Federal Center in Battle Creek. 15 inches. Photo of Hispanic astronaut involved in festivities.

Hire: Applicants for teaching or support positions will be given preference if they live in the district, according to a residency policy being considered by the Battle Creek Board of Education.

Park: Parking rates for special events at Kellogg Arena are changed, from 25 cents per ticket to a flat $2 a car. 7 inches.

Guns: Guns n' Roses' first release in four years is selling like hotcakes in Battle Creek. Music store owners open to lines of customers. 7 inches. Photo: Color shot of music store owner with album display.

Lake: City commission approves $95,000 for a man-made lake. 10 inches.

Cold: The Arctic Express is making a summer visit to the area. Temperatures are expected to fall into the 30s by tomorrow night (assume this is summertime). 4 inches.

Steve: Stephen Sroka says nothing is too serious for humor; not sex, drug abuse or even AIDS. Sroka, a health educator who is on a mission to educate schoolchildren about AIDS, is here speaking as part of today's "Just Say Know" conference on AIDS. 14 Inches. Black and white shots of Sroka.

Photo budget:

Crime scene in Bedford where body was found/ color.

AIDS speaker/black and white.

Guns and Roses/color.

Photo of Hispanic astronaut involved in festivities.

Head shots of county commissioners

Exercise and information: courtesy of Ellen Leifeld, former executive editor of the *Battle Creek* (Mich.) *Enquirer.* Used with permission.

2-2. Qualities of news

Some of the main qualities of newsworthiness are timeliness, proximity (news in or near your community), unusual nature, prominence (stories about celebrities or prominent people), human interest and conflict. Some other newsworthy angles include entertainment, helpfulness (such as consumer news), trends (stories that show patterns in society). Using these qualities as your guide, identify the newsworthy elements in the following items; some items may have several qualities:

a.   News qualities:_____
Ninety-eight alligators were found the bedroom of a man who lives in Omaha, Nebraska.

b.   News qualities:_____
The police department on your campus yesterday released crime statistics for the first six months of the semester.

c.   News qualities:_____
A study released yesterday says that women who smoke at least a pack of cigarettes a day are more likely to have children with behavior problems than children of non-smokers.

d.   News qualities:_____
Residents in your community are protesting plans by a developer to build a landfill on the outskirts of town.   They will express their feelings at a public hearing tonight.

e.   News qualities:_____
Prince signed a $100 million deal with warner Bros. Records. The deal makes him the highest paid player in pop music. Warner Bros. agreed to pay the singer-composer $10 million per album plus royalties.

f.   News qualities:_____
A man in your town was gardening, but he didn't dig up weeds. He dug up his gold wedding band that he had lost 30 years ago.

g.   News qualities:_____
The average age of college students is increasing. One out of four college students is over age 30.

The Basic News Story

3

The following exercises will give you practice writing basic news stories. First find the focus, the main point of the story. Your focus sentence may also be your lead. If you want to use a creative lead, your focus statement should be your nut graph. Before you write your story, think about the order of the information you will use. Then write your story using the tell-a-friend technique. Consider the most important facts, and place them high in the story.

3-1. Fire

Write a news story based on the following information. Write your focus sentence at the top of your story. Decide what material needs to be attributed.

This information comes from Lynn Wilbur, University Place assistant fire chief: A fire occurred in a Tacoma suburb called University Place in Washington. Wilbur said that the fire started in a corner unit at the Meadow Park Garden Court apartments. It spread to a two-bedroom apartment next door through a common attic the two apartments shared. Both apartment units were destroyed and two others were damaged. Four families were left homeless. About 12 people had to be relocated. It was a two-alarm fire (which means two fire companies responded to the fire.) Investigators have not confirmed the cause of the fire. The blaze may have been started by a stove that was left on in one unit. "The pots were melted down on it." No one was injured. A pet cat died in the fire.

Information from apartment manager Steve Edwards: He said he couldn't relocate the families in the apartment complex because it was filled to capacity. He said some residents may have to seek shelter with the American Red Cross.

Information from Rosemary Hurlburt, who lived in one of the apartments: Her apartment was gutted. She said she and her two daughters were at a convenience store when the fire started. She said she lost a lot of new possessions. "We just got new stuff," Hurlburt said. "My 5-year-old daughter just had a birthday party. We just got her a brand-new bunk bed set."

Based on a story from *The Oregonian.* Used with permission.

3-2. Survey

Write a brief news story based on this information. Write a focus sentence on top of the story. Consider whether you would use a chart or other graphic for some of the statistics. If you plan to use a graphic, write a paragraph under your focus sentence explaining what information your graphic will contain.

This information comes from a survey that was published in a book, *The Day America Told the Truth.* The book was just released and is arriving in area book stores this week. The survey says 90 percent of people in the United States lie routinely. Thirty-six percent confess that they tell important lies.

Co-author James Patterson says in an interview with you: "Americans are willing to lie at the drop of a hat. Lying is part of their lives. People say what others want to hear."

He classifies lies as "dark lies," the ones that hurt other people, and "trivial lies," those that include insincere compliments on dinner or clothes.

Here are some of his findings:

■ 86 percent lie regularly to parents, 75 percent lie to friends, 73 percent lie to siblings and 69 percent lie to spouses.

■ 81 percent lie about their feelings, 43 percent lie about their income, 40 percent lie about sex.

The survey also asked people what they tell the truth about. These are the findings: 51 percent say there is no reason to marry, 29 percent say they aren't sure they still love their spouse, and 31 percent admit they are having or have had an extramarital affair.

Based on a story from *USA Today,* Copyright 1991. Used with permission.

3-3. Program advance

A program about date rape will be offered at your school tonight. Your editor hands you a press release and tells you to write a story about the upcoming program. This type of story is called an advance. You interview one of the panelists who will be on the program. You also get comments from people involved in the organization sponsoring the event. Instead of writing a lead announcing the program, try writing a lead based on something that one of your sources tells you. Ask yourself what you find most important or interesting. Use that in your lead. Then write a nut graph giving the basic information about what, where, when and so forth. You do not need to use all the quotes from each source in one block. Here are your notes:

Notes from a press release: There will be a forum tonight about date rape. The program is called "Date Rape, Acquaintance Rape." It is sponsored by the Emily Taylor Women's Resource Center. The program will be held in the Pine Room of the Student Union on your campus. It will be conducted from 7 to 9 p.m. It is open to men and women. The forum will feature a film, "Campus Rape." Panelists will discuss issues in the film and an audience-participation discussion will follow.

Notes from interview with Sherill Robinson, graduate assistant in the Resource Center: SHe said the forum would address problems that contribute to date rape, such as miscommunication, drugs and alcohol. "Regardless of those things, unless a woman says 'yes,' it's rape," she said. She said she hoped people would become aware of what date rape was.   She shows you an advertisement for the forum that defines date rape as forced sexual intercourse by someone you know.

Notes from interview with Barbara Ballard, director of the Resource Center: She said the center sponsored an outreach program which brought sexual assault programs to residence halls, scholarship halls and fraternities. "When I came here there was no such thing as date rape or acquaintance rape," she said. "Those things didn't even have a title. Now it's a topic that's discussed and people are a lot more educated about it."

Notes from interview with Sharon Danoff-Berg, a graduate assistant in the Emily Taylor Resource Center: At least one in four women will be sexually assaulted in their lifetime. About 90 percent of college rape victims are violated by someone they know. She says that is why she agreed to be one of four student panelists on the program. "There's this myth that most rapes are stranger rapes, where someone attacks you from out of the dark. That does happen, but not in the majority of rapes. People need to understand it's not the fault of the woman. Nobody deserves to be sexually assaulted or does anything to ask for it. The rapist is the one who needs to be held accountable."

Based on a story from *The University Daily Kansan*. Used with permission.

3-4. Burglary

Write a news story based on the following information. Write a focus sentence on top of the story.

You are a reporter for a Louisville newspaper and you interviewed this man after you read the report of the burglary in the police records. Be careful to attribute any material that you can not substantiate as factual. You do not have to use the quotes in one block. Use them where you think they fit best.

Information from Louisville police Sgt. Frank Lavender: No one has been arrested. The item that was stolen has not been found. He said that this misfortune reinforces a point that police have been trying to convey to citizens: It's not enough just to lock your car. "We're trying to encourage people to look into their cars and see what's in there and put it in the trunk. People need to be more careful."

Information comes from Roy L. Jones, 60: He was having lunch with a friend at a Shoney's restaurant, 811 Eastern Parkway in Louisville. He parked his 1980 Oldsmobile in the restaurant parking lot. Inside the car he had a package wrapped in a plastic bag on the floor. When he returned to his car about 30 minutes after he entered the restaurant, the package was gone. The back door was open and the glove compartment had been rifled. Inside the package was an $8,000 artificial leg. He had gone to Falls City Limb and Brace Co. before lunch to have his hip-to-floor prosthesis adjusted. He reported it to the police yesterday, but the leg has not turned up.

"I'm disgusted as hell, is all I can say. I bet whoever took it, when they opened the package is as disappointed as I am. I just hate to go through all the hassle of getting another one made. You have to go down there for a fitting, then you have to go down there again."

He said the leg is probably covered by insurance but that doesn't make him feel any better. He lost his left leg more than 30 years ago in an industrial accident. He uses a wheelchair when he goes out. He uses the artificial leg to move around his house. He had another one but it no longer fit. He needed further amputation two years ago. That's why he needed the new leg. He lives at 950 Samuel St. in Germantown.

Based on a story from the (Louisville, Ky.) *Courier-Journal.* Used with permission.

3-5. Telephone bill

You are a reporter for your local newspaper and your editor asks you to interview this man who has an unusual story. You call him and he gives you this information. Write a focus statement on top of your story and organize the material by the tell-a-friend method, placing the most interesting information high in the story.

The man's name is Jim Tyler. He says he received a monthly telephone bill for July that amounted to $110,099.44. The bill said there would be a late penalty of $1,650.27 if payment were not received by Sept. 2.

The bill was from Southwestern Bell Telephone. Tyler lives in Herington, Kansas. The calls of the longest durations were from Boston to China. One call lasted seven hours. It began at 10:36 p.m. on July 26. The charge for it was $690.

The majority of the calls originated from coin-operated phones in the Boston area. Calls had been placed to 53 foreign countries and to several locations in the United States, primarily along the East Coast.

The bill is about a thousand times higher than his normal bill. It was 386 pages, 1 3/4 inches thick and required postage of $2.90. The bill listed 3,261 calls. Only 44 of them were made by Tyler.

The operator assured Tyler that he would not have to pay for calls to foreign countries or places in the United States that he had not called.

Tyler thinks the problem resulted from someone illegally using his telephone credit card number. He says it is possible that his credit card number was stolen when his daughter, Trisa, used it to call home from a coin-operated phone in a Pittsburgh airport. She was returning from a church group trip to Kentucky when she tried to call home, but there was no answer. Tyler says someone at the airport apparently saw her punch in his credit card number. He says the number may have been sold several times since then.

He said he doesn't know how much of the bill he actually owes for his own calls. He thought something was strange when he received a call at 2 a.m. on July 27 from an operator asking him if he would authorize a credit card call to China.   "I said, 'No, I don't even know anyone in a foreign country." He said the operator informed him that several calls to foreign countries had been made using his credit card number during the past several hours and that he could expect an astronomical phone bill. "By astronomical, I thought maybe $2,000 or $3,000."

Tyler is an administrator at the Lutheran Home care center in Herington. This telephone bill was for his home.

Based on a story from *The Topeka* (Kan.) *Capital-Journal*. Used with permission.

3-6. Style quiz

This quiz will test your knowledge of Associated Press style for ages, percentages, addresses, money, numbers and titles, time and geographical regions. Some sentences contain more than one error. Cross out the errors and write your corrections above them.

1. The police officer in charge of the investigation was Sergeant Frank Lavender.

2. Women will make up forty seven % of the work force in the twenty-first century.

3. Fire officials said that twelve people had to be relocated because of the fire.

4. The survey showed that ninety % of the American people lie routinely.

5. The artificial leg cost the man 8,000 dollars.

6. The 60 year old man lives at 950 Samuel Street in Louisville.

7. Jim Tyler's phone bill last month was 110 thousand, ninety nine dollars and 44 cents.

8. Most of the telephone calls were to places along the east coast of the U.S.

9. Tyler said 3261 calls were on the bill, which required postage of two dollars and ninety cents.

10. One of the calls was placed at 5:51 P.M. on July 27 and another was at 8:00 A.M.

Story Ideas 4

These exercises are designed to help you develop ways of thinking about story ideas. Although many story ideas at newspapers, magazines, television stations and corporations are conceived and assigned by editors, reporters are expected to suggest their own ideas as well. Remember to include ideas for visual presentation with your story ideas.

4-1. Coaching

Pair up with a partner in the class and coach each other on the idea.
Coaching questions:
What is the main idea of your story? Answer in one sentence.
What is new about this story? What is the "so-what" factor?
What makes this story newsworthy now?
Is there anything unusual, helpful or informative such as news about a trend or material that is consumer-oriented in this story?
What effect will this story have on readers?
What makes this story of interest to your readers?

4-2. Localizing national news

You are the editor of your campus newspaper. You are scanning the wire service and find the following national stories. How would you localize them for your campus newspaper? Write a few sentences to develop the local angle for each issue, identifying experts or leaders of groups on campus and in your community whom you would interview.

a. The U.S. Department of Labor released a study predicting that from now through the first few years of the 21st century, the number of college graduates would exceed the number of jobs to match their skills. The report said that about 25 percent of the 25 million college graduates in the last year were working in jobs that did not require the degrees they held. The report predicted that by the year 2005, 78 percent of all the jobs available will not require a college degree and that 30 percent of all college graduates would take a job for which they were overqualified.

b. A report by the College Board says that tuition at public universities increased by an average of 10 percent this fall. The study of tuition at 2,800 public universities found that the average tuition at a four-year school was $2,315. Average tuition at a four-year private college was $10,498. The report also said that in the last 15 years, financial aid represented by loans instead of grants increased from 17 percent to 50 percent.

c. Next week is National Coming Out Day, a day dedicated to encouraging gays and lesbians to accept their sexual orientation and to discourage discrimination.

4-3. Holidays and special events

Choose any one of the following holidays, preferably the one that is coming up soon, and devise three story ideas for your campus or community newspaper. Make sure you ideas are clearly focused and include sources and graphic ideas. Thanksgiving, Christmas/Hanukkah, Valentine's Day, Easter, or Spring Break.

4-4. Special sections

a. Your campus newspaper is planning a special section about fashion, primarily aimed at male and female college students. Plan at least five story ideas that would appeal to this audience.

b. Your campus newspaper is planning a special section about entertainment for college students. The section will feature ideas about places in your community such as restaurants, bars and nightclubs, local bands and other recreational activities that students would enjoy. Plan at least five story ideas for such a section.

4-5. Classified advertisements

Read the following classified advertisements that appeared in campus newspapers and identify newsworthy angles for a story in your campus newspaper. (Each ad was followed by a phone number.) Discuss or write a budget line identifying sources you might contact and a focus you would develop.

a. Need cash? Help others while helping yourself. We need men and women to donate valuable plasma. We provide TV entertainment, two hours free parking, $15 for each donation.

b. Therapeutic hypnosis. Gentle, non-coercive, holistic. Also therapeutic Tarot readings for problem solving, insight. Certified hypnotherapist.

c. Seized cars, trucks, boats, 4-wheelers, motor homes, by FBI, IRS, DEA. Available in your area now.

4-6. Design a competing newspaper

This exercise is an extension of the first three exercises in your textbook. Imagine that you are trying to establish a newspaper to compete with your local or campus newspaper. Gather information from your chamber of commerce or city planning commission about the demographics of your community. If you decide to devise a campus newspaper, gather information about the demographics of your university from the public relations department or university administration. You will need basic information such as total population, age groups, marital status of residents, income levels and so on.

Working individually or in small groups, brainstorm the kinds of stories you would include in your newspaper. If you are working in groups, divide the responsibilities for sections in your newspaper. For example, you could have the following editors: city editor responsible for local news, sports editor, business editor, national/foreign news editor and a lifestyle/entertainment editor. Then write a plan explaining your concepts. Include an overview to explain your purpose and general ideas and then write a few paragraphs for each section specifying the changes you recommend.

Consider the following questions:

What kinds of stories would you include in your newspaper that your competition does not? What kinds of stories would appeal to the demographic groups in your market? Are there special groups you would try to reach, such as high school students? Would you include more news of interest to women and minorities, and if so, what kinds of stories would you suggest? Does your entertainment section provide the kind of stories that appeal to your readers? How could you improve this section or others?

What new sections or new beats would you recommend to appeal to readers in your community. Include design features such as columns of briefs, suggestions for graphics and other visual tools that would make your newspaper more enticing than your competitor's.

4-7. Choosing press releases

You are the city editor of your local newspaper. You have received the following press releases this week. Which ones will you assign to a reporter for a story or a brief announcement to include in your newspaper? Justify your decision by identifying the newsworthy angle: consumer interest (news you can use), proximity, unusual nature, human interest or other angle that makes the release relevant to your readers.

a. The Senior Services Center in your community will hold an Information Day for Older Adults this weekend (date, time and location). The program will feature a health care crisis panel and a panel on financial issues of interest to older adults.

b. Approximately 60,000 builders and associates in housing-related businesses will converge on Las Vegas this month to kick off the new year at the National Association of Home Builders' Annual Convention and Exposition.

c. Five citizens in your community will receive awards this weekend for outstanding (names enclosed) volunteer work in helping disabled residents. The awards will be presented by Independence, Inc., an organization in your community devoted to helping disabled people.

d. McNeil Consumer Products Company reports that Tylenol has introduced a new "No Drowsiness Cold & Flu" medication. The release states that this new nonprescription cold remedy is the first product in the hot liquid cold medication category available in a non-drowsy formula.

e. A press release from your county Department of Public Works announces that Route 123 from U.S. Highway 20 (assume this is in your area) will be closed to through traffic this Saturday due to reconstruction.

f. Busy holiday shoppers and travelers may purchase fewer Christmas gifts this year, but they'll spend more cash. Use of cash machines during the holiday season has increased steadily over the past several years, and this season should prove no exception, according to Plus System, Inc., an international network of automated teller machines.

4-8. Using a press release

Press releases should be used to give you ideas and information for a story, but you should add to them with interviews of your own. Using the following press release from the University of Kansas about an increase in residence hall rates, imagine that this information related to your university. In addition to the source named in this release, who else would you interview for a story on this subject? Make a list of sources you would interview from your own school if residence hall rates were increasing on your campus. This press release from the university's public relations department presents this issue in the best light possible. Write a list of questions you would ask to add balance and other points of view. Also, add a suggestion for graphic presentation.

University of Kansas residence hall rates will increase $396 annually beginning next fall under a proposal presented to the Kansas Board of Regents Thursday.

If approved, KU's rates will remain less than those of KU's peer institutions and below average for Big Eight Conference universities, Kenneth L. Stoner, director of housing at KU, said.

KU's peers are considered to be the universities of Iowa, Oklahoma, North Carolina and Oregon. The average 1991-92 residence hall rate at those schools was $3,133.

The national average for college residence hall rates in 1991-92 was $3,235.

At KU, 1992-93 residence hall room and board rates are proposed to be $3,080. In 1991-92 the rate was $2,684.

The regents took no action Thursday and are scheduled to discuss rate increases proposed by all regents universities at the board's December meeting.

The rate increase KU is seeking this year is larger than those sought by other regents universities. Additional funds are necessary to maintain KU's halls in good condition and to offset increased operating costs, Stoner said. KU does not require students to live in residence halls. About 3,700 students chose this form of housing at KU this year.

"KU residence halls remain a bargain," Stoner said. "The proposed KU residence hall room and board rate for 1992-93 equates to slightly less than $13 a day for room and board for the entire academic year."

KU residence hall rates have increased 25.7 percent over the past five years, compared to a national average increase of 32.3 percent.

Press release from Office of University Relations, University of Kansas. Reprinted with permission.

Curiosity and Observation 5

Your senses of sight and sound are important reporting tools. To a lesser degree, what you smell, touch and taste also can provide information for your story. This chapter is intended to help you learn how to use your curiosity and observation to report and write your news stories. Although much of your information for news stories comes from answers sources give to your questions, what you see, hear, and smell at a scene may also be included in a story. Your observations will generate information for the writing technique known as "show-in-action," meaning you can show what your sources are doing as well as tell what they say. The following exercises are designed to help you understand how to combine your observations with information from your sources.

5-1. Observation analysis

Analyze the following story for information the reporter gained by observation and sources. Discuss how the writer used details and whether you would have included this information in the story if you had been on the scene. This event occurred in April 1992, eight months before George Bush was defeated in his bid for reelection as president. Underline the material that came from direct observation.

500,000 march on capital to support abortion rights

WASHINGTON – Hundreds of thousands of women and men – mostly women – marched past the White House on Sunday to protest the decline of abortion rights.

In the largest demonstration to hit Washington in many years, National Park Service police estimated 500,000 marchers filed down Pennsylvania Avenue chanting "Bush Must Go," and "Free Barbara Bush" en route to a massive rally in front of the U.S. Capitol.

"We are tired of begging for our rights from men in power," National Organization for Women president Patricia Ireland told the crowd. "We are going to take power."

The turnout, which organizers claimed was closer to a million, apparently was helped by sunny, cool weather and recent controversies that activists said went to the heart of respect for women and who controls their bodies: the sexual harassment charges Anita Hill brought against Clarence Thomas and the Palm Beach and Mike Tyson rape trials.

"This is my first time in Washington marching," said Jayne Gall, who arrived from Cincinnati wearing a "William Kennedy Smith . . .meet Thelma and Louise" T-shirt.

"I'm overwhelmed," Gall said. "It's wonderful."

Buttons and shirts advising "I believe Anita Hill" were common. Marchers said the rough treatment Senate Republicans showed the former Thomas aide, and the full Senate's eventual approval of the man she credibly accused, galvanized women, especially since Thomas is assumed to be anti-abortion.

Again and again the call went out for women candidates in fall elections, with a goal of a 50 percent female Congress, up from about 5 percent today.

"Look what happened in Illinois," said Carol Moseley Braun, the black woman who upset an incumbent Democrat in that state's primary. Sen. Alan Dixon had voted to approve Thomas' nomination.

Of the many Hollywood celebrities who spoke, Callie Khourie, who won an Oscar for writing "Thelma & Louise," got one of the warmest receptions.

"I always thought, 'Gee, I'd like to write a movie some day. I'd like to make a difference,' " Khouri said. "And you know what? I made a difference."

The day's official sign carried the National Abortion Rights Action League threat, "We will Decide, November 3."

But, as usual at an abortion rights event, the best standards were homemade: "Witches for Choice," "M.I.T. Nerds for Choice," "Menopausal Women Nostalgic for Choice," "Support Vaginal Pride."

Not everyone was feeling chipper.

"It makes me sad to come down here to march about something so personal and so sad," said Patti Flowers, a student from Baltimore.

And Kris Taylor of Bethesda, Md., toted a sign that on one side read, "I wish I had been aborted," and on the other: "And so does my mother."

He said he meant it.

"It's a joke, but it's based in fact," Taylor said. His natural parents were forced to marry and have both him and his older brother, he said, even though his mother was mentally ill and kept the boys in a closet. He was 8 months old when "normal people" adopted him, but his brother was 2 and barely spoke. "People thought he was autistic.

"We should have been aborted," he repeated. "Neither one of them was suitable parents."

The rally had a paradox of its own.

Both NOW organizers and speakers at a small anti-abortion rally nearer the capitol expect the Supreme Court to continue undermining Roe vs. Wade, the 1973 decision that made abortion legal nationwide. Polls consistently show a majority of Americans reluctantly support abortion rights, but most of the current court, whose members serve for life, apparently do not.

"We Won't Go Back," was the march's slogan.

One speaker recalled that abolitionists actually welcomed the high court's ruling in the Dred Scott case in 1857. By declaring slavery legal, American Civil Liberties Union president Nadine Strossen said, the court stirred the majority that believed otherwise.

"This is going to be our Dred Scott," she said. "It is going to galvanize us, and we will win in the legislatures and in the streets."

Karl Vick, *St. Petersburg* (Fla.)*Times*. Reprinted with permission.

5-2. Observation writing exercise

You are covering a speech. Outside the hotel where the speech is being given, picketers are protesting. Using these notes, which contain observation and information from sources, write a news story. Decide what material that you observed should be included in the story. Write the story in the order you think is best. Put your quotes in separate paragraphs unless you have two related quotes from the same speaker. Here are your notes:

Bill McCartney, University of Colorado football coach is giving a speech at the Westin Hotel Tabor Center. Use yesterday (but name the day) as your time frame. You count the members of the audience and decide there are 330 men. McCartney was the guest speaker for the Shaka Franklin Foundation for Youth. The foundation was established by Les Franklin, director of the Governor's Job Training Office. Franklin started the foundation in honor of his son who committed suicide 18 months ago. The foundation attempts to head off young suicides.

Outside the hotel you observe about 30 people who are picketing the speech. They are carrying signs and chanting slogans to protest a comment McCartney made last month against homosexuals. At that time he called homosexuality an "abomination." Some of the signs say, "McCartney is Satan," "Bill McCartney, NOT!, "Homophobia Kills Kids."

You hear the protesters chanting this refrain:

"Bill, you're lying. Kids are dying.

"Two. Four. Six. Eight. How do you know your kids are straight?

"We're here. We're queer. Get used to it.

"Bill. Bill. Take a chill. Your rhetoric is making me ill."

Cheryl Schwartz, coordinator of youth services for the Gay and Lesbian Community Center of Colorado, tells you that the protesters represented various gay and lesbian groups in the state. "Gay and lesbian youth are three times more likely to commit suicide than heterosexual youth," she said. She said comments such as McCartney's about homosexuals undermine the low esteem of homosexual youths. "They think they're no good. So why not just die?"

McCartney praised Franklin for creating the foundation. "In the midst of his pain, he wanted to be part of the solution," McCartney said. "His pain is really the potential gain of so many young people who are out there."

McCartney's speech was about parenthood and its responsibilities. He told the men in the audience that they need to be good fathers by listening to their children and spending wholesome time with them. "We need to take regard and responsibility for those in our homes," he said. "We as men need to be spiritual leaders in our home. We can make a difference, not only in our homes, but in all of the homes we touch." McCartney did not comment on the protest or about homosexuals.

Based on a story from the *Rocky Mountain* (Colo.) *News*. Used with permission.

Sources

6

Your campus and local libraries contain a wealth of information you can use to check accuracy in your stories and to find sources. Libraries subscribe to many directories with which you should become familiar. Many libraries now have a wide variety of resource information on data bases, which are very easy to use. You should familiarize yourself with these resources; they can save you time when you are researching background for a story. The following assignment is based on information from these printed directories: *Reader's Guide to Periodical Literature, The Wall Street Journal Index, Facts on File, Encyclopedia of Associations, Statistical Abstract of the United States (1991), Consultants & Consulting Organizations Directory, National Trade & Professional Associations of the U.S.,* and the *Contemporary Authors* index, *Familiar Quotations* by John Bartlett, *Standard and Poor's Register of Corporations, Directors and Executives,* and *Gale Directory of Publications and Broadcast Media.*

6-1. Library research

1. The rap singer Ice-T is going to perform in your area, and you are writing a concert "advance" story about him. You know that in 1992 Ice-T had a very controversial song, "Cop Killer," that the performer pulled from his album because of the furor it created. You want to include some background material about this issue, and you plan to check articles in some of the major news magazines, but you aren't sure of the exact dates they were published. Using a resource directory, find the article in *Newsweek* about the controversy in 1992.

Write the name of the directory and the heading under which you find the item:

Directory:_____

Heading:_____

a. Title of article: _____

Source:_____ Date_____

2. You are writing a story about AIDS and you want to include some information from the Eighth International Conference conducted in 1992. You can find out some basic information quickly using Facts on File, a weekly world news index. Provide the following information about the conference:

a. Where was the conference held?_____

b. Give the dates of the conference:_____

c. Who gave the opening speech?_____

d. How many adults are expected to have AIDS by the year 2000?_____

3. In your textbook, you read about the (Louisville,Ky.) *Courier-Journal* reporter Scott Thurm who wrote a Pulitzer-Prize winning story about school bus safety following an accident in Kentucky. Your community also had a tragic accident involving a school bus, and your editor wants you to do a similar story. Using a directory, find a phone number for a national association that deals with school transportation:

Directory used:_____

Name of association:_____

Address of association:_____

Phone number:_____

4. You are writing a story about child abuse in your area. You want to add some national perspective. Find the following information:

Directory used:_____

Total child abuse and neglect cases in 1980: _____

Total child abuse and neglect cases in 1987:_____

Area of country with highest number of these cases:_____

5. You are writing a story about gender differences in life expectancy. Find the rates for men and women from 1980 and the projections for the year 2010.

Directory you used:_____

1980 projections: Men_____   Women_____

2010 projections: Men_____   Women_____

6. For your story about gender differences in aging, you want to quote a consultant who deals with matters of health care for people over age 50. You have found the name of a consulting firm, Age Wave, in one of the clips you researched, but you don't know where it is based or how to contact a source from there. Find the address and telephone number:

Directory used:_____

Address of consulting firm:_____

Telephone number:_____

7. Many newspapers write advance obituaries about famous people who are elderly so that they have the information on file in case the person dies. You are doing research for an obituary about author James Michener. You want to start with some basic facts, and later you may check data bases for news stories about him. To start your research, use a directory and answer these questions:

Directory used:_____

Where was he born?_____

Date of birth:_____

Name of his third wife:_____

Date he married her:_____

8. You are writing a story about garlic supplements for the food section. You want to include some business facts about the growing market for these pills, which became very popular in 1992 and were sold like vitamins at drug stores and health food stores. You decide to check if *The Wall Street Journal* had any articles about these supplements, and you find just what you need.

Directory:_____

What date did an article appear?_____

Give the section and page number in the paper for the article:_____

What was the increase in drug store sales of these supplements during the year ending Aug. 31, 1992?

_____

9. Writers often begin stories with famous quotations. For example, in Chapter 24 Tad Bartimus wrote a story about three brothers who died, and she began it with a quote from Shakespeare. You are writing a story about horses, and you remember this quote, "A horse! a horse! My kingdom for a horse," but you don't know who wrote it or the title of the work in which it appeared. Using a directory, find the proper citation:

Directory:_____

Author of the quote:_____

Work in which the quote appeared:_____

Specific reference for quote (act, scene and line):_____

10. You are writing a business story about annual income tax returns, and you want to include some information about the profitability of a firm that prepares income taxes. One of the main companies in this business is H&R Block. You also want to check with the company's law firm to ask about a lawsuit filed against the firm. Find the following information about this company:

Directory:_____

Chairman of the company:_____

Number of employees:_____

Law firm:_____

Sales for the company:_____

11. Using the same directory, find out this information about Gannett Co. Inc., the company that publishes *USA Today* and about 80 other newspapers.

Number of employees:_____

Sales reported (preferably as of 1992):_____

12. You are considering pursuing a graduate degree at the University of Montana in Missoula. You would like to work part-time for a daily newspaper or trade magazine in the area, excluding the campus newspaper. What newspaper and what trade magazine (not including scholarly publications) are published in Missoula?

Directory:_____

Daily Newspaper: _____Circulation:_____

Trade magazine:_____Circulation:_____

6-2. Writing a news story from research

Using the most recent *Statistical Abstract of the United States* you can find, write a news story based on any interesting figures you find. Choose items that you think might be of most interest to readers. Be careful not to fill your story with too many statistics. When you want to use several statistics, use the list technique (described more fully in Chapter 12). Just itemize several numbers in a list preceded by a dash or a dot and an overview sentence such as: Here are some findings. Use a creative lead based on one or two interesting items you found and follow with this nut graph: The latest issue of the *Statistical Abstract of the United States* was released today. The 979-page paperback printed by the Government Printing Office contains more than 1,400 tables of data and costs $29. (This information is based on the 1992 edition; change the number of pages and cost if they differ in a later edition.)

Graphic: In addition to your story, write a highlights box listing some of the key facts about the book and/or some of the interesting items that you have not included in your story.

For example:

Americans who exercise like to walk or swim more than run, and in their leisure time the majority watch cable television or their VCR.

Those are some of the facts in the latest Statistical Abstract of the United States, which goes on sale today for $29. . . .

[Then back up your lead with the substantiation.] The book reports that more than 71 million people walk but only 24 million prefer running as a form of exercise.

Other facts include:

• Fifty-nine percent of all household watch cable television and 72 percent own a VCR.

• College students studying the Japanese language numbered 45,700 in 1990, an increase from 11,500 in 1980.

Listening and Note-taking Skills

7

Do you struggle writing full quotes in your notes when you interview sources? Are you thinking of what you will say rather than listening to what the source says? These exercises are designed to help you identify your listening problems and improve your concentration so you can take better notes.

7-1. Your listening profile

The prerequisite for taking good notes is good listening. This is an unscientific test. It is meant only to help you identify your strengths and weaknesses in listening skills. Rate yourself for your listening skills by circling the answer that best describes you.

a. On a scale of 1 to 10 (1= terrible to 10 = excellent) rate yourself as a listener.

   1   2   3   4   5   6   7   8   9   10

b. On a scale of 1 to 10, (1= terrible to 10 = excellent) how do you think your friends would you rate you as a listener?

   1   2   3   4   5   6   7   8   9   10

c. When you are talking with friends, do you interrupt?

   Often   Sometimes   Rarely   Never

d. When you receive instructions verbally in a class, how often do you need to have them repeated so you understand them?

   Often   Sometimes   Rarely   Never

e. When you listen to your favorite songs with words, how often do you know the score by heart?

      Often   Sometimes   Rarely   Never

f. When you are in your lecture classes, what factors inhibit your listening skills?

    (1) Boredom
    (2) Thoughts of personal problems
    (3) Difficulty hearing
    (4) Lack of interest in the subject matter
    (5) Limited attention span
    (6) Other
    (7) None of the above

g. When you are conversing with your friends, what factors inhibit your listening skills?

    (1) Boredom
    (2) Thoughts of personal problems
    (3) Difficulty hearing
    (4) Lack of interest in the subject matter
    (5) Limited attention span
    (6) Other
    (7) None of the above

h. When you are interviewing a source for a story, what factors inhibit your listening skills?

    (1) Boredom
    (2) Thoughts of personal problems
    (3) Difficulty hearing
    (4) Lack of interest in the subject matter
    (5) Limited attention span
    (6) Other
    (7) None of the above

I. When you are interviewing a source for a story, how often do you concentrate more on what you are going to ask next instead of what the source is saying?

      Often   Sometimes   Rarely   Never

j. Now look at the answers you have circled. Do you notice any patterns? Are you thinking about personal problems or questions you might ask when you are conversing with friends or sources? Is your major problem a limited attention span, indicating lack of concentration or boredom? Using these answers as a guide or others that characterize your listening habits, identify your weaknesses:

I need to work on improving my listening skills by overcoming:

_____   _____

_____   _____

_____   _____

_____   _____

7-2. Concentration

If you want to remember quotes from your sources, you have to concentrate when you hear them. Test your concentration skills:

a. Read these numbers and then cover them with your hand or a piece of paper. Write them in your computer or on a piece of paper in the order they appeared.

       1   3   5   9   7   5   8   1

b. Read one of these two paragraphs quickly. Then turn the book over or cover it with a piece of paper. Try to write it as exactly as you can. (Alternative method: Pair up with a partner in your class. Ask your partner to read one of these two selections to you. Then write as much of the selection you heard as accurately you can. After you have completed your portion, read the next selection to your partner.

These passages are from *The World Is My Home: A Memoir* by James Michener, Random House, 1992.

"I am always interested in why young people become writers, and from talking with many I have concluded that most do not want to be writers working eight and ten hours a day and accomplishing little; they want to *have been* writers, garnering the rewards of having completed a successful manuscript, and seeing it become a best-seller. They aspire to the rewards of writing, but not to the travail." (p. 349)

"If I were a young writer today starting over, I would focus my attention on the changing relationships between the sexes; despite my age I am fascinated by this and the other subjects but do not feel myself qualified to write about them." (p. 507.)

c. This is a famous passage from "Hamlet" by William Shakespeare. Read it quickly and then cover it or turn the book over. Write it as exactly as you can.

To be, or not to be, that is the question:
Whether 'tis nobler in the mind to suffer
The slings and arrows of outrageous fortune,
Or to take arms against a sea of troubles
And by opposing end them. To die: to sleep
No more; and by a sleep to say we end
The heart-ache and the thousand natural shocks
That flesh is heir to: 'tis a consummation
Devoutly to be wish'd.

Interviewing Techniques 8

The best way to learn how to interview sources is to do it. You will improve your skills the more you interview people. Some of the fears you might have will also diminish as you gain more experience. These exercises are intended to give you some practice and make you aware of your own strengths and weaknesses in interviewing.

8-1. Coaching

Pair up with a classmate and take turns coaching each other on the story idea (similar to coaching in Chapter 4) and on the interview. If you are coaching before the interview has been conducted, brainstorm some questions with your partner. If you are coaching after the interview, use the suggested questions. Your role as the coach is to listen and ask guiding questions. Here are some coaching questions, but you may add more:

Coaching on the idea:
1. What is the story about – answer in one or two sentences.
2. What is the focus? Is it what you just told me or do you have an angle you will pursue on the topic you just described?
3. What's the point – the "so-what" factor?
4. Why are you writing about this now? Is there a timeliness factor?
5. What's new, unusual, different, helpful or indicative of a pattern/trend in this story ?
6. If this idea is for a feature about some previous event, what makes it newsworthy now?
7. What effect, if any, will this story have on readers? Why would they want to be informed about this topic?
8. What strikes you as interesting about this topic?

Coaching for the interview:

1. What are the main points the reader needs to know to understand this issue?
2. Do you have sources to confirm, react or provide other points of view? What sources should you contact?
3. Do you have background about the person or issue? Is there any previous related story you should check?
4. What do you want to know? (The coach can add some questions here.)
5. What difficulties are you anticipating? Do you have any alternative ways of getting this information?

Coaching after the interview:

1. What struck you as most interesting in the interview? Was it related to the focus?
2. Do you have enough information to back up your focus? If not, should you change your focus?
3. What interesting anecdotes or facts did you learn from the interview?

For the writer: If you are still struggling with your focus, try writing a hard-news lead; that lead could be your nut graph if you plan to use a soft lead.

8-2. Class reunion

You are attending a class reunion – your class 25 years from now. Interview your classmates. Ask them how old they are now, their occupations now, check spelling of their names (some of the women may be using married names; if so include their maiden names) and ask them about some of their favorite memories of college. While you are interviewing different members of your class, you must take notes standing up. You may find it easier to work in small groups and rotate to different groups during the time allotted for interviewing (about 30 minutes). Your nut graph something like this: The class of ----- for your university or journalism school met for its 25th reunion in the (give a location). Although you may make up information and quotes for this story (contrary to what you may do in a real news story), keep your story consistent so that you give the same information to everyone who interviews you. Write the story as though you were a reporter for your local newspaper. Do not use the first person (I,we) voice; pretend you were just an observer, not part of the reunion.

8-3. Observing interviewing techniques

Work in groups of three. One person will be an observer while the other two interview each other. Then switch, letting the observer be an interviewer and so on until each person has had a chance to be an observer. While you are observing, do not say anything. Just jot down notes about the interviewer's techniques. You may fill out the following sheet or just use it to guide you. When you are finished interviewing each other, discuss the strengths and weaknesses you noticed. Analyze your own interviewing weaknesses and strengths.

Observer's Form – Reporting Techniques

Rate the interviewer on the following traits by circling the appropriate adjectives:

1. Manner (pleasantness, politeness, friendliness).........Good   Fair   Poor

2. Eye contact with the source......................................Good   Fair   Poor

3. Interviewer's interest in subject................................Good   Fair   Poor

4. Quality of the questions...Good   Fair   Poor

5. Listening skills...Good   Fair   Poor

6. Control of interview ....Good   Fair   Poor

7. Note-taking skills..Good   Fair   Poor

8. List the interviewer's strengths:

9. Briefly describe the interviewer's weaknesses:

10. What recommendations do you have for the interviewer?

8-4. Interview a news source

Interview a source who has been in the news or one who frequently deals with the media. The purpose of your interview is to ask the source about his or her experiences with the media. You are responsible for learning some background about your source. You will need to ask follow-up questions, and you should seek specific examples of good and bad experiences the source has had with the media. For example, if your source says some person or some newspaper or television station never treats him or her fairly, get examples of what the source means – questions asked, specific stories, and so on. After you conduct your interview, write a report (make sure you include background about your source). To encourage candor from your source, you may tell the source this report is for a class assignment and not for publication. Here are some questions to guide you:

1. How often do you come in contact with the media?

2. With whom are your contacts (local newspaper and radio, regional newspapers and TV, state media, national media)?

3. How long have you had press contact? Is it steady or intermittent?

4. Have you had other roles in the past in which you had press coverage? Please explain.

5. Have you been interviewed primarily for hard-news or feature stories?

6. Are most of your interviews in person or by telephone? Which do you prefer and why?

7. Do you ever contact the press? Why or why not? Give examples, if you do.

8. Overall, how do you view your coverage by the media so far (fair, accurate, complete)? Please specify if the coverage differs for newspapers, radio, television or magazines.

9. Have you had bad experiences with interviewers? Would you cite examples of interviewing techniques and reporting that you considered bad interviewing techniques? (Here you will need to seek specifics from your source for the most complete explanation you can get.) Have you experienced poorly stated or ignorant questions, misinterpretation of your position, inaccurate quotes, personality conflict with the interviewer or bias by the interviewer?

10. In situations in which you might not have been presented as positively as you would have liked, was the coverage fair and accurate? Explain.

11. Do you have any general complaints about interviews?

12. If you were involved in any good interviews, what made them good? Did the interviewer do something new that you though made him or her more effective?

13. What suggestions about interviewing do you have for beginning reporters?

8-5. Analyze the interview

You are interviewing Dixy Lee Ray, author of *Trashing the Planet: How Science Can Help Us Deal With Acid Rain, Depletion of the Ozone and Nuclear Waste*. Ray is a former governor of Washington and was assistant secretary of state at the Bureau of Oceans, International Environmental and Scientific Affairs in 1975. She favors the use of pesticides and is very critical of environmentalists who want to ban the use of these chemicals. Your background research includes a poll in 1990 in which more than four of five people in the United States want organic fruits and vegetables (grown without pesticides). The primary focus of your interview is to determine why Ray is such a staunch supporter of the use of pesticides in light of increased interest by consumers for organically grown foods.

Before you read the following interview, devise at least five questions you might ask her.

1._____

2._____

3._____

4._____

5._____

Now read the following interview conducted by *USA Today* reporter Wendy Benedetto. Analyze the type of questions she asked: open- and closed-ended questions, follow-up questions, background questions and whether the questions elicited good quotes and answers that you think might interest readers. Circle key words the reporter used to frame follow-up questions. Discuss whether the follow-up questions are based on conversational interviewing. Since you didn't have the benefit of the answers, you couldn't be expected to devise follow-up questions; however, compare some of Benedetto's questions with the ones you devised. Benedetto's questions are identified by Q, and Ray's answers follow.

Q: Environmentalists have raised consumer consciousness about pesticide dangers. Why do you criticize their efforts?

A: They get all the publicity because they make the charges, and it's sort of an unwritten law of journalism that making an accusation is a lot more newsworthy than saying, "Hey, look, everything is all right." So they get the coverage, but the fact is they're wrong.

Q: Why do you say the environmentalists are wrong?

A: They make accusations without giving you any evidence. They will say, for example, "Pesticides cause cancer." There's no evidence whatsoever of any cancer having been caused by pesticides used on food. They make claims that there is a lot of pesticide residue because of pesticides being used during the time that food is being grown.

Q. And you say that's not true?

A: In 1989, the Food and Drug Administration made a very extensive survey of foods on the market and found that 61 percent of all the food that we eat had absolutely no pesticide residue at all. And, of the remainder, only 1 percent had enough pesticide that it actually exceeded the very, very conservative standards that are set.

Q: What do you mean by "conservative"?

A: The Environmental Protection Agency bends over backward to be conservative. And that's right. But the risks are vastly exaggerated. A Stanford University study showed the risks of any pesticide residue on tomatoes is exaggerated 2,600 times. And so it goes with lots of other foods.

Q: When did all this begin?

A: It started with the campaign against DDT in the early '70s and grew rather slowly until it reached a crescendo just two or three years ago. I think the climax was reached with the Big Green initiative in California.

Q: Why shouldn't consumers be concerned about pesticide residues? After all some of them are known to cause cancer in laboratory animals.

A: They have to feed them such enormous quantities that they actually poison the animals with the amounts of materials they feed them in order to have tumors.

Q: Then doesn't that show pesticides could be dangerous to people?

A: Human beings are not mice; human beings aren't rats. We respond differently to many of these substances. The problem is this: Whenever anybody makes an accusation, if they accuse a person or an organization of doing something wrong, that gets lots of news coverage. Later, if the charge is shown to be not correct, hardly anybody ever hears of that.

Q: Are you saying this happens often?

A: Especially when a laboratory comes up with a result that the crusader types don't like, they'll always accuse it of fraud. It's the easiest thing in the world to do. It doesn't cost them anything to make an accusation. They don't have to prove it.

Q: How should a pesticide's safety be determined?

A: It should be decided on the basis of testing and evidence, and that does play a part. Unfortunately, as William Reilly, the administrator of EPA says, they are more sensitive to public opinion than they are to scientific information.

Q: Who tests pesticides, manufacturers or the EPA?

A: Both. To apply for a license to be able to sell a pesticide, the company that manufactures it has to go through a long, long series of tests and to provide that information to government agencies. And then they double-check it.

Q: Has fear of pesticides become so great that even safe pesticides are taboo?

A: Some people have been unduly frightened and are refusing to eat certain types of fresh fruits and vegetables, which are very good for them, for fear of pesticides. That's a very tragic thing.

Q: But how can consumers be sure what is safe and what is not?

A: As a rule of thumb, you can assume that everything is safe until it's proven not to be.

Q: So you're saying we can go into any grocery store and feel safe about buying the food?

A: That's right. And if it's fresh fruits and vegetables, and you want to feel even safer, then wash them before you eat them. Or if it's a fruit, then peel it. But the fact is, the systems that we have set up, the Food and Drug Administration and the various food inspection services, really do a good job.

Q: What do you think of organic foods? Many people at Earth Day celebrations this weekend urged consumers to buy them.

A: In my opinion, they are wasting their money. Many of the foods they buy are less safe because, not having been protected with pesticides, many of them have fungus growth, bacteria, which make them less healthy than the ones not organically grown.

Q: You're saying pesticides make food healthier. Do they protect people from diseases?

A: From salmonella, the most common type of food poisoning, from botulism and from various rots and fungus that cause food to decay.

Q: What else?

A: They also prevent plant pests and prevent lots of crops from being spoiled before they reach the market.

Q: Any other advantages?

A: The use of a plant pesticide, generally called herbicides, against weeds, reduces the amount of plowing that has to be done and thus reduces soil erosion.

Q: But there are dangers.

A: Pesticides have to be used wisely. It's like everything else; you can't use them unwisely or in excess.

Q: But aren't those who handle and work with pesticides likely to be overexposed, and doesn't that put them in danger?

A: People where these materials are manufactured are very carefully tested and protected. Those who have been exposed have medical checkups. Where there have been problems with pesticides has been where people don't read the directions and have been exposed to large amounts. But that's been tightened up.

Q: If pesticide dangers are so minor, why are there so many legislative proposals made to restrict or ban them?

A: There are very few people elected to office who know anything about science at all. They get their scientific information from lobbyists and pressure groups. What's happening is that a long campaign by the political and anti-everything environmentalists is showing up in legislation that is not only unnecessary but will be very costly.

Wendy Benedetto, *USA Today*. Copyright 1991. Reprinted with permission.

The Writing Process

9

This chapter will reinforce the four-step concept of the coaching process — conceive, collect, construct, correct. The exercises will give you practice in thinking about what makes stories work and in revising stories.

9-1. Coaching the writing process

Revision is an important step in the writing process, but revision doesn't just mean cleaning up grammar and style. In the coaching process, revision means analyzing your whole story from the idea to the final written version. Many writers have problems with focus, and lack of a clear focus can lead to a story that rambles. The following story was a student's first attempt at writing a news story, and it has many problems. Using the coaching method, analyze the problems with this story and offer suggestions for improvement.

Public Relations Student Society of America is a campus organization that encourages professional development and provides educational opportunities for college students.

This organization, known as PRSSA, offers diversity among students, and it builds relationships between students and professional public relations practitioners.

PRSSA was formed in 1968 as a nationally recognized pre-professional organization. There are more than 5,000 members in 160 chapters across America. Participation is on chapter, district and national levels.

The many opportunities offered in the PRSSA chapter include: building a portfolio/resume, meeting professionals by attending the meetings and PRSSA events, attending workshops and touring public relations firms. All of these activities can lead to a better business sense as a students.

Referring to a better business sense, PRSSA invited a speaker to attend the meeting last night. The president of Gilbert, Christopher & Associates, Christopher Carter, spoke on developing a good business sense. Carter said, "You have to be able to read and write well.

He elaborated on this statement, saying that a person does not have to be a master writer to write well and to have a photographic memory to read well. He said that one should use the tell-it-to-a- friend approach to write naturally well and to just read as much as you can.

"It makes you look smarter," he said.

Carter listed a few of his key points of developing a good business sense including: be patient, learn to lose, be smart and truthful, have an opinion, keep your opinion to yourself until you have discussed it with the boss, follow your instincts, try to be the kind of person that other people want to see succeed, work and understand that all business is personal.

This information that Carter relayed to the audience is an example of the direction that members of PRSSA are striving for. The faculty/professional liaison of PRSSA, Tamara Plush, commented, "I think he comes across as harsh, but the world is also harsh. He gave a straightforward approach to the business world way of thinking."

Conceive: What is the most newsworthy idea and how should it be developed?

Collect: What additional reporting would you suggest?

Construct: What suggestions can you offer to improve focus, organization and sentence structure?

Correct: What revision would you suggest?

9-2. Revision to tighten and correct style

This story has many extraneous words and style errors. Edit or rewrite it by eliminating the wordiness and correcting the style errors.

A woman named Shirley Anne Hall has up until December 8 to clear up her Garden Grove house of rotten oranges that have gone bad, cobwebs, vehicle parts, musty newspapers and a year's worth of dirty dishes that have not been washed.

Hall, who is age 54, must remove overgrown weeds in her yard and other debris from her yard, which is located in the 12,000 block of Barlett Street, Orange County superior court judge Randell Wilkinson said on Wednsday. If she fails to comply with the order which judge Randell Wilkinson made on Wednesday, the city will bring in work crews and send Hall the bill for the work the crews have done.

The city has been trying to persuade Hall to sort through her mess since the year of 1988, city attorney Stuart Scudder said.

Hall, a woman who is diagnosed with cronic depression, said the city is harrassing her and that the stress that the city has caused her by harrassing her has prevented her from making any progress.

The Dayle McIntosh Center for the Disabled in Anaheim is looking for volunteers who of their own volition will offer to help Hall to clean up.

Adapted from a story in *The Orange County* (Calif.) *Register*. Used with permission.

9-3. Revision to correct grammar and style

These sentences are poorly written, and they contain grammar, spelling and style errors. Rewrite these sentences as directed.

Change these sentences from passive to active voice. In some cases passive voice is preferable. Which do you prefer in these sentences?

1. Fourteen months later, in the fall of 1986, a marriage proposal came from Bob Goldman in the form of a diamond ring tucked inside a fortune cookie.

2. Expectations by Barbara Wasserman and Bob Goldman that their blind date would work out were low.

3. A speech was given by Christopher Carter, an officer in a public relations firm.

4. A 24 year old man was arrested last night and charged with possession of an illegal substance by police.

5. A survey of students to determine weight gain among college freshmen was conducted by two university professors.

Circle and correct the grammatical and style errors in these sentences; rewrite sentences as needed.

6. The professor gave the books to my roomate and I, but we used poor judgement and sold them.

7. The two lovers sat on the bench, sharing a coke.

8. Before leaving for his 2:00 P.M. class, the books were left on the desk by the student.

9. A student filed a complaint charging her professor with sexual harrassment, but the professor, who has taught at the university for twenty years, claimed the acussations were false.

10. The students were honored for thier acheivements, and they recieved special priveledges.

11. The thirty year old man was killed by lightening.

12. When the incident occured, she was embarassed. She admited she had used marihuana, but she claimed she did'nt inhail.

13. When you compile your portfolio but sure to seperate your homework from the outside assignments you wrote.

14. Editors definately want you to know grammer and correct style.

15. City council decided to cancel their meeting, they rescheduled it for 9:00 a.m. tommorow.

16. This assignment will not effect your grade, it should help you recognise the need for checking you're stories.

17. After the council passed it's motion, the audience applauded.

18. He has been teaching economics to sophmore for fourty years.

19. After adopting the ordinence, the meeting was adjourned by the officials who had voted.

20. Everyone did their homework, but the professor said that none of the papers were perfect.

9-4. Story organization

The following story is about a controversial new law in Washington state. The story includes several sources and points of view. The information that follows is not in good order. Read these paragraphs and plan an order for your story. Then reorganize this information using the FORK method described in your textbook. Label your nut graph. You do not have to change the wording in these paragraphs; this exercise is intended only to help you organize a story. You might find it helpful to number your paragraphs when you begin writing.

Under that controversial provision of the state's new Community Protection Act, a sexual offender may be imprisoned even after he has completed his sentence if a case can be made that he continues to represent a threat to the public. The offender may also be ordered to undergo therapy.

Framers of Washington's new statute have said they preserved the rights of both the individual and society. But opponents of the law, including the Washington State Psychiatric Association and the American Civil Liberties Union of Washington, have said those rights have been perverted to appease a frustrated and fearful public. And they have dubbed the law "legal voodoo" and "bad medicine."

Rapist Andre Brigham Young, 49, will go on trial in King County Superior Court this week for crimes he has yet to commit.

Alleging Young is a violent sexual predator who may attack again, prosecutors will ask the court to order Young committed indefinitely under a civil procedure, approved by the Legislature last year.

"There is no clinical basis for determining predatory sexual behavior," said Dr. James Reardon of the Washington State Psychiatric Association.

"There is no reliable data indicating we can forcibly rehabilitate these very violent sexual offenders. And there is absolutely nothing to suggest a mental-health professional can predict with certainty when it is safe to release such individuals," he said.

Young, who was to be released from prison last October, has remained in custody pending the outcome of the proceeding.

Both the psychiatric association and the ACLU have filed briefs in the Young case, opposing the law as medically unfounded and in violation of the U.S. Constitution.

Said David Summers, an attorney who helped prepare those briefs, "I don't think anyone would argue with the motives and aims of the Legislature. But both groups are saying that this is not the way to do this."

Young's trial is expected to take two weeks. However, it is all but certain that the state Supreme Court will hear the case at a later date.

Defense attorneys have already lost an important round in the case. Superior Court Judge Lloyd Bever recently ruled on pretrial motions that the new law is presumed constitutional in light of the Legislature's responsibility to "create laws in the public interest."

King County Deputy Prosecutor Timothy Blood and Assistant Attorney General Jeanne Tweten will argue for the people. Blood was instrumental in development of the civil-commitment law. Defending the statute, he said, "It has some unique aspects, but many are similar to other states' statutory schemes for the civil commitment of sexually dangerous persons."

Summers, whose clients include women who have been sexually exploited or abused, said the law smacks of the same logic that led the federal government to intern Japanese Americans during World War II. "And we since have reached the conclusion that it was the wrong thing to do," he said.

Based on a story by Marla Williams and Julie Emery, *The Seattle Times.* Used with permission.

Leads and Nut Graphs 10

The following exercises will give you practice writing a variety of leads. Before you write your lead you should identify the focus of the story. If you want to write a soft lead, your focus should be your nut graph. If you think the story should have a hard-news lead, your focus should be in your lead. You may find it helpful to write a focus sentence before you write your lead. Instead of struggling to write the perfect lead, try writing several leads and then choose one after you have written more of the story.

10-1. Hard-news (summary) leads

These leads summarize the main point of the story. Choose the most important elements of who, what, where, when, why or how, but don't clutter your lead with all these elements. Place points of emphasis at the beginning or end of the sentence. Read the following information, and write a one-sentence summary lead for each item.

1. A survey was released yesterday by the Child Abuse Prevention Center in Baltimore. The survey shows that three to four children die every day in the United States from child abuse or neglect. Statistics in the survey show that the number of child abuse or neglect cases reported in 1991 rose to 2.7 million, from 2.5 million in 1990. More than half of the children who died were under age 1. Seventy-nine percent of the deaths were among children under age 5.

2. MILWAUKEE – For the past three days nearly 2,500 people have been demonstrating outside of abortion clinics here. Some demonstrators support the clinics and others oppose them. Yesterday nearly 150 of the anti-abortion protesters were arrested. Police said they were arrested on disorderly conduct charges of blocking the entrance to the clinics. The protesters said they planned to demonstrate for six weeks.

3. This information comes from police. A delivery driver for a Chinese food restaurant was taking food to an apartment in your town yesterday. The apartment complex was at 718 S.W. Western Ave. The driver was robbed of the Chinese food at gunpoint. The driver works for The Great Wall of China Restaurant at 1336 S.W. 17th St. A man opened the outside security door for him, and then the man disappeared. A short time later, the man came back and pointed a gun at the delivery driver. The man threatened to kill the driver unless he handed over the food. The driver gave it to him and ran out of the apartment building. Police weren't sure what specific food dishes the driver was carrying.

Based on a story from *The Topeka* (Kan.) *Capital-Journal*. Used with permission.

4. A fire in your town caused $45,000 in damages to a two-bedroom home in the 2300 block of Main Street. Fire officials said the fire was started by a lighted cigarette on a sofa. Firefighters arrived at the house at 3:30 a.m. and found it on fire. They had the blaze under control in five minutes. The homeowner, Kathy Mahoney, was awakened by the smoke and flames. She suffered minor burns on her hands and feet.

5. The state Bureau of Investigation [in your state] yesterday released a report of crime rates for the first three months of the year. The report says murders in your state are up 53 percent and violent crime increased 2 percent. The state bureau officials said the number of rapes and robberies decreased significantly.

6. A United Nations scientific panel released a report yesterday. Researchers of the United Nations Environment Program found that damage to the earth's ozone layer is increasing. They predicted that ozone levels could drop 3 percent in the next decade, which would lead to a 10-percent increase in skin cancer. The ozone layer above the earth absorbs some of the sun's cancer-causing ultraviolet rays.

7. Information comes from police in Santa Ana, Calif. A woman was charged with attempted murder yesterday. She was being held in the Orange County Jail after being unable to post $250,000 bond. Police said the woman, June Carter, 71, doused her husband, who was wheel-chair bound and had cancer, with rubbing alcohol and set him on fire. Police said she was angry because he ate her chocolate Easter bunny. She called paramedics six hours after the attack on her husband. Paul Carter, 62, was taken to the University of California Irvine Burn Center with third-degree burns, police said.

Based on a story by Reuters news service.

10-2. Delayed identification leads

When the person in your lead is not well-known, you can delay identifying him or her until the second paragraph. Instead of using a name, you can identify the person by age, occupation (or affiliation with a group), location or some description, such as, "A man, wearing pantyhose over his head, robbed the grocery store." Write delayed identification leads as directed.

1. Use age as your delayed identification factor. Use your city as the location and yesterday as your time frame. This information all comes from police. Police said a boy's tears may have saved him. The boy was 13. He was walking in the 2700 block of S.E. 10th St. about 5:25 p.m. when a car containing four people pulled alongside. The driver displayed a blue semiautomatic handgun and demanded the boy's jacket. The boy was wearing a Chicago Bulls jacket. The boy started crying. The driver said, "Never mind," and the car left. No one was hurt and no arrests have been made.

Based on a story from *The Topeka Capital-Journal*. Used with permission.

2. Use occupation or affiliation as your delayed identification factor. Mike Haney spoke at your university yesterday. He is a member of the American Indian Movement and one of its founders. He urged the audience to support a ban on using Indian names and symbols as mascots in sports. He said that using Indians as mascots promotes racism. "If all the kids see are those guys out there in the parking lot with makeup on their faces and dyed chicken feathers doing the war whoop, or they just see those TV westerns, that's how they'll perceive us," he said.

Based on a story from *The Topeka Capital-Journal*. Used with permission.

3. Use location as your delayed identification factor. John Sony was in critical condition at St. Francis Hospital and Medical Center yesterday. He just turned 69 yesterday. He is from Emporia (you may substitute your town). He has been diagnosed with Legionnaires' disease, which state health officials suspect he contracted at an Emporia High School reunion. Legionnaires' disease can cause a severe form of pneumonia. The disease was first identified in July 1976 when 34 people died after attending an American Legion convention in a Philadelphia hotel.

Based on a story from *The Topeka Capital-Journal*. Used with permission.

4. Use a descriptive identifier for delayed identification. Information is from police reports. A man unsuccessfully tried to rob an eastside grocery store last night. The man was armed with a handgun. The man was wearing a white sack over his face. He entered the store and demanded money from the cashier at Food 4 Less at 3110 S.E. 6th. St. The cashier leaned against the alarm button. Other customers started coming to the front of the store. The robber fled.

10-3. Advance leads

Advancing the lead means you give the most current information, what is happening now or what will happen next, in the lead. It is also called forward spin. It is a technique often used in broadcast journalism. If an event happened Saturday and you are writing for Monday's newspaper, chances are your editor will want you to advance the lead. Using the following information, write advance leads.

1. The faculty senate voted to require all undergraduates at your school to take courses in cultural diversity. The requirement goes into effect next fall and will begin with the freshman class.

2. (Use a delayed identification as well as an advance lead.) Police report that a man in your town was stabbed in a convenience store in your town last night. He is in fair condition at the hospital in your town today. Police said that Aristide Roberto, 43, was shopping in the Stop and Shop on 450 Elm St. at 2 a.m. last night when a man wearing a jogging suit stabbed him and fled. The assailant has not been found.

10-4. Impact leads

An impact lead tells readers how the story will affect them. Sometimes you may use the word "you" in your lead to personalize the impact, but you also can use a noun, such as "residents" or "voters" or whoever will be affected by the action in the story. Write impact leads for the following information.

1. The U.S. Army Corps of Engineers is conducting a program to install free plastic covering for roofs of homes damaged during Hurricane Andrew. There are five more days to apply for the program. Homeowners whose roofs were damaged during the storm may sign up for the free roof repair at any of the corps offices.

2. Topeka City Council is considering an ordinance to outlaw parking of vehicles in front yards and unpaved side yards. The ordinance would allow vehicles to be parked on private property only if they are on asphalt or concrete driveways. If residents have a gravel driveway, they would be forced to park in the street if the ordinance is adopted. Councilwoman Carol Schimmel, like more than 50 percent of the homeowners in her district, has a gravel driveway. She is opposed to the ordinance. "Where am I supposed to park my car?" she said. The council took the ordinance under consideration and will discuss it again at its next meeting.

Based on a story from *The Topeka Capital-Journal*. Used with permission.

3. The Missouri Board of Curators approved a new tuition rate for the University of Missouri. The tuition will increase 12 percent. That's equivalent to $240 more a year. The increase affects students at all four campuses of the university: Columbia, St. Louis, Rolla and Kansas City. The increase was necessary to help cover a $14 million increase in expenses, said University President C. Peter McGrath. Under the new rate schedule, full-time students who are Missouri residents will pay $67.20 a credit hour. They now pay $60 a credit hour. Juniors and seniors will pay $74.30 a credit hour. They now pay $66.30.

Based on a story from the *St. Louis Post-Dispatch.* Used with permission.

10-5. Attribution in leads

Decide whether attribution is or is not needed in the following leads by writing yes or no:

_____ **1.** An employment workshop for foreign students will be at 3:30 p.m. today in the student union.

_____ **2.** Students will receive their enrollment permits in the mail this fall instead of waiting in line for them.

_____ **3.** A fire that caused an estimated $150,000 damage to a home in the western part of the city was caused by a lighted cigarette on a sofa.

_____ **4.** A man shot and killed his wife because he was convinced she was having an affair with his best friend.

_____ **5.** A woman was arrested and charged with hitting a police officer in the face with her key ring.

_____ **6.** A 28-year-old man bashed a relative's car with a baseball bat Saturday night in a dispute over a baseball card.

10-6. Soft leads

Soft leads usually can be classified as descriptive, anecdotal or narrative. Many times a soft lead will have a combination of these qualities. Using some of the leads in your textbook as models, write soft leads for the information that follows.

1. Write a soft lead, using any technique you wish.

A man in your town was charged yesterday with battery to a law enforcement officer and obstructing official duty. The man was named Harley Dudley Surritte. He was 42 years old and lived at 2313 S.W. Mission Road. He was released on $1,000 bond last night from the Shawnee County Jail. Police said he threw a 2-by-3-foot velvet painting of Elvis Presley off the wall and threw it at officer Chuck Haggard's head. Police said they were sent to Surritte's home at 3:49 p.m. on a report of a domestic fight. Police said Surritte told them he didn't like police officers. "It's the only known Elvis sighting by law enforcement officers in this area," a Topeka police officer said yesterday.

Based on a story from *The Topeka Capital-Journal*. Used with permission.

2. Using the focus-on-a-person technique, write an anecdotal lead for this information and include your nut graph.

Your focus is about the frustrations students experience trying to park on campus because the parking department has oversold the number of permits to students. Nancy Pauw circled the parking lot east of the computer center three times before she found a parking space. Last year there were 7,565 student parking permits sold for the 3,930 spaces. "I have to get here an hour early so I can get to class on time," said Pauw, a graduate student. She is one of many students (on your campus) who experience the daily frustration of not finding a parking space even though they have purchased $30 and $50 permits.

Based on a story from *The University Daily Kansan*. Used with permission.

3. Using the focus-on-a-person technique again, write an anecdotal lead for this information and include your nut graph.

Your community has a home renovation program called Model Block. It is for homeowners who are elderly or disadvantaged and unable to repair their homes. This past weekend 45 people in three neighborhoods in your community were treated to free exterior home remodeling as part of that program. Robert Thompson was one of them. He stood on his newly repaired porch and watched as volunteers, with tools and paintbrushes, scurried around his neighborhood. Thompson and his wife, Flora, were unable to pay for repairs to their home after a van hit the side of their house more than a year ago. Matters became worse when Flora Thompson suffered a stroke that left her paralyzed on her left side. About 400 volunteers took part in the program to give free repairs during the weekend.

Based on a story in *The Topeka Capital-Journal.* Used with permission.

4. Write a descriptive lead and nut graph for this information.

You are writing a story about apartments that violate city codes and are considered hazardous but are often rented to students anyway. You are interviewing a student who lives in an attic apartment. His story is similar to the stories of many other students in this neighborhood, known as Oread. As you climb the steps to his apartment, you notice that duct tape keeps the banister in place on the stairs. You see that the kitchen is infested with mice and roaches. The student, Ted Flis, takes you to the bathroom and says it has no electricity. "It's a dump," says Flis, a senior majoring in architecture. "But it was the cheapest thing I could find." This apartment is located at 1032 Tennessee St.

Based on a story in *The University Daily Kansan.* Used with permission.

5. Write a descriptive lead, using the show-in-action technique. Include a nut graph.

You are writing a story about an Earth Day celebration by students from Topeka High School. The focus is that 75 students spent their first-hour class at Lake Shawnee picking up trash as part of the school's sixth annual Earth Day celebration. You went to the lake and observed the students in action. Star Stickles, one of the students, was walking slowly with her head down as she scanned the ground for litter. Three girls walked alongside her. A strong autumn wind was blowing across the lake and against the backs of the girls. It was 54 degrees, but it felt colder. The four girls continued slowly. Their heads were bowed as they bent periodically to pick trash off the ground and deposit it in a white plastic trash bag. Susan Yeh, a freshman at Topeka High School, is one of the four girls.
"Sock?" she said as she held a water-logged tube sock up for inspection.
"Ooooh, gross," the others chorused.
Star Stickles tells one of the teachers who is supervising the cleanup at the lake, "We also found a belt and a blanket."

Based on a story in *The Topeka Capital-Journal.* Used with permission.

6. Write a narrative lead (reconstructing the event) for the following information:

You are writing an anniversary story about Pearl Harbor, Dec. 7, 1941. On that day, Japanese fighter pilots bombed Pearl Harbor in Hawaii, killing 2,471 Americans and drawing the United States into World War II. The Japanese lost 55 men. You interview a World War II veteran. His name is Earl Schaeffer. On that date he was 19 years old and he was Pvt. Earl Schaeffer. He was stationed at Hickam Field in Oahu, Hawaii. He is a member of the Pearl Harbor Survivors Association, a national organization with about 115 members in your state.

He tells you what he was doing on Dec. 7, 1941. He says it was a quiet Sunday morning. He was sitting at the switchboard at Hickam Field in Oahu, Hawaii. He says not a single phone call came across the wire. The only sound was the voice on the radio, speaking during the "Lutheran Hour." He says he was studying a book about aerial navigation. He wanted to be a fighter pilot. He began to hear sounds of bombing. It hardly drew his attention. Practice maneuvers were common around the base. But the noise grew louder and louder.

"I ran out of the hangar and I saw aircraft swooping down and dropping black objects, and it still didn't dawn on me, because I wasn't expecting anything like that." Then he saw the large red circles painted on the side of the planes, the symbol of Japanese fighter planes.

Based on a story from *The Salina* (Kan.) *Journal*. Used with permission.

7. Change this lead into a narrative lead.

A man threatening suicide kept police at bay for more than nine hours Sunday before he was pulled back from the ledge of a parking garage rooftop.

The man, a 36-year-old Topeka State Hospital patient and Wichita resident whose name wasn't released, threatened to jump from the south ledge of St. Francis Hospital and Medical Center's three-story parking garage at S.W. 6th St. and Mulvane.

Louis Cortez, St. Francis public safety officer, spotted the patient walking toward the ledge on the roof of the garage about 8:40 a.m. Sunday. Cortez stopped his vehicle and told the man over a public address system to move away from the ledge. The patient shook his head no.

"I stepped out and asked him, 'Can I help you, sir?' and he said, 'I'm going to jump,' " Cortez said.

Shortly before 6 p.m., several teenagers in front of St. Francis House, 701 S.W. Mulvane, began shouting, "Don't jump!" and "It's not worth it." The patient shouted back, "You want to see me jump?"

But the teens distracted the patient just long enough for Cortez to grab him around his waist and pull him from the ledge.

Based on a story in *The Topeka Capital-Journal*. Used with permission.

8. Write a mystery teaser lead for this information.

The County Commission in your community voted 2-1 yesterday to pass an ordinance banning the sale or ownership of 16 species of animals "not normally domesticated." Banned were tigers, lions, cougars, leopards, bears, elephants, wolves, wolverines, badgers, rhinoceroses, primates, prairie dogs, foxes, skunks, alligators and crocodiles. The commission's action was prompted by complaints from neighbors of Delores Sampson. To Sampson, her pet named Marriaha is "like any other kitten." She says Marriaha is always trying to jump up on her lap and until recently, she made a habit of sleeping on Sampson's bed. But there is one big difference between Marriaha and other 22-month-old cats. Marriaha is a 300-pound Bengal tiger. Marriaha made a reputation for herself in December when she escaped from a cage on the back porch and traipsed around her front lawn, separated from the neighbor's property by just a 4-foot high chain-link fence. . . .

Based on a story from *The* (Louisville , Ky.) *Courier-Journal.* Used with permission.

10-7. Style quiz

Circle the style errors and correct them in the following sentences.

1. The survey shows that 3 to 4 children die every day from child abuse; more than half of those who died were under age one and seventy-nine % of the deaths were among children under age five.

2. A fire started at 3:00 p.m. and caused 45 thousand dollars worth of damage to a home in the 2,300 block of Main St.

3. Murders in the state are up 53% and violent crime increased two %.

4. A man who threw a two-by-three foot velvet painting of Elvis Presley at officers was 42-years-old.

5. Almost 2500 Americans were killed at Pearl Harbor on December 7, 1941.

6. Tuition will increase twelve % at the University of Missouri and will effect students at all four campuses.

7. 45 people volunteered to repair homes for disadvantaged people.

8. The 36 year old patient said, "I'm going to jump".

9. The two to one vote by the county commission to ban non-domesticated pets will effect Marriaha, a 300 pound Bengal tiger.

10. The tiger lives in a house that has a four-foot fence in the front yard.

Body Building

11

These exercises will give you a chance to see if you can use some of the techniques of award-winning writers like Ken Fuson, featured in your textbook. The exercises will test your abilities to organize middles and endings. Although some day you will develop your own style, if you can learn some of the methods that other writers use successfully, you will be able to decide which ones work best for you

11-1. Story analysis

The following story by *Des Moines Register* writer Ken Fuson includes many of the elements discussed in the text to keep the middle moving. Analyze this story by identifying the following techniques: pacing (mix of short and long sentences), parallelism, natural transitions of quotes, repetition of key words for transitions, and the type of ending – circle, quote or factual kicker. Write your comments in the column next to the story.

Amid euphoria, town mourns soldier's return

PANORA, Ia. – This small town welcomed home one of its soldiers Friday.

But instead of jubilant well-wishers, there were 525 mourners who packed every corner of the United Methodist Church.

Instead of a parade down Main Street, there was a stream of cars that stretched from the church to the West Cemetery outside of town.

There were flags – at half-staff. There were red, white and blue ribbons – tied to flower sprays that surrounded the altar. There were tears – of grief, not joy.

To the rest of the country, Army Spec. Michael Mills was one of 191 Americans killed in the Persian Gulf War, one of 28 people killed Feb. 25 when an Iraqi Scud missile leveled a barracks in Dhahran, Saudi Arabia.

To the 1,100 people here, Mike Mills was the 23-year-old hometown boy who carried on a family tradition by joining the Army.

His funeral Friday provided a somber contrast to the joyous reunions held for returning troops throughout the country.

"It's difficult to stand before you this day when coming-home celebrations for the troops have just begun, knowing they will continue to be held for days ahead," the Rev. Mark Young said. "Yet we believe with all our strength and heart that Michael, too, has come home, in a most victorious way. He has gained the victory of eternal life."

Mills' death, coming so late in a war that was so decisively won with so few casualties, struck hard in Panora and surrounding communities.

Many shook their heads Friday as they recalled the tragic series of events. Mills had been discharged from the Army for 45 days when the war prompted military officials to recall him to duty. He had been in Saudi Arabia just six days when the missile struck. He leaves a wife, Pamela, who is eight months pregnant. She lives in Jefferson with another son, Matthew, who turns 2 next month.

"It's like one of the family is lost," explained Panora Mayor Maryln Adams. "It's a sad day in the community."

That sadness was expressed in the center of town, where 30 flags waved at half-staff, and in a storefront display, where Mills' name was the largest of the two dozen names of area troops, and on the faces of mourners some of whom arrived an hour before the funeral to secure a seat.

"This jarred a lot of people," said Dodie Davis, 18, a high school senior. "They were really upset. We know that people died there, but it just kind of stunned us that someone so close did."

Area communities responded with an outpouring of affection for Mills' parents, David and Rilla, of Panora.

"You really can't say what it means," David Mills said. "You can't put it into words. The whole community is behind us."

For him, Michael's death seemed particularly eerie. Twenty-five years to the day before his son was killed in the missile attack, David Mills was blown out of a tank in Vietnam and burned over almost half of his body. Two other men in the tank were killed.

"But that's all Michael ever wanted to do was to join the Army," his father said. "Ever since he found my uniform."

Inside the church, family members filled one section, while representatives of veterans groups filled another. Friends who couldn't find chairs upstairs were directed to the basement. As they entered, all were given red, white and blue lapel ribbons and a funeral program that featured on its cover an eagle and an American flag.

"Michael will not be forgotten," pastor Young said. "Michael will be remembered being a loving husband and father, out riding a motorcycle, being a sports fan, wrestling and playing football with high school teammates."

Michael died sacrificing his life while serving his country for others."

Two taped songs were played – "From a Distance " and "Mother's Pride." Both gained popularity during the war, especially among the families of troops serving overseas.

Pamela Mills sat near the front, escorted by Tom Bogle of Wellsville, N.Y., who served with Mike Mills in the same platoon at Fort Drum, N.Y.

Seven other platoon members, still in the Army, served as casket bearers. They sat in a row in the middle of the church, their backs square, their jaws firm, their uniforms crisp.

"He was loyal and dependable," said Sgt. George Morgan, Mill's platoon leader. "If the man told you it was done, it was done."

Other platoon members recalled Mills as an upbeat soldier who rarely let the sometimes trivial demands of military life overcome him.

"He was thoroughly considerate, a family man who backed his friends in everything he did," Spec. Joseph Caldwell said. "He'd drop what he was doing in a second to help you out."

At West Cemetery, the platoon members stood to the side of the canopy that covered the burial site. They shivered as fierce winds pounded cold gusts at them.

They saw about 50 veterans salute as six soldiers fired three rifle volleys into the chilled air. They listened to the slow, sad sound of "Taps." They watched as two officers from Fort Sheridan, Ill., folded the flag that covered Michael Mills' casket and presented it to his widow.

Pamela Mills placed three roses on the casket, – one for her, one for their son and one for their unborn child.

After it was over, shielded from view by the canopy, the seven platoon buddies from Fort Drum let down their guard. Huge tears streaked down their faces as they stared at the ground or comforted each other with a pat on the back.

War is a tough business. Even when you win.

"He's home," Caldwell said.

Ken Fuson, Copyright 1991, *The Des Moines* (Iowa) *Register. & Tribune Co.* Used with permission.

11-2. Analyze story style

This story by Patrick Beach, also from *The Des Moines Register,* is an example of how a writer can turn what might have been an ordinary police story into an extraordinary one by using short sentences to build drama, a cliffhanger approach, and good pacing. Study the following story as a model. Label sentences that demonstrate pacing, foreshadowing for the cliffhanger, key words used for repetition in parallel structure and sentence fragments used for effect to build tension. Write your comments in the column next to the story.

Mystery call has police barking up wrong tree

The following nail-biting police drama probably won't find its way onto the "Rescue: 911" TV show, but it's had some folks around Eldridge talking about it since it happened at the end of last week:

A call comes to the Eldridge police dispatcher over the 911 emergency line. The dispatcher answers and asks what the problem is.

No response. Silence. The dispatcher can hear very heavy breathing. That's all. Pretty obvious somebody's in trouble.

Police Chief Martin Stolmeier, on patrol in the area, takes 20 seconds to get to the Frank and Paula Griggs residence, where the dispatcher's computer says the call is originating.

The caller is still on the line. Still breathing heavily. Still needing help.

Stolmeier arrives. Announces loudly that the police are there, begins a room-by-room search. Stolmeier knows somebody needs help. He enters the situation assuming someone may have broken into the house. Maybe some sort of struggle.

Stolmeier nears a downstairs bedroom. The dispatcher hears him over the phone getting closer. On the other side of the door is the situation – the burglar, killer or heart attack victim.

Right about now, if this were a movie, the camera would zoom in very close on Stolmeier's perspiring face and the music would be building to a crescendo of tension and you would be going crazy as Stolmeier at last comes face to face with . . .with . . .

Blaze. A 6-month-old black Labrador who seemed very energetic and very happy to see Stolmeier. In a fit of rambunctious puppyness, Blaze had knocked the phone off the wall and somehow dialed 911.

No word on whether Blaze's phone privileges have been restricted since the incident. But they'd better not tell him about 900 numbers of the Home Shopping Network.

11-3. Copy a style

This is a story that lends itself to the dramatic, lighthearted style that Patrick Beach used in the previous example. Imitate that style by rewriting this story. Include dramatic action and consider building the story to a climax ending — whether or not the skunk is caught. Consider using a mystery lead and try inserting a cliffhanger in the middle.

What's the big stink?
A skunk in the store!

A skunk wandered through the open door of National Furniture Liquidators on Monday afternoon. Throughout the day store employees tried to catch it. By 8 p.m. the store closed and the skunk was still at large. Efforts to capture it had failed.

But when the skunk first walked in, with thousands of dollars' worth of overstuffed chairs, sofas and loveseats at stake, Dennis Goke, acting assistant manager, wasn't taking any chances. So for the first hour, the skunk was allowed run of the place, which is at 1202 Maple Grove Road. It wandered up and down warehouse aisles while employees eyeballed it warily from the doorway.

As customers pulled into the parking lot, they were greeted by the unsettling warning of "Hey – we got a loose skunk in here!"

When three strong and brave employees first saw the skunk, they did what anyone would do. They hid.

Although the employees stayed outside more than in, the store didn't close. Business continued throughout the afternoon, if not exactly business as usual.

"If it would have been a squirrel, I would have chased him out with a broom," said acting assistant manager Dennis Goke.

But it wasn't a squirrel. It was something more powerful – or at least, something with a more powerful weapon.

At one point, the employees tried to lure it out with a trail of whole wheat bread crumbs, but the skunk wasn't hungry.

However, the crumbs attracted dozens of gulls, who screeched and screamed and flapped and gorged until most of the bread was gone.

Store manager Bill Frolichman, who had been on vacation, arrived late in the afternoon to oversee the situation. He decided to wait until closing, then try to spook out the skunk with bright lights and rock music.

Earlier in the day, after the attempts by employees to lure the skunk out failed, Rich Ulkus of Animal Allies arrived to see what he could do. By then the skunk had had enough. There were too many people around, and too much commotion. It disappeared into hiding somewhere in the bowels of the store.

That made employees more nervous than watching it roam the aisles.

Ulkus spent a few minutes on his hands and knees, shining a floodlight under some of the couches and drawing gasps of admiration and comments about his bravery from the others but he couldn't find the skunk so he and Goke baited a trap with tuna, wrapped the tuna in several layers of plastic, then wrapped the whole thing in a blanket and stuck it in a corner.

"I've worked in strange situations before," he said. "I've worked in floods. I've worked without any power in the building." But none of those circumstances had the opportunity to wreak as much havoc as a skunk.

Based on a story from *The* (Duluth, Minn.) *News-Tribune.* Used with permission.

11-4. Endings

Write endings for these stories as directed. The information given is not in good order. The idea (or the actual paragraph) for the ending is in the body of the material.

1. Write a factual kicker for this information:

Marcel Tomio Stahl is a homeless man. On Easter Sunday many residents of South County celebrated the day at church with a large brunch after the service.

Stahl said he thought Easter would be a bad time to seek help. Everyone was too busy and everything was closed. He was wrong.

Some Boca Raton police officers told the 44-year-old that he should try the First United Methodist Church on Mizner Boulevard for some food. Stahl quietly and patiently waited for the Easter Sunday service to let out in hopes of receiving a small meal. After hearing Stahl's misfortune, the Rev. Aaron Ankeny immediately went into the church storage room and got Stahl a bag of canned vegetables. He then referred Stahl to the nearby Salvation Army branch on Northwest Second Avenue for a place to stay.

Nearly 20 centuries have passed since the Crucifixion and Resurrection of Jesus Christ, but on this Easter Sunday, his memory, his deeds and his teachings were not forgotten.

Based on a story from *The* (Boca Raton) *News*. Used with permission.

2. Use a combination factual and circle kicker (a statement that refers to the beginning of the story.) The first two paragraphs are in order; the rest of the story is not. Use one of the paragraphs for your factual/circle kicker.

In seventh grade, Christine Arguello read a magazine article about lawyers. The article specifically mentioned Harvard Law School. She decided at that moment she wanted to be a lawyer and she wanted to attend Harvard.

In fact, Harvard was the only law school she applied to after receiving her undergraduate degree in elementary education in 1980 from the University of Colorado.

After practicing law for 11 years, Arguello decided she needed another challenge. Plus, she always had wanted to teach, she said. Arguello, who is now a University of Kansas law school professor, received the 1991 Hispanic of the Year Award in Colorado and was involved in the Colorado springs community.

She often wonders where she would be if she had not read the magazine article about law school.

Arguello, who specialized in bankruptcy and commercial litigation, was the first minority to become a partner in the prestigious Denver-based law firm, Holland and Hart.

She was also the first Hispanic to be hired by any of the four biggest law firms in Denver.

Being Hispanic was an advantage, Arguello said.

"At times, I had to be twice as good as the next person," she said. "I used it positively and did not dwell on it."

"I want law students to be able to look back and say I made an impact on them as an attorney," she said.

Based on a story from *The University Daily Kansan.* Used with permission.

3. Write a quote ending that serves as a circle kicker for this story. Use the lead, which is the original one for this story, as your clue to find the right ending quote.

David Gottlieb chews out a student on the phone for missing class, telling the teen he's on thin ice. Then Gottlieb turns around and lends another student his car keys.

It's part of an approach Gottlieb uses to teach the 17 Florida Atlantic University students in the Lois Pope National Institute for Teaching Commitment that they have to be responsible for themselves to make it in the world

The 2-year-old program, funded by Lois Pope, widow of *National Enquirer* founder Generoso Pope, offers full $50,000 scholarships to FAU for low-income high school dropouts who have returned for their diplomas. The students promise one thing to get the grant, that upon graduation they will teach kids at risk of dropping out.

"I'm tough. But I'll wrap my arms around the biggest kid, too," Gottlieb said. "I tell them, 'I don't want to figure out what you can't do. I want to figure out what you can do.' "

Eric Davis is an 18-year-old from Baltimore. He dropped out of school in 10th grade because he found it unchallenging, but family and a special teacher urged him to go back for his equivalency degree. A freshman in the Pope program, he believes he'll be able to make a difference.

"If you can give a kid a reason to learn, they will," Davis said.

"We're literally taking these kids off the streets," Gottlieb said. "Some of these kids have been out of school since ninth or 10th grade. Some lived in their cars."

Based on a story from *The* (Boca Raton) *News*. Used with permission.

4. Write a future kicker; select a paragraph from the story or write your own ending.

Topeka resident Gary Henson may have the largest Batman collection in the world.

He hasn't met anybody with more Batman merchandise. His collection contains about 4,000 items.

Henson, who has owned Quality Carpet Cleaning since 1975, would like to eventually open a Batman museum. He would charge $1 admission only for one reason – so he could buy more Batman merchandise.

Henson, 47, does have a wide variety of Batman memorabilia, including several rare items from the 1960s, such as Batman and Robin bubble bath containers and a Batman lamp.

Most of Henson's collection consists of Batman merchandise that was made in conjunction with the 1966-68 television show. A new generation of Batman merchandise was produced when the 1989 Batman movie was released.

Henson believes Batman's mortality is one reason for his popularity.

Based on a story from *The Topeka Capital-Journal*. Used with permission.

5. Write a cliffhanger as though this were part of a series and the next installment will be tomorrow. This information is from the Pulitzer-Prize winning series by Jane Schorer of *The Des Moines Register* about a rape victim's ordeal (a portion is in Chapter 26 of your text). Choose a paragraph or sentence from this abbreviated portion that might work as a cliffhanger if you wanted readers to continue reading the series the next day.

> She would have to allow extra driving time because of the fog.
>
> A heavy gray veil had enveloped Grinnell overnight and Nancy Ziegenmeyer, always methodical, always in control – decided to leave early for her 7:30 a.m. appointment at Grand View College in Des Moines.
>
> It was Nov. 19, 1988, a day Ziegenmeyer had awaited eagerly, because she knew that whatever happened during those morning hours in Des Moines would determine her future.
>
> If she passed the real-estate licensing exam that Saturday morning, she would begin a new career. If she failed the test, she would continue the child-care service she provided in her home.
>
> At 6 a.m., Ziegenmeyer unlocked the door of her 1988 Pontiac Grand Am and tossed her long denim jacket in the back seat. . . .
>
> The digital clock on the dashboard read 7:05 a.m. as she pulled into a parking lot near Grand View's Science Building.
>
> Suddenly the driver's door opened. She turned to see a man, probably in his late 20s, wearing a navy pin-striped suit.
>
> "Move over," the man ordered, grabbing her neck. Then he took her denim jacket from the back seat and covered her head.
>
> "Is this guy going to kill me?" Ziegenmeyer wondered. "Is he going to rape me? Does he just want my money?" She thought about her three children – ages 4, 5, and 7 – and realized she might never see them again.
>
> The man talked constantly. He asked what she was doing in the parking lot. He asked where she worked.
>
> Ziegenmeyer wriggled under the coat, trying to see out, and the man pushed her down.
>
> They drove for a few minutes and pulled into a driveway. . . .
>
> Jane Schorer, *The Des Moines Register.* Used with permission.

66

Story Structures 12

These exercises will give you more practice with various story structures. Before you write your story, think about the type of structure that best suits your material.

12-1. Inverted pyramid

An incident of vandalism at a local middle school has forced the school to close. Reorganize this story in inverted pyramid order, placing the most newsworthy information first and the rest in descending order of importance. Use a summary lead. You may substitute your town or use the places in this story, taken from *The Oregonian*. Put your quotes in separate paragraphs, unless you have two quotes from the same speaker.

Information from the Portland Fire Bureau: A canister of tear gas was set off by vandals (yesterday morning) at the Gregory Heights Middle School. Three students are being sought for questioning. At least 48 children and two teachers were taken to a dozen Portland hospitals for treatment. The fire department was called at 9:31 a.m. A second alarm was sounded at 10:32 a.m. The problem caused no evacuation of homes in the neighborhood around the school. The school is located at Northeast 73rd Avenue and Siskiyou Street.

Students and teachers vomited and suffered a number of other problems, including a burning sensation in the lungs, nose, throat and eyes, due to the gas that apparently was released in a school corridor. The school was closed for the day. The Fire Bureau began allowing staff members to return inside about noon.

From Don Mayer, spokesman for the Portland Fire Bureau: He said the trips to the hospital were precautionary. He didn't know if anyone was in serious or critical condition. "The symptoms the kids are exhibiting are consistent with Mace." He said a Mace-like container was given to investigators by a parent who said it was sold to her son on the school grounds yesterday morning. Mace is a type of tear gas. He said school officials gave investigators the names of three possible suspects. He said investigators were trying to reach those youths.

From the school Principal John Alkire: He said the substance was in the science and math hall area in the northwest corner of the school's first floor. He said the substance was odorless. "It was like walking into an irritating wall."

From Nguyen Do, an eighth grader: He was in class during the morning break. He said he and others went out in the hall and started coughing. "So I covered my mouth and ran out of the building. It's Mace. I know that. It was a set-up to get out of class or something."

From Michael Grice, spokesman for the Portland Public Schools: Students who were not affected by the fumes were sent home about 10:45 a.m. The school district sent buses to take the students home. Classes at the school will resume tomorrow [use the day of the week].

From Jessie Doty, 12, a seventh-grader: "I started coughing. It just stung my throat. My eyes watered and turned red."

From Jeff MacMillan, 12, a seventh-grader: He said he got a headache from the chemical. He said other classmates were worse off, including one girl who fainted and had to be carried from the building.

From Autumn Gierlich, 13, an eighth-grader who suffers from asthma: She was coughing and receiving oxygen shortly after the incident when you arrived at the school. You notice her waiting for an ambulance and you get these comments from her: "I got the stuff into my lungs, and I could barely breathe. I had to gasp for air. I was dizzy. Now I'm feeling better. They gave me oxygen. I coughed and coughed, and spit up phlegm."

From Richard Harder, a paramedic with the Portland Fire Bureau: He said he was one of the first to arrive. He said he saw about 15 children on the ground. Some of them had severe respiratory problems. Others were coughing, vomiting and sneezing.

From Carol Palumbo, an eighth-grade teacher: She was consoling crying students in front of the school after the evacuation. "The kids are really upset. It's just horrendous, whatever it was."

From your observations and basic questions: Students were taken to an area on the front lawn of the school. They were carried by stretcher or walked to ambulances. The children were ages 12 to 15. More than a dozen ambulances were sent to the school. The school is located at Northeast 73rd Avenue and Siskiyou Street. It has more than 900 staff members and students in the 6th, 7th and 8th grades.

Based on a story from *The Oregonian*. Used with permission.

12-2. The High Fives

Rearrange the paragraphs in this story to follow the "High Fives" method described in your textbook. Label the paragraphs for the following factors and place the paragraphs that contain these elements in the first four paragraphs: the news (what the story is about); context (the background of the issue); scope (the national impact, if any); edge (what happens next); impact (how it affects the reader). You may have more than one element in the same paragraph. This story was written for a local newspaper. Consider that when you decide what is the news.

Public health officials investigate all AIDS cases, said Dr. Glenn Davis, medical director of the state's AIDS program.

The case of a Nashville surgeon who reportedly contracted AIDS from an infected patient highlights a continuing debate about balancing professional responsibility and personal safety.

The American Medical Association and the American College of Surgeons have issued statements saying the doctors have a professional responsibility to treat all patients, including those with AIDS.

Only one of the nation's 84,503 confirmed cases of AIDS has involved a health care worker infected on the job, said Charles Fallis of the U.S. Centers for Disease Control. However, there have been several other health care workers who have been infected with the AIDS virus through their work but have not yet developed the disease. Dr. Gary Swinger of the Tennessee AIDS program said there are no documented cases of a doctor becoming infected with AIDS by treating a patient.

"It's always in the back of your mind," said Dr. William Pridgen of Baptist Hospital in Memphis.

Dr. Pridgen said he favors routine testing of all surgery patients, surgeons and operating room staff.

"This would enable us to limit the fee," he said. AIDS tests currently are done only with the patient's consent.

Dr. Pridgen predicted national guidelines on the issue within several years.

AIDS is caused by a virus that attacks and destroys part of the body's disease-fighting immune system. The virus can be transmitted through sexual intercourse and blood from an infected mother to her newborn child.

On Wednesday, Baptist Hospital of Nashville released a statement confirming that Dr. Harold Dennison, a 56-year-old Nashville general surgeon is hospitalized for AIDS.

It is believed he contracted the disease in the course of his surgical practice. He is currently critically ill, the statement said.

Dr. Dennison, his family, Baptist and other hospitals and members of the medical community are cooperating fully with a study of his illness by public health authorities, according to the Nashville Hospital's statement.

State officials believe that Dr. Dennison is the first doctor nationwide to contract AIDS from treating patients but it's something Memphis surgeons have worried about since the epidemic began.

But several local surgeons said they know colleagues who would refuse to operate on AIDS patients or people infected with the AIDS virus.

"I think it boils down to a personal choice. Since I don't refuse to operate on them, (AIDS patients), I get them sent to me all the time," said Dr. Guy Voeller, a University of Tennessee, Memphis, surgery instructor. He also is on the staff at the Regional Medical Center at Memphis trauma center.

Based on a story from *The Commercial* (Tenn.) *Appeal.* Used with permission.

12-3. *The Wall Street Journal* formula

The Wall Street Journal formula is based on the principle of going from a specific to a general point to entice the reader. A story written in this formula usually starts with an anecdote about a person who exemplifies the main point of the story, explained in the nut graph. The story is then organized by backing up the nut graph with specifics and elaboration. The ending is often an anecdote that comes full circle to make the point expressed in the lead. Read the information and write a focus sentence. Then organize the story around that focus. You do not have to change the wording in this story; just reorganize the paragraphs in *The Wall Street Journal* formula order. Plan your order topically, and use the kiss-off technique, blocking information from each source.

Voice-mail systems – manufactured by companies such as Octel Communications, AT&T, Rolm and Northern Telecom – basically are one step beyond the household answering machine. They store messages on fingernail-size computer chips, not the cassette tapes you find in answering machines.

About 85 percent of Fortune 500 firms and 2 million smaller companies are using voice mail, and the $1 billion-a-year voice mail business is still growing 20 percent a year.

Many companies use voice mail as an electronic gatekeeper, routing calls through a main number and an automated attendant. You hear a recording and choose from a menu of departments or services. But it can take a minute or more to go through all the options. This can result in a hefty tab if you happen to be calling long distance. And the 19 percent of U.S. households that still have rotary telephones as opposed to touch-tone phones are really stuck. They can't push buttons to make choices so they're left on hold indefinitely.

Delta Air Lines experimented with voice mail, and some departments – including public relations – discarded it. Says Delta spokesman Bill Berry: "We quickly decided we wanted nothing to do with it. If you call, I don't want you to speak to a mechanical voice."

A company can buy a voice-mail system for $10,000 to $800,000 and can often recoup that investment within 24 hours. Or it can pay the phone company a flat monthly fee for a voice-mail service. Baltimore lawyer Wilbur Jensen, 67,

pays C&P Telephone $5 a month and saves the $1,500-a-month cost of a secretary.

"Once you get used to voice mail, it's irreplaceable," says spokesman Bob Powers of the Institute for Electrical and Electronics Engineers.

Melinda Ayala, 40, of Hollywood, Fla., tried to call the Better Business Bureau every day for a week. "I just couldn't get through," says Ayala. "They say, 'Press 2.' You get a busy signal. A recording says, 'Press 5' to be put on hold. You could go on and on with this all day. I don't think it's any way to run a business."

But others argue that nothing can soothe a customer like the human voice. Phyllis Rosen, 48, a receptionist and phone operator at Lyons Financial Group in Charlotte, N.C., says, "I can make or break sales that come into this company by speaking directly to the people that call, by trying to console them. I don't think a machine can do that. It's a very cold way of dealing with people."

NBC-TV tried using voice mail featuring a lengthy electronic menu at its studios in Burbank, Calif. "It was awful," says Rick Romo, West Coast producer of "Today." It infuriated publicists, advertisers and anyone else who called. Two weeks ago NBC dumped it and returned to live operators.

After Karen Malloy, 48, of St. Louis fell down steps recently and wrenched her back, she phoned her doctor. All she got was voice mail – a computerized recording that said the doctor wasn't available.

Because she couldn't get the

doctor's OK for an emergency-room visit, her insurer refused to pay the $350 charge.

Her frustration with voice mail, shared by millions daily, reflects a growing disenchantment with the technology.

Complaining about voice mail isn't easy either. Who do you call? The Federal Communications Commission The Better Business Bureau? Both use voice mail.

Despite its drawbacks, voice mail seems here to stay. As companies downsize to cope with tough economic times, many use voice mail to trim payroll costs or shift operators into other roles.

Hickory Printing Group in Hickory, N.C., has axed voice mail because "customers hated it," says CEO Thomas Reese. His revenue is running 10 percent ahead of the $27 million level a year ago, and he credits the human touch.

Beyond saving money, voice mail makes message taking more accurate because it eliminates human error. . . .

But customers increasingly complain about being stuck on the phone listening to a computerized voice or leaving messages that are never returned. A recent survey by Plog research found that 56 percent of consumers have at some point given up trying to reach a company because of frustrations with voice mail. Those concerns are forcing some companies to rethink or abandon voice-mail technology.

12-4. Hourglass exercise

Write this story in hourglass form, starting with a hard-news lead. Then proceed in chronological order for a portion or the rest of the story. You do not have to use all the information and quotes from the girl in one block. The point of this exercise is to decide when and where you will begin the chronology. Here are your notes.

You are checking records at the Pasco County Sheriff's Office and you see a report containing this information. A 13-year-old girl shot and wounded her stepfather with a BB gun. She was not charged in the incident. She attends a local middle school. The report says she shot the man, Edward M. Petley of 8031 Lazy Lane in Hudson, after he hit her mother on the head with a frying pan. He is 29. Use yesterday as your time frame. Sheriff's officers will not release the girl's name in order to protect her identity. Her last name differs from her stepfather's.

Petley is being held at the Central Pasco Detention Center in lieu of $15,000 bail. He was charged with aggravated battery against his wife, Jeannette Petley, 33. She is the girl's mother. Before he was jailed, Petley was treated and released from HCA Bayonet Point/Hudson Medical Center for BB wounds in the left side of his face and his back, according to the Sheriff's Office.

You check clips in your newspaper files and discover a story from last May (eight months prior to this incident) that says Mrs. Petley was charged with aggravated assault and battery against her husband after she allegedly tried to run him down with a car and stabbed him in the shoulder with a fillet knife, causing a minor wound. That information was attributed to the Sheriff's Office in the story. You are unable to find out the resolution of those charges before your deadline for this story.

You get the following information from the Sheriff's Office reports:

Petley came home about 5 p.m. He is a commercial fisherman. He began to shout at his stepdaughter. His wife was in the kitchen. She asked him to lower his voice. He took a frying pan and hit his wife twice in the head, hard enough to dent the pan. He then began to kick his wife, who was on the floor.

You interview the daughter and she tells you the following information, some of which is the same as in the sheriff's report.

He (the stepfather) was drunk and he began to shout at her (the girl) and called her names. She says her mother, who is seven months pregnant, was holding her 10-month-old daughter as she stood in the kitchen. The mother asked her husband to lower his voice. The girl says that she and her 12-year-old brother ran to separate neighbors' houses to call 911. When she returned, her stepfather was collecting his belongings, as if to leave. "He was like, wrecking the whole house."   She says he began to chase her around the yard. He was throwing rocks at her. Then she says she took her brother's Daisy BB gun and shot him twice.

"He was coming after me, so I pumped it up and I shot him. It was, like, strange.

"The first time, I didn't know if I hit him. Then I shot him again; then he was holding his neck and said, 'Ohhh.' I did it to help my mom and me."

She tells you that her mother was bleeding from her right ear but declined medical attention when paramedics arrived. She says her mother has been married to her stepfather less than a year.

Based on a story from the *St. Petersburg* (Fla.) *Times*. Used with permission.

12-5. List technique

Itemizing information in a list form can help the reader move though a story. You can use lists in the middle or the end of a story. Lists are often used to clarify bureaucratic stories, especially those containing numbers. Try to keep your lists in parallel construction. You may use more than one list in a story — but usually no more than two. With the information that follows, write a story using the list technique.

The U.S. Census Bureau released a report today. The report was based on a study the bureau conducted in 1990. The study was a survey of 23,000 households in the spring of 1990. The study was called "What It's Worth." It was a study of the value of a college degree. The study revealed that if you get a college degree, your income will increase by about $1,000 a month. The study said any post-high school degree, whether it is a trade school certificate or a professional degree, will increase earning power. The study said that more adults than ever – 25.2 percent – now have a post-high school degree. The author of the study, Rebecca Sutterlin, said that's up 20.7 percent from 1984. But the study showed some racial disparities as well as other differences.

People with post-high school degrees earned an average of $2,231 monthly, compared with $1,280 for those with some college but no degree. People with just a high school diploma earned $1,077 a month and those who don't have a high school education averaged $492 a month.

In engineering, 15 percent of men had degrees but only 2 percent of women.

The average monthly earnings for professionals were $4,961. People with a doctorate averaged $3,855 a month. People with a master's degree averaged $2,822 a month and those with a bachelor's degree averaged $2,116 a month.

On the average, blacks earn significantly less than whites at each educational level, with the exception of blacks with master's degrees. Blacks with bachelor's degrees earned an average of $1,814 a month, compared to $2,149 for whites.

Of the adults over 18 who hadn't finished high school, 19.4 percent were white, compared with 31.9 percent of blacks and 43.8 percent of Hispanics. For college degrees, 26.4 percent of whites have college degrees, compared to 14 percent of blacks and 11.6 percent of Hispanics. (See chart next page.)

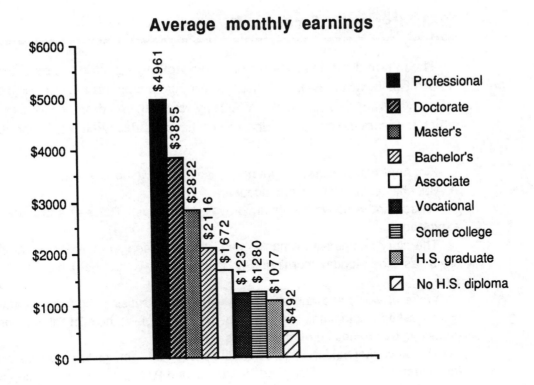

Average monthly earnings

- Professional — $4961
- Doctorate — $3855
- Master's — $2822
- Bachelor's — $2116
- Associate — $1672
- Vocational — $1237
- Some college — $1280
- H.S. graduate — $1077
- No H.S. diploma — $492

12-6. Pyramid form

The pyramid form is old-fashioned storytelling – in chronological order from start to finish, which is the climax. Rearrange the paragraphs in this exercise to follow a pyramid-order story. You may retain the lead and second paragraph, which are from the original story, so you have an idea what this is about.

Kim Amack says she was sure her house had blown up Monday.

But she couldn't tell anyone about it.

Amack and a co-worker finally drove to the house Tuesday and found it hadn't exploded.

The story begins with Amack setting off insect foggers inside her house on the city's east side Monday morning. She then went to work at her job on the city's west side.

While at work, she and a co-worker began discussing the foggers and the co-worker asked whether she had remembered to extinguish the pilot lights on her natural gas stove before setting off the foggers.

The co-worker said the flame from the pilot light might ignite the fogger and cause the house to explode. Panicked, Amack dialed 911 to send the fire department to check on her house.

Between 10 a.m. and noon Monday there were 80,000 more calls than usual to the downtown Topeka telephone circuits, Southwestern Bell reported Monday.

The first day of ticket sales for November performances of the Broadway musical "Cats" at the Topeka Performing Arts Center prompted the 70 percent increase over normal numbers of calls.

She was calling from the business phone at the Sonic Drive In, 1151 S. W. Gage. Dudley Havens, a restaurant patron, said he used the pay phone at the business to try to call 911 for Amack. He, too, got a busy signal.

The calls were placed from approximately 10:45 a.m. to approximately 11:15 a.m.

Instead of a fire department dispatcher, Amack says she got a busy signal.

Over and over – for nearly 30 minutes.

Southwestern Bell is investigating the apparent 911 malfunction.

Fire department officials said Tuesday the pilots lights likely wouldn't have ignited the bug spray, but as one fire department veteran said, "Anything's possible."

She said police and fire department administrative phone lines also were busy.

"You couldn't get through to anybody," she said. "It was pretty scary."

Based on a story from *The Topeka* (Kan.) *Capital-Journal.* Used with permission.

12-7. Sections technique

The use of sections for stories is usually reserved for long, in-depth stories. Breaking a story into sections offers the reader some visual relief from a long block of type, and it also serves to organize the story into parts. The most common ways to divide a story into sections are by time frames (present to past to present to future) or by points of view. You can also use sections for a story that has different elements – such as different settings or a mix of anecdotes and research material. Ideally, each section should end with a kicker, almost as though each section were a separate little story. Read the excerpts from following story, which was published in sections. Decide where you would split this story in sections; write the lead and ending for each section. That will help you recognize how sections are structured with good leads and kickers. This story had five sections, but you may decide you want more. Analyze how this story is divided. What topical order did you use to define sections?

Lost souls

Alzheimer's disease extracts an exceedingly high price – physical, emotional and financial – from both sufferers and care givers.

Five weeks ago, 75-year-old Winnifred Dasher fell and broke her arm. She lay on the floor while her 79-year-old husband stepped over and around her for two days.

John Dasher had been a talkative, outgoing salesman. But Alzheimer's disease has robbed him of his ability to telephone for help.

For his family, it was the turning point in a gradual process, the revelation that caring for him at home was no longer possible.

"It's insidious," said his daughter, Linda Printz. "We thought Mom was coping, because it all happened so gradually. Suddenly, it was obvious that his illness was endangering her."

Dasher is just one of the estimated 76,000 Oregonians suffering from Alzheimer's disease, a brain disorder that steals victims' minds, personalities and, eventually, their lives.

Alzheimer's is an incurable, untreatable disease with unknown causes. It is the fourth leading cause of death of American adults.

The disease has commanded almost unprecedented attention since a Portland Alzheimer's patient was found abandoned last week at an Idaho dog track. Authorities are investigating John Kinger's removal from a nursing home and the finances of a daughter who lives in Hillsboro.

The abandonment focused attention on the strain the disease can place on families of Alzheimer's sufferers. According to one estimate, up to 70,000 elderly parents may have been abandoned last year by family members who were unable or unwilling to care for them any longer.

"I can't see abandoning kittens, let alone a grandfather," Printz said. "Everyone has a different threshold, different abilities to deal with other people's illness. After a while the frustration and anger can make you irrational.

"But there is no excuse to dump anyone," Printz said. "There is too much help available on every level – medical, legal, financial, care-giving options, counseling."

The Alzheimer's Association, informally associated with Good Samaritan Hospital & Medical Center, is the clearinghouse for information on the disease in Oregon. It offers workshops, runs support groups and maintains a communications network with the many public and private care and counseling services in the Northwest.

"Until medical science comes up with something, all we can do is stand by the families who are dealing with it," said Liz McKinney, executive director of the association's local chapter.

Printz was alerted to her parents' plight after an uncle tried unsuccessfully to reach her mother. . . . [Story continues with comments from Printz about her father]

". . .He's like a 3-year-old in a man's body,"

Printz said. "But a 3-year-old can learn. He can't."

The number of people over age 65 is expected to double, from 30 million now to nearly 60 million by the year 2030. People over the age of 85 make up the fastest-growing segment of the elderly.

A generation of baby boomers is being squeezed between caring for elderly parents and their own children. Sometimes, however, the healthy spouse must assume the responsibility of care.

Daryl Walton, 80, lived with his wife for 58 years, but he knew he could no longer keep her at home when she fell one night and he could not lift her.

[Story continues with anecdotes and quotes from Walton about his problem, the emotional and financial burden.]

The financial burden can be crushing. Caring for a patient at home can reach $30,000 a year. If there are other medical complications the costs can get bigger.

Anne Walton now lives in a private foster home.

Sen. Mark O. Hatfield had to make a similar decision to find help outside the family when Alzheimer's afflicted his father, Charles Dolan Hatfield.

"You can deny this disease as long as you can," Hatfield said. "But after a while you can't. At first, the behavior is peculiar, like neglecting to flush the toilet or drain the bathtub. My father was 80, so a little forgetfulness seemed normal.

"But then he would wander and couldn't get home. A neighbor two blocks away would call my mother and say he was at their house. . . . "

Hatfield recently initiated a program to identify Alzheimer's sufferers who wander and get lost, a frequent symptom.

Just last week, Hatfield led a policy forum for the National Alzheimer's Association. Hatfield said he would seek another $1 million for the "wanderers" program next year and $8 million for respite care.

"I can tell you from experience, he told the forum "that it's frightening when a family member wanders from home."

At Marylhurst Care Center, 24 nuns are receiving care from their family, their religious community.

"There can be a terrible loneliness with this disease, so we try to involve them to the greatest extent possible," said Sister Clare Murphy, the care center administrator.

One patient with Alzheimer's, Sister John Mary Lane, cannot wander as she once did. Born Kathleen Lane 87 years ago, she was a daily swimmer and strong hiker. Now she trudges endless sentry duty up and down the halls of the Marylhurst Care Center.

[Story continues about Sister John Mary Lane.]

Lynn Szender, Marylhurst director of nursing, said patients are considered part of the community.

"There are different ministries," Szender said. "Teaching, care-giving, prayer. We feel that these women are still part of the prayer ministry, even if we can't seem to reach them. They are still nuns, still praying in some area of their being."

Prayer is a major part of the lives of Barbara Savage, 68, and her husband Virgil, 71. They have been married 49 years.

He is a retired Baptist preacher with Alzheimer's, and she cares for him full time. Aided by their four grown children and three foster children, she intends to keep him with her in their manufactured home in a Clackamas mobile home park.

[Story continues with more information about Virgil Savage and returns to the person in the lead for circular reference.]

Like John Dasher and Anne Walton, Virgil Savage is a "sundowner." He gets nervous at twilight and dislikes the night.

"Their brains process what their eyes see differently from us," Barbara Savage said. "He can think that what he sees on TV is happening in the room with him. For some reason, 'Star Trek' really bothers him.

"But he loves music, and tracks it. We had 'Monday Night Football' on without the sound and had 'Swan Lake' on the turntable. He loved that. He's always had a great sense of humor, and he said those were the clumsiest ballerinas he'd ever seen."

Ted Mahar, *The Oregonian*. Reprinted with permission.

Storytelling 13

This chapter will help you develop ways to make your writing more colorful by using descriptive and narrative writing techniques. You can apply storytelling to news, such as crime and court stories, as well as feature stories.

13-1. Analyze a story

The following story by Matthew Purdy of *The Philadelphia Inquirer* is an example of how a reporter used storytelling techniques for a court hearing. This story uses description based on observation and show-in-action techniques. Gene Foreman, deputy editor of *The Inquirer*, said this story "illustrates how a reporter, by listening sensitively and observing carefully, can give readers a glimpse of human drama. A lesser reporter would have made this a routine news story."

Indeed, it could have been written in a hard-news fashion without any drama, something like this version:

An inspector in the Philadelphia Housing Authority was sentenced yesterday to eight months in prison, a $5,000 fine and two years' probation for extorting money from the city.

Virgil Mariutti, 38, was caught shaking down contractors whose work he was supervising. Sometimes he asked for and received as much as $250 a week. Other times he got a bicycle, carpeting for his house or a radar detector for his car.

Although a grand jury is conducting an extensive investigation of corruption at housing authority, Mariutti, a low-level inspector in the housing authority, is the only employee to be charged so far.

Yesterday more than 70 friends and family members attended his sentencing hearing in U.S. District Court.

Several friends pleaded for leniency.

The Rev. Edward Kelly described the Mariuttis as a loving family. He told the judge that if Mariutti were taken away, even for a short time, "it would be like death."

But Barry Gross, assistant U.S. attorney, said federal investigators had documented more than 100 incidents of Mariutti's extortion scheme. He said Mariutti continued extorting money from contractors even after he was informed by hand-delivered letter last summer that he was a target of a federal probe.

U.S. District Judge Robert F. Kelly sentenced him to serve eight months in prison, plus a $500 fine and two years' probation. Kelly said that Mariutti didn't invent the system which allows corruption.

"It is something that takes place in large government projects," he said. "But when it is found out, it has to be dealt with."

Compare that version with the following written by Matthew Purdy. Underline the details that come from observation. Analyze the type of story structure – inverted pyramid, pyramid, hourglass, or whatever you think the writer used. Discuss which version you prefer. Note that the writer referred to the priest as "Father Edward Kelly" to create a more familiar tone instead of using the Associated Press style, "The Rev. Edward Kelly." Unless your editor and newspaper allow such exceptions, stick to the AP style.

A family man faces sentencing

The crime seemed so far away yesterday. Reduced to typewritten citations of laws broken, it was carried in lawyers' square briefcases, destined to be filed with so many thousands of other lifeless documents.

The charge was extortion, and months ago the defendant had pleaded guilty. Now he was in court to receive his sentence.

Virgil Mariutti, who worked at the Philadelphia Housing Authority as an inspector, was caught shaking down contractors whose work he was supervising. Sometimes he asked for and received as much as $250 a week. Other times he got a bicycle, or carpeting for his house or a radar detector for his car.

Mariutti, 38, worked in public housing, a dismal world of leaking pipes and collapsing roofs, of patronage and poverty. An unpleasant stew, to be sure.

Mariutti's life in Philadelphia is defined by more pleasant certainties – his wife and three children, Sunday Mass at Saint Monica's, Friday night bowling with the kids. His misdeeds have made a tragedy of Mariutti's life since his arrest last year. And yesterday, as the final act of his sentencing was upon him, an opera of voices filled the courtroom, nearly crowding out the facts that made all this necessary.

Friends who have known him for 20 years say they were shocked at the news of his arrest. The feds found him early one September morning as he sat at work eating a lemon pie, and took him away in handcuffs.

There's a big investigation of corruption at the housing authority, volumes of information have been subpoenaed, witnesses have told their stories to the grand jury under threat of prison. But so far, Mariutti, a low-level inspector, is the only employee to be charged.

Mariutti sat with his lawyer as behind him more than 70 friends and family members filed into court like parishioners, wearing everything from suits to leather jackets, hair neat, their eyes expectant, their voices whispers.

Just a few witnesses, attorney Anthony List assured U.S. District Judge Robert F. Kelly.

Anita Ciccotta, a friend of the Mariuttis', put her left hand on the Bible and raised her right hand clutching a piece of yellow Kleenex. "It didn't seem like the kind of person I knew," she said. "It's a heartache."

Ciccotta said Mariutti and her husband coach youngsters on the ballfield. . . .

Father Edward Kelly described the Mariuttis as a loving family who live in an immaculate home. "They're a very close, traditional family," Father Kelly said. "If he were taken away, even for a short time, it would be like death."

There were other witnesses, who described Mariutti's caring for his grandmother, helping his brother overcome a drug problem, ferrying his ill father to appointments for radiation and chemotherapy.

His wife, Diane, testified that in the middle of the night, when he thinks she is asleep, Mariutti whispers apologies to her. "He's just so sorry it happened,' she said. "His eyes are sad. He's sad. I'm sad."

She said that he gave the money he extorted to her and that she thought it came from his grandmother. She said she spent it on their three children.

"I thought it would put a little culture in their lives, a little piano, dance lessons for my daughter," she told the judge.

She pleaded to keep her husband out of jail. "We would fall apart. We would totally fall apart," she said. "My children don't know anything. I would like to keep it that way."

Mariutti, his eyes indeed sad, told the judge that when he began working at PHAA, he found that contractors were making payments to inspectors. "It was very easy money," he said. "I was motivated by my desire to provide my kids with the finer things in life."

He said he meant no harm. He figured he was only taking part of the profits from contractors. He apologized and asked for a sentence that would punish him alone, and not his family.

Finally came Barry Gross, a tall assistant U.S. attorney who disputed nothing that had been said.

"We've heard the giving part," he told the hushed courtroom. "Now we must describe the taking part.

He said federal investigators had documented more than 100 incidents of Mariutti's extortion scheme. He said Mariutti extorted as much as $250 a week from contractors whose work he was overseeing.

Gross said that Mariutti continued extorting money from contractors even after he was informed by hand-delivered letter last summer that he was a target of the federal probe.

Documents filed in court yesterday said that Mariutti is cooperating in the investigation.

Judge Kelly took a break. The courtroom cleared and a cloud of cigarette smoke erupted in the hallway.

Kelly, who sat impassively during the hour of testimony, was struck by what he had heard.

"This is one of the most difficult sentences I have to impose," he said, after returning to the bench.

"On the one hand we have large segments of some of the most respected members of a community who have come to vouch for Virgil Mariutti," he said. "On the other hand, we have had, for a period of five years, extortion."

Mariutti stood facing the judge.

"Virgil, I know you didn't invent the system. You came into something already in progress," Kelly said.

"It is something that takes place in many large government projects. But when it is found out, it has to be dealt with."

Kelly gave him eight months in prison, a $5,000 fine and two years' probation. Mariutti could have faced two years in prison.

There were only muffled tears. Briefcases shut. The sentence spoken was accepted. Mariutti walked out of the courtroom with a blank stare.

Matthew Purdy, *The Philadelphia Inquirer*. Reprinted with permission.

13-2. Storytelling for a crime story

The following information could be written as a basic crime story or it could be presented in more dramatic storytelling form. Write this story using narrative writing style to reconstruct the event. Here are your notes:

It is the Christmas season. A woman was shopping at the Galleria shopping mall in Fort Lauderdale. A man robbed the woman after she got into her unlocked car. The suspect has not been caught. Police described him as a white man about 27 years old, 5 feet 7 inches tall, with brown hair and brown eyes. He was described as clean-shaven but unkempt. He stole her wallet.

You interview the woman who was robbed. Her name is Pauline Cayia and she lives in Fort Lauderdale.

She said she finished shopping about 7 p.m. Sunday and returned to her unlocked car at the Galleria mall. She said she had been shopping for about an hour and a half. She manages a recording studio. She said the robber was polite and well spoken.

She said he took her wallet but on Monday (a few hours before you interview her) she received a phone call that her wallet had been found. It was returned along with her credit cards and driver's license. Only her $85 in cash was missing.

She said as she got into her car, she smelled a strong body odor. She drove away from the shopping center at 2700 E. Sunrise Blvd. and a man popped up in the back seat and demanded her purse. She said the robber went through her purse as she was driving south along Federal Highway toward Broward Boulevard.

"Before I got in the car, I looked around and didn't see anything. I smelled an odor when I put my packages in the front seat, and I checked the back seat, but I didn't see anybody. I suppose he was sleeping, because he didn't say anything until I got to Federal Highway.

"He said, 'Ma'am, give me your purse and let me off here.' I started going fast to try to attract the attention of a policeman, but I didn't find anybody to stop me. I was going fast, and he said, 'You're going to kill us.' "

When she was driving toward Broward Boulevard, the robber returned her purse. "He said, 'Here's your purse' and threw it into the front seat, but he kept my wallet."

At Federal and Broward, Cayia slowed to turn and ended up hitting a car. At that point, the robber jumped out and ran, even though the car was still moving. She drove directly to the police station. "I don't know if I was scared or in control. I just wanted to get the police."

Based on a story from the *Sun-Sentinel* (Fort Lauderdale, Fla.). Used with permission.

13-3. Descriptive writing

You are writing a feature about a school for homeless children in Spokane, or you could substitute your community. Use the show-in-action technique and other description to let the reader see and hear the children at this school. Some of the information is presented here as the writer, Diana Dawson of *The Spokesman-Review* in Spokane wrote it. Here are your notes:

This school for homeless children is designed as a collaborative effort between the YWCA, Spokane School District and the city's shelters. District 81 provides two certified teachers and a teacher's aide. The school is among only about a dozen such classrooms nationwide for an estimated 220,000 children. Washington state has three of these schools and another five are planned. Last year shelters took in 18,000 children in Washington and turned away another 37,000.

Classes are open to children from kindergarten through the eighth grade for however long they are without a home. One student stayed only a few hours. Another stayed 46 days.

Marylu Wade, one of the teachers, said, "You know you don't have them for long, so you do more for them. It's being open, friendly and giving them lots of hugs. The less response I get, the more I know they need."

Program coordinator Ann Morling tries to keep track of the families. She tells you that some disappear without leaving a forwarding address. Others fill up the gas tank and don't know where they'll stop. She says that a few weeks ago, a 10-year-old girl living in a car with her mother moved to California for warmer parking grounds.

"As she left, she waved goodbye and said, 'See you next year,' " Morling says. "You don't know whether you'll see her again. But you figure that while she was here she had at least two meals a day, she got a new coat and some education. The rest is out of our control."

School supplies, breakfast, lunch and bus transportation are provided. Everyone gets a shower at least three times a week on the days the children swim. Parents may pick through the donated clothing and take all they need for their family.

You visit the school and you observe children playing. One of them is Rose Wilt. She has crooked bangs. She sweeps them from her eyes and bites her lip as she presses another Lego block into place. She says, "I'm building a house, my house. I want a stove in it."

She sits up tall on her knees so she can see into the Lego barrel to find just the right pieces. You continue watching. She slowly begins pushing six red blocks into the floor of her house. You ask her what they are. She says, "These are the beds. Mom and Daddy and my two brothers and sisters and me will live here."

A study by the Washington State Coalition for the Homeless in 1988 found that 19 of 80 homeless families kept their children out of school because they lacked the money and transportation, clothing and school supplies.

The 127 children who have come through this school's doors since May have been from families shattered by domestic violence and from families who have just run out of luck, either for the first or the 50th time. They've been sleeping in shelters, transitional housing, their parents' cars.

Teacher Kim Schultz blows through the room like a warm breeze. Children cling to her legs and pull at her fingers as she brings to order 25 students of the school. It's known as the YWCA School. She pulls an American flag from its stand. "OK, time for the opening. Let's push those toys into nice, neat piles."

She sweeps her hand and without knowing it, Rose's house falls to pieces.

After breakfast, the little girl darts back to the Lego barrel. She risks receiving a disciplinary warning so she can jam extra blocks into another house.

A "Where Have We Been?" map is tacked to the office wall with red pins marking the last place each child lived. They dot most states, West Germany and the Virgin Islands.

The children are on the third floor of the YWCA. Schultz calls the roll. The children tell her what has become of her students who disappeared overnight.

"The other girl ain't here," one child says.

"They got a house," a boy pipes up.

"They're all living on a bench in a park," a kindergartner argues.

"No, silly," explains an older student. "They got a house with a friend in Deer Park."

Their lives are as varied as their reasons for being homeless. Some have Nintendo games at home and others have never eaten pizza. One mother takes used textbooks donated from a public school and tries to help teach her children. Another mother sends her little girl to school wearing soiled adult underwear and bearing suspicious bruises. The YWCA must meet all their needs.

Schultz peels a label off a desk bearing a former student's name and slaps a new name on top of it. This week, school started on Tuesday with 25 students, went down to 20 by the end of the day and up to 30 on Wednesday. One day during lunch a mother fleeing an abusive husband comes to the school and taps her daughter on the shoulder. "Today's your last day," she says softly.

The girl has been eating a corndog drenched in mustard. She pauses between bites. "Today?" she asks. Then she says, "OK," shakes her bangs from her eyes and turns back to her lunch.

Eleven-year-old Hank Boblitz squints his eyes, furrows his brow and strains to read about a frog and a toad. He's considered a bright child who simply refuses to work. His attention wanders, turning from story time to mischief.

"Hank, that was wonderful," says Sandra Ingebritsen, a teacher's aide. "I want you to read this one more time and then whip in there and surprise Miss Schultz by reading to her. Can you do that?" He breaks into a not-on-your-life grin, leans forward and spreads his fingers across his face. He casts his chestnut eyes down to his oversized Seahawks T-shirt. "I don't want to," he says.

Based on a story from *The Spokesman-Review* (Spokane, Wash.) Used with permission.

13-4. Narrative writing

A young boy named Jacob Wetterling disappeared from a community in St. Cloud, Minn. a year ago. (The boy actually disappeared on Oct. 22, 1989.) He is still missing. Imagine that this story occurred in your community and your editor wants you to do a major story about how the child's disappearance has affected his family, friends and the community a year later. You decide to do a series from the points of view of people who were close to Jacob or involved in the search for him. The first story will focus on the father. Write this in narrative form, reconstructing the events of a year ago. For this story, you may take the liberty of calling the father by his first name to prevent confusion with his son's names and establish a more intimate tone. Here are your notes; you may copy some of these paragraphs; just rearrange them in narrative order. Try a lead that reconstructs the event.

The father of the boy is Jerry Wetterling. He says he is haunted by the disappearance of his son, Jacob. He had taken his boys, Jacob, 11, and his other son, Trevor, 10, ice skating at Municipal Ice Arena on the afternoon of Oct. 22. That was the day Jacob disappeared. He later learned that his son was kidnapped by a masked gunman on the rural road near his home. His boys had gone to a Tom Thumb store to rent a video while he and his wife were at a party. Jacob never returned. Jerry has questions: Was the man who abducted Jacob somewhere in the arena that afternoon watching Jacob? He asks himself why didn't he think to check the bleachers. Did the man follow him and his boys home? Jerry shakes his head. He doesn't know. He has wrestled with those questions and more since the night his son was taken.

There is much he doesn't understand. People accuse him of taking his son. They say he smiles too much. He doesn't break down on camera. And he belongs to an unusual religion. He's a Baha'i. A rumor spreads that Baha'is sacrifice their first-born sons.

He says those people don't know him. They don't know his spiritual nature. He seeks solace in prayer more than in people. They don't know that he is a quiet man. It's not easy for him to share his feelings.

And, most of all, those people don't know how much he loves his son.

He says it hurt him when people accused him of abducting his son. "Still does," he says.

He says he will run in today's Twin City's marathon and wear a "Jacob's Hope" T-shirt to remind people that his son is still out there, waiting to be rescued.

He says he tries to understand. People, he reasons, don't want to think that this was random violence. They don't want to think that it could happen to anybody.

He says people want to think that he took him. That way their kid is safe.

Jerry keeps up the hope in his own way. He believes Jacob is alive. He is sure he is going to be found. "Statistics," he reasons. "Of 800 people who have been abducted, half of them are found. Half of those are found alive.

"I know that's only one in four." His voice trails off.

You ask him to recall the events of the day Jacob disappeared.

He remembers when he got the phone call that night that his son was missing. He and his wife, Patty, had gone to a party in St. Augusta, about 15 miles from their rural St. Joseph home. Jacob was going to babysit for his sister, Carmen, 8.

The boys called their parents at the party. Patty took the first call from them. They wanted to bike to the Tom Thumb store to rent a movie. Patty said no. But she told Trevor, who was calling, to ask his father.

On the second call, Jerry caved in. He says he gave them permission but he told the boys to use the reflective vest he wears jogging at night and to take a flashlight. The daughter of a neighbor would watch Carmen, the boys told him.

Then the third call came from his neighbor. Jerry remembers his neighbor's words: "Jerry, the boys went to the store for a video. Jacob didn't come home. He was taken by a masked gunman. I want you to get Patty and come home."

He says he and his wife drove home in the family's blue Toyota in silence for the 20-minute drive. Patty cried.

The rest of the night is a blur of police, people, the press and more people.

You ask him to recall the afternoon before Jacob disappeared.

He says the night before Oct. 22, he had talked with his boys about an early morning fishing trip. Trevor decided to sleep in. Jacob would go. He loves to fish and is good at it.

That morning, Jerry recalled he was the first one up. Before the rest were up, he jogged about four miles. It was a nice day; the temperature was in the 40s.

Jacob was waiting for his dad when he returned. They loaded the fishing boat and headed for nearby Big Fish Lake.

He says the walleye were nowhere to be found, though. Jerry says he and his son said little, but they shared much. They quietly searched the shoreline and marshes for blue herons. As noon approached, the pair reeled in the lines, packed up and hustled for home. They wanted to be home in front of the TV for the Vikings/Lions noon kickoff. The action was so lopsided, Jerry, Jacob and Trevor left for the ice arena. Hockey season was under way and the boys wanted to put in some extra practice time.

He says he remembers that when he took his sons ice skating, he had a feeling that day that Jacob was in danger. He says the feeling hit while he and his boys, Jacob and Trevor, skated at the Municipal Ice Arena. He says from his spot on the ice, he searched through the Sunday afternoon skaters for a bully. He didn't see one, nor any reason to be alarmed. He says he brushed the feeling aside. He didn't remember having it, until five days later – five days after his son was kidnapped by a masked gunman on the rural road near their home. He says they came home from the rink and played football for a while before he and Patty went to the party.

Based on a story from the *St. Cloud* (Minn.) *Times.* Used with permission.

The Art of Brevity   14

This chapter will help you improve your selectivity for all stories, not just for writing briefly. If you can decide what the most crucial elements are for a brief, you will be able to tighten your writing.

Briefs are abbreviated stories that usually range from one or two sentences to one to three paragraphs. Some briefs may be longer, as many as five paragraphs. Brights are briefs with a strong kicker. They are usually written about humorous or unusual subjects. Read the following information and write briefs and brights as directed.

14-1. Briefs

a. Write a brief of one or two sentences based on the following information:

A Colorado State University professor of environmental health has studied the lifestyles of 51 dogs with lung cancer. John Reif, the researcher, found that dogs with short noses are 50 percent more likely to develop lung cancer when they live with owners who smoke. The researchers also studied 83 dogs with other forms of cancer. Reif is using the dogs as models to study the environmental effects of smoke on human beings. He said the study confirms findings that exposure to environmental tobacco smoke increases the risk of human lung cancer. Reif found that long-nosed dogs, such as collies and retrievers, seemed to be protected against passive smoke. The study appeared in the American Journal of Epidemiology. Reif is also studying the effects of pesticides on dogs.

b. Write a two-paragraph brief based on the following information.

   A University of South Florida professor is operating the country's first solar-powered vehicle. The professor is Lee Stefanakos. He is chairman of USF's electrical engineering department. He is operating the vehicle at the university's Tampa campus, which is the test site for a fleet of 12 electric vans, cars and trucks. The vehicles get their energy from the sun. The vehicles have solar panels mounted in a carport roof. The solar-powered cars come equipped with air conditioning and other options. The vehicles cover up to 60 miles on a charge and can reach speeds up to 55 miles per hour. The cost of operating the vehicles is about 4 cents per mile. The cost of operating a gasoline-powered car is about 40 cents a mile. The solar-powered cars have 36 batteries mounted under the vehicle. They weigh a total of 1,200 pounds. "Florida does not have any energy resource of its own except the sun, so it makes sense to use it," Stefanakos said. The university received a $1 million grant from the U.S. Department of Energy to study ways to make motorists less dependent on gasoline.

Based on a story from the *Sun-Sentinel.*, (Fort Lauderdale, Fla.) Used with permission.

c. Write a two-paragraph brief based on the following information:

   The National Organization for Women is sponsoring a conference this weekend in your town. The conference is called "Women Victorious." It will be held in The Holiday Inn on 2500 Main St. in your community. The conference is open to the public. The keynote speaker is Alicia Partnoy, an activist with the human-rights group Amnesty International. Some of the events on Friday include: A discussion on gender bias from 2 to 4 p.m.; a workshop on coping with breast cancer from 4:30 to 5:30 p.m. and a discussion of recent U.S. Supreme Court decisions on abortion from 7:30 to 9 p.m. On Saturday: A workshop on issues of family leave and gay and lesbian rights, from 2 to 4 p.m. and a workshop on sexual harassment from 4:30 to 6 p.m. On Sunday: a brunch for $20 per person. The money will be used to support female political candidates.

d. Write a one-paragraph brief based on the following information:

   The Institute of International Education reported this week that the number of foreign students attending U.S. colleges and universities rose 5.3 percent to a record 407,500 in the last academic year.
   At your university, the number of foreign students increased 2 percent in the last academic year, said Daphne Johnston, assistant director of the Office of International Services. The number of foreign students increased from 1,870 in the fall of 1992 to 1,908 in the fall of 1993. She said the increase has been steady since 1958 when your school had only 203 foreign students.

The People's Republic of China has the largest representation on your campus, with 221 students, Johnston said. Other foreign countries represented are: from Malaysia, 194; from Taiwan, 141; from Japan, 122; from India, 118; from South Korea, 107. The number of students has decreased from countries such as Iran, Israel, Jordan, Kuwait, Syria and the United Arab Emirates, she said.

Nationally the most popular major for foreign students is business, according to the Institute's report. On your campus, the most popular major for foreign students is engineering.

e. Write a brief of one to three paragraphs based on the following information:

The Office of Academic Affairs at your university informed faculty members this week that posting grades with students' identification numbers is illegal. David Shulenberger, associate vice chancellor for academic affairs, said his office had distributed fliers to all faculty members and graduate teaching assistants to notify them that posting grades with the students' ID numbers is an invasion of privacy. It is a violation of the Family Education Rights and Privacy Act, more commonly known as the Buckley Amendment, he said. The amendment has been in effect since 1974, but some faculty members may not have known that it applies to posting grades with student identification numbers, he said. Other violations of the amendment would include posting information with a student's name, social security number, personal characteristic or any other information revealing a student's identity, said Rose Marino, associate general counsel for the university. Instructors have the option to devise a secret identification code with the student so the grade can be posted, Shulenberger said. "It's very difficult to get grade information back to students except by posting it," he said.

Based on a story from *The University Daily Kansan*. Used with permission.

14-2. Brights

a. Write a bright of two paragraphs based on the following information:

A man in your community died last month. After his death, your local County Department of Social Services sent him a letter. The man's name was Albert Maxwell. The man's brother, Jason Maxwell, said the letter is "living proof of how screwed up the system is." The letter said: "Your food stamps will be stopped effective January 1993 because we received a notice that you passed away. You may reapply if there is a change in your circumstances. May God bless you." Rose Josephson, director of the county's social service system, said it's not the fault of her agency. She said the form letter was generated by a computer. She said a caseworker added the "May God bless you," because the employee wanted to soften the message.

b. Write a bright of one to three paragraphs based on the following information:

The information comes from a police report in your town; attribute to the report. Police have arrested a 24-year-old man from your town on charges of burglary. The suspect broke into a Domino's pizza parlor on 1700 W. 23rd Street Sunday night. The man was drunk. He told police that he had not had anything to eat since Friday night. He said, "I was hungry." It was not known whether the suspect got anything to eat. A store manager heard the disturbance. The manager lives across the street from the pizza parlor. The manager called police. The man had raided the restaurant cooler. The cooler contained three plastic containers of pizza sauce, 10 pounds of mozzarella cheese and two sacks of flour.

c. Write a bright of up to five paragraphs based on the following news story; use your own wording.

A little tender loving care was all she wanted

A Colorado Springs male gorilla sensed what a Pittsburgh male gorilla didn't, provided what the Pittsburgh gorilla wouldn't, and now there's a chance he'll be what the Pittsburgh gorilla won't – a daddy.

A 22-year-old female gorilla at the Pittsburgh Zoo had punched one male and ignored two other suitors before the Colorado Springs gorilla came to town in November 1990.

Now she has taken to the genteel 27-year-old westerner, a 400-pound Silverback. He was loaned by the Cheyenne Mountain Zoo in the nationwide Species Survival Plan to breed endangered species in captivity.

"She's going through all the appropriate behavior with him. When she comes into an estrus cycle, she'll come close to him to show that she feels comfortable with him and give him the opportunity to mate," said the zoo's general curator, Lee Nesler.

"She's going to him and eliciting for companionship and whatever comes with that," she said.

Officials at the Pittsburgh Zoo have been watching these hirsute players in the story of love for the past 14 months as they attempted to breed the zoo's first gorilla born in captivity.

The gorillas no longer are given names in order to encourage respect for them as wild creatures, zoo officials said.

But wild was not what the Pittsburgh female wanted. Outweighed 2-to-1, she fought off the advances of her former roommate, a 21-year-old, 400-pound Silverback with the aggressive high-strung manners of a bodybuilder on steroids.

"The male from Colorado is very laid-back, very easy-going," Nesler said.

Different females like different types, Nesler said, and they are more likely to conceive and carry their pregnancy to term without aborting when they have chosen their mate. That is why zoos exchange the animals and also why Nesler is optimistic this time after previous disappointments.

"He had been in a social group in the wild and had sired offspring before. He knew how to breed and how to protect the female and the offspring," Nesler said. "We're hoping she can understand this and feel comfortable, and hopefully we'll have a baby gorilla."

Dick Foster, *Rocky Mountain* (Colo.) *News.* Reprinted with permission.

d. Write a bright of three paragraphs based on the following story:

Woe to Lois. Woe to Metropolis. Woe to every freedom-loving being alive. Superman is dead.

Well, not quite yet. But, alas, his days are numbered.

The Man of Steel finally will meet his match in issue No. 75, due to hit stands Nov. 18, DC Comics spokeswoman Martha Thomases announced Friday.

Superman, in what DC is billing as his most brutal battle ever, will successfully defend Metropolis against Doomsday, a maniacal villain escaped from a cosmic lunatic asylum.

But deliverance for Metropolis will come at the cost of life for Superman.

Now, be honest. At least once, as a child or later, you joked with a friend by looking into the sky and yelling, "It's a bird! It's a plane! No, it's Superman!"

Maybe there wasn't anything in the sky at all. Maybe you just fantasized that *you* could move faster than a speeding bullet, that *you* could bend steel with your bare hands, that *you* were the hero of generations.

Then again, maybe *you* aren't a Superman fan. But countless people are or have been.

In "The Overstreet Comic Book Price Guide," author Robert Overstreet boasts that Superman is the "quintessential hero with extraordinary powers. Arguably the most imitated character in all of fiction.

Are last rites really in order for the awkward Clark Kent, mild-mannered reporter for the Daily Planet?

Death for Superman is certain. But the door for a superheroic return appears to be open.

Thomases said she had received calls from around the world lamenting Superman's flight to superhero heaven. One caller even claimed to be organizing a boycott of Time Warner, DC's parent conglomerate.

After issue No. 76, "Funeral for a Friend," readers will be closer to knowing whether the Man of Steel is truly immortal.

Even Thomases said she doesn't know what Superman's death means for the comic now.

"I don't know the schedule through all eternity," she said. "But I know it through March, and there's no Superman."

Erik Schutz, *The Topeka Capital-Journal.* Reprinted with permission.

14-3. Tightening a full-length story

Write a story from the following information, using the guidelines of *USA Today* and tips from Richard Aregood.

A new study was released yesterday. The study was conducted by the American Council on Education and the University of California, Los Angeles and it is the 25th annual survey of college freshmen which the council and the University have conducted. The study shows steadily changing attitudes among college freshmen. The council and the university surveyed attitudes of 194,182 freshmen at 382 colleges who were included in the study and the basic finding was that U.S. college students, who were criticized as being over-materialistic in the decade of the 1980s are now showing increased interest in social causes such as the environment and they are showing less interest in making money, according to the latest study.

Frank Burtnett of the National Association of College Admission Counselors says the findings suggest there is now a freshman class living through – and responding to – social concerns of the 1990s. "That's a very healthy signal," he says.

Some of those findings of the survey conducted by the Council on Education and the University of California include that 18.4 percent chose a business major and that is down from 24.6 percent in 1987 which was the peak year for students who chose a business major.

Another finding was that college students' need for "being very well off financially" declined for a second straight year, falling from 75.4 percent last year to 73.7 percent in this year. And that drop followed 17 consecutive years of increases in the numbers of college students who had needs for being very well off financially.

Forty three percent of the college students in the survey said it's essential or very important to "influence social values," and that is an all-time high for students who felt that way.

Eighty eight percent of the college students surveyed said the government isn't doing enough to control pollution, which amounts to an increase from 86.3 percent last year, and 77.6 percent in 1981.

Of the students in the survey, 38 percent said it's essential or very important to help promote racial understanding, and that is an increase from a low of 27.2 percent of the college students who were surveyed and had that response in 1986.

14-4. Style quiz

Correct the errors in the following sentences:

1. The cost of operating the vehicles is about four cents a mile.

2. The Institute of International Education reported this week that the number of foriegn students attending colleges in the U.S. rose 5.3%.

3. The number of foriegn students increased in the Fall of 1992.

4. The 22 year old female gorilla had punched one male and ignored two other suiters.

5. The female gorilla was from the east, but the male she wanted was from the western part of the country.

6. The Department of Social Services seems too have believed in reincarnation.

7. Students were criticized as being overmaterialistic in the 1980's.

8. The day after Earvin Magic Johnson signed his one year extension, he changed his mind and decided not to play professional basketball.

9. The Buckley Amendment has been in affect since 1974, but many faculty members did not know it applied to posting grades.

10. Posting students grades with thier identification numbers violates a Federal law.

Public Relations Writing 15

15-1. Rewrite a press release

This press release about an event is poorly written and is not in proper form. It also has spelling and style errors. Rewrite this release using proper form (name of organization, address, your name as contact and your telephone number on the left; date the release, write a headline and write "For Immediate Release" on the right or below the headline. Double-space the release and type – 30 – at the end. Write one or two paragraphs and eliminate extraneous information.

<u>News Release</u>

<u>To whom it may concern:</u>

Big Brothers/Big Sisters of Douglas County, Inc. will host an informational meeting for perspective volunteers at 10:00 a.m., Saturday, (add Saturday's date). We would be so happy to have you attend, and we would welcome news coverage. The meeting will be at the organization's office at 220 Main st. in Lawrence, 04040. The meeting will last approximately 2 hours and officers of Big Brothers/Big Sisters will discuss how you can become a volunteer to a child who needs adult companionship, which is the purpose of the organization. If you would like more information, call 454-1222 anytime during the week. We are hoping to gain more volunteers for the organization, and will appreciate anything you can do to help us.

I am George Hand, contact for the organization, and I would be happy to talk with you about it. You can call me at the organization's office, 454-1222. P.S. If anyone can't make this meeting, another informational meeting is scheduled <u>for Tuesday, [add Tuesday's date].</u> That will be at 6:00 p.m.

15-2. News release

Assume this is a news release issued by the Office of University Relations at your university, which has a total enrollment of 24,500 students. Use a hard-news lead and write it in inverted pyramid style. Limit it to one page. Write a headline and use standard press release form. Label it "News Release" and put the University and contact information at the top; use your phone number. You may use today's date and "For Immediate Release." Consider a chart or list format for some of the statistics. Here is the information, which is poorly written.

The university has released figures for its minority enrollment for this fall. The enrollment categories are based on self-reported student data. The minority enrollment has increased. In fact, it increased 8.7 percent this fall. This increase came in a year when overall campus enrollment grew less than 1 percent.

"This university has taken a significant step forward," said [Use the name of your university president or chancellor]. "Our many efforts of recent years are beginning to produce the desired results."

Enrollment of black students increased by 34 students to 678.

"The increase in minority students is a gratifying sight indeed for the many students, faculty and administrators who have worked for it," the chancellor (use his or her name) said. "We still have more to do. This is only the beginning."

In other categories, American Indian student enrollment showed the largest increase of 46 students to a total of 204. Asian student enrollment increased by 44 to 565. Hispanic enrollment grew by 28 to 452.

Comparing minority enrollment for previous years, the statistics show that minority enrollment for 1989 was 1,540 and 1,597 in 1990 and 1,694 in 1991 and 1,747 in 1992 and 1,899 in 1993.

Based on a press release from the Office of University Relations, University of Kansas. Used with permission.

15-3. News feature release

You are working for the Office of University Relations for your university. A professor of anthropology has written a book about the hidden consequences of tests. You are writing a feature press release that you hope will be reprinted in newspapers throughout your state. This exercise is based on a press release from the University of Kansas, but you may substitute the name of your school. Label this a news release, include contacts, your phone number, date of the release and "For Immediate Release." Write a headline, as well, and double space your copy. If you use a soft lead, make sure you get to the point very quickly, preferably in the second paragraph; news editors are busy people who do not want to wade through your prose. First write a brief that can be used as a teaser in a "News Tips" release to accompany this release. Then write the full release, which can be one to two pages.

F. Allan Hanson, professor of anthropology at the University of Kansas, has written a book. The book, "Testing Testing: Social Consequences of the Examined Life" is published by University of California Press and is available at local bookstores or by contacting Denise Cicourel at UC Press, 2120 Berkeley Way, Berkeley, CA 94720.

In the Feb. 28, 1993 New York Times Book Review, Richard Flaste writes of Hanson's book: "What he brings to the arguments is surprising vivacious writing. He is splendid in pointing out absurdities hidden in the various testing systems. The author brings to his often impassioned discussion of testing a fine humanism that accepts the need of societies' institutions to know something about people but that deplores the warping of the tools of assessment into prying, fearsome, demeaning instruments."

The book is about American society's addiction to tests. Hanson uncovers a variety of hidden consequences – many of them unsavory – of tests commonly used in business and education. He recommends eliminating most drug tests, intelligence and aptitude tests, and lie detector or integrity tests.

Employers use drug testing and integrity testing to screen applicants and monitor employees.

Hanson recommends eliminating integrity testing and using drug tests only when people are suspected of using drugs.

An exception is testing for anabolic steroids. Because the effects of steroids remain long after the drug can be detected by tests, Hanson says, "random testing is about the only way we can discover the use of the drug in athletic competition."

"The American preoccupation with testing has resulted in a panoply of techniques dedicated to scanning, probing, weighing, perusing and recording every last detail of our personal traits and life experiences," Hanson said.

Hanson says it should be possible to eliminate much of the testing used to predict behavior and aptitudes. For example, some college admissions offices no longer require scores from aptitude tests such as the American College Test, or ACT, or Scholastic Aptitude Test, or GMAT, as an application requirement.

Of all forms of testing, Hanson finds lie detectors the vilest, a pornographic gaze into a person's private thoughts. The test taker is powerless to conceal or control anything, and the test results are often unreliable, he says. Yet people whose character may be under public scrutiny, such as Anita Hill or Woody Allen, submit to and even request polygraph tests to establish credibility.

The future is likely to produce even more detailed knowledge of each individual as new genetic tests and DNA fingerprinting are developed, he says.

Hanson says tests that measure performance, such as what a student has learned in class or skills mastered for a job, are useful.

But tests that predict behavior or aptitude – IQ tests, for example – can have unintended and undesirable consequences, he argues. Scores from IQ tests can become life sentences for children with very high or very low scores. Tests assign people to various categories – genius, slow learner, security risk – "Where they are then treated, act and come to think of themselves according to the expectations associated with those categories," Hanson says.

"People are examined and evaluated less for qualifications or knowledge they already possess than for what the test results can predict about future actions or potential behavior," Hanson says.

"Decisions are made about people not on the basis of what they have done, or even what they certainly will do, but in terms of what they might do."

Because tests provide information about people, they serve as devices of power for agencies – employers, educational administrators, insurance firms, law enforcement agencies – to determine whom to employ, to admit to college, to take on as a risk or to arrest.

Based on a press release from the Office of University Relations, University of Kansas. Used with permission.

15-4. Product promotion

Your textbook contains a press release from Binney & Smith to promote Crayola new washable crayons. Now the company has come out with another new product – its first highlighters for kids. They, too, are washable. Write a press release to promote this product. Use standard double-space form, and limit your release to one page (approximately three to four paragraphs). Make sure you include the company name, address, telephone number and use your name as the contact person with your telephone number. Label your release "For Immediate Release." Write a headline at the top of the release, and use Easton, Pa. as your dateline. Here is the information:

The company uses "From Crayola Products" above its name, Binney & Smith, Inc., 1100 Church Lane, P.O. Box 431, Easton, Pennsylvania 18044-0431 [use your phone number].

Binney & Smith is the maker of Crayola products, which include crayons and markers and paints and a variety of other products. The company is introducing a new line of products which it says is its first set of highlighters specifically designed for kids. The product will be called Crayola Screamin' Neons. These are washable school highlighters that were designed especially for school children. The products are bright, neon colors. Bright, neon graphics on each highlighter "screams" kids and fun. The highlighters feature a special rounded nib that allows a smooth flow of ink without noise or squeaking. They are washable. The washable formula is patented. It allows the highlighter ink to be washed from hands, face and most children's clothing. They are non-toxic. They are available in a pack of four colors: glowing green, neon yellow, hot magenta and electric blue. The suggested retail price is $1.99. The highlighters were developed after research conducted by Binney & Smith revealed that children start using highlighters around the age of 8. The research also revealed that they continue using highlighters throughout their school use. The research also indicated that children use highlighters for a variety of activities. Some of those activities include school papers, study sheets, plays, maps and reports. Tailoring a highlighter to the needs of children resulted in the development of Screamin' Neons.

In addition to the press release information for this product, you are including this background about the company; decide if any of this should go in the press release or should be packaged separately:

Binney & Smith, maker of Crayola Products, was founded by C. Harold Smith and Edwin Binney in 1885. Slate pencils and chalk preceded the company's introduction of Crayola crayons in 1903.

Each year Binney & Smith produces more than 2 billion Crayola crayons.

Tests reveal that the smell of Crayola crayons is one of the 20 most recognizable aromas to American adults. Coffee and peanut butter top the list.

One the average, children ages 2-7 color or draw 28 minutes a day.

In a given year, Binney & Smith manufactures enough Crayola paint to cover all of the major league baseball and football stadiums, the Brooklyn Bridge and the World Trade Center combined.

In addition to crayons, Crayola products include markers, watercolors, tempera paints, chalk, clay, washable paints as well as fabric paints.

Each year American children spent 6.3 billion hours coloring – almost 10,000 human lifetimes.

Crayola crayons are currently sold in more than 60 countries from the island of Iceland to the tiny Central American nation of Belize. Crayola product boxes are printed in 11 different languages including English, Spanish, French, Dutch and Italian.

The first box of Crayola crayons sold for 5 cents.

Based on a news release from Binney & Smith. Used with permission.

15-5. Media kit

Using the previous product as a base, design a media kit. In addition to the press release, what else will you include? How will you package background about the company? Decide what type of folder you would use and plan a cover, although you do not have to draw the design. Write a list of all the information (including creative ideas for enclosures) you will package in this kit.

Broadcast Writing

This chapter will give you some practice writing basic broadcast stories for the anchors to read (on camera readers) and for a reporter package. For the following exercises, assume you're working in a large- to medium-sized market. These stories are interesting but they're not the most important stories in tonight's newscast, so you must keep them "tight" − focused on the important and interesting elements that your audience will want to know. These exercises were written by John Broholm, broadcast journalism professor at the University of Kansas.

16-1. Church embezzler

Write a television news story from the following notes. First decide the focus of the story. Then write a lead (either direct or indirect) related to your focus. Write the story as a :20 (20 second) anchor on-camera reader (a story with no video, only the anchor reading on camera).

A trial has just ended in Johnson County District Court. The defendant, Ron Poteet, 26, 1010 Wellington Rd., was caught pocketing monies from the collection plate at Presbyterian Fellowship Church, 2416 Clinton Pkwy. Both addresses are in Overland Park. He was arrested on June 6, 1991. He had been entrusted with counting the daily donations, and was sentenced earlier today (just after 2:00 p.m.) to three years in prison. That was his job since 1986.

The pastor of the church, Gordon Price, said yesterday that he had been impressed from the beginning with Poteet's work and thought he was "extremely nice. Polite. Reserved. Gentle-hearted. I assumed everything was OK. I was wrong." Poteet was caught when discrepancies between the amounts entered on the donation envelopes and the actual amounts of money contained inside the envelopes were noticed by another church employee. The investigation was then handed over to the K.B.I. (Kansas Bureau of Investigation). In all, about $70,000 was taken by Poteet, although the exact amount isn't known. Price said he debated a long time over whether or not to prosecute.

Poteet was sentenced in courtroom D by Judge Jane Shepherdson to serve 3 years and pay a fine of $10,000. He had pleaded guilty earlier. He made no statement to the court, either when he pleaded or was sentenced.

16-2. Lumber fire

Write a brief "voiceover" story – a story with accompanying videotape – for this "follow" story. Follow stories run a day or more after the event covered to update viewers on recent developments. Your story will run on your station's 6:00 evening newscast. The fire happened in a small, nearby community, which received aid from the fire department at another nearby community. Your station was able to obtain videotape of the fire but no interviews from the scene, and your information comes from a wire story. The first sentence of your story will be "on camera" and then the director will go to the videotape.

(DELTON) – Investigators continued to search for the cause of a fire last night that heavily damaged the Delton Lumber Co., while the lumber company's owner worked to get back into business.

The blaze was fought by firefighters from Springfield and Delton as part of a mutual aid pact signed by the two cities.

A 4 p.m. meeting was scheduled for today by fire and law enforcement officials from Springfield and Delton at the Springfield/Hamilton County Law Enforcement Center to discuss the fire that destroyed two buildings at the lumberyard and a nearby historic railroad depot, which was used for storage by the lumber company.

No one was injured in the fire that began at approximately 8:30 p.m. in one of the lumberyard buildings, spread to the depot and burned brightly in the night sky until it was brought under control at about 11:00 p.m.

"We're just going to discuss the investigation and where we need to go from here," Springfield Fire Chief Herman McMahon said today.

McMahon said he, Hamilton County Sheriff John Chavez, Delton's acting police chief, Kenny Gault, and Larry Westerman, a Springfield firefighter in charge of the investigation, would be among officials at the meeting.

Dennis Salyer, lumberyard owner, said he hoped to be doing business in a limited way within one or two days, depending on how much the fire episode had disrupted power and lights to the lumberyard office, which suffered only smoke damage.

"We'll do the best we can because we've got some contractor customers who need lumber for building projects," said Salyer.

Officials haven't determined the cause of the fire, which resulted in at least $200,000 in damage.

An official estimate of the damage is being withheld pending inspection by insurance adjusters, McMahon said.

16-3. Acid arrests

From the following notes, write a short package news story, with an anchor intro and with your recorded voice delivering the main section of the story. Use one or two soundbites with news sources from the quoted material in the notes. You may substitute the names of your community for the ones in this story.

You have been told by Otto Privette, the regional director of the Drug Enforcement Administration, the arm of the U.S. Justice Department that is concerned with illegal drug trafficking, that the D.E.A., the F.B.I., and local law enforcement agencies in northeastern Kansas have seen a significant hike in arrests for sale and/or use of LSD. All told, there have been 10 arrests since the beginning of the year, up from just three all of last year, according to Privette, and the year still has four months to go. LSD was a popular hallucinogenic, countercultural drug in the 1960s. (Phone calls to local law enforcement offices confirmed Privette's assertion of an increase in arrests.) Privette predicted 10 more arrests during the remainder of the year.

Privette said that overall in the Kansas City and Lawrence areas:

"More people are using acid, and we're sure arresting more people these days. It's a good bet we'll make some more arrests because we've got three investigators running down leads full-time. In a way it's discouraging because there's so much of the drug around, but I think we're making some headway on the problem." (:12)

Privette said police in the region were looking to arrest manufacturers, sellers, and users, and they're particularly on the lookout for clues leading to the apprehension of a probable local manufacturer of the drug. Privette said it was common for LSD to be manufactured locally.

Lynne Harris, who works for the state of Kansas as a counselor for juveniles who have been arrested on drug-related offenses, said police were arresting many teenagers on LSD-related offenses. She said the drug was popular with teenagers because it was relatively inexpensive and provided a longer "trip" or high than many other drugs. LSD manufacturers have always added one of many varieties of stimulant to the drug to accelerate its entry into and assimilation by the human metabolism, according to Harris. She said the intended purpose of the stimulant was to enhance the sensation of euphoria, or "rush," caused by the drug. She said she didn't know whether the strychnine contamination was for that purpose, or was simply a by-product of drug production:

"A lot of the LSD we've been seeing has impurities in it. Now the drug's dangerous enough as it is because it can really unhinge people who are already emotionally unstable. But once you add something like strychnine, you can wind up with some pretty toxic stuff. So it's doubly dangerous." (:10)

Harris guessed that if LSD was in Lawrence, it was also showing up around the rest of the country. He said that it was possible there was a manufacturer in Kansas, but that it took a fairly skilled chemist to make the drug, more so than for metamphetamines, a manufacturer of which was recently discovered in Kansas City by police. Harris said that there were no local reports of the drug falling into the hands of children in grade school, although she had seen reports from elsewhere of acid-impregnated stamps showing cartoon characters.

You have the following videotape:

■ Privette showing you evidence bags containing LSD capsules, shot at Kansas City DEA headquarters (up to :30).

■ A group counseling session run in Lawrence by Harris, with six teenagers who are recovering drug users, whose faces you can't show on camera (up to :20).

■ The police testing lab in Kansas City, which determines the chemical makeup of confiscated drugs and material (up to :30).

Accuracy and Libel 17

This chapter will give you practice checking for accuracy and will test your knowledge of some very basic principles of libel. No exercise can substitute for the fact checking you should do before you turn in your stories. You should always check the spelling of names and make sure that you have spelled one source's name correctly in all references. You should also check facts, such as dates, and make sure your quotes are used in the proper context.

17-1. Accuracy checks

This story contains several factual inaccuracies. Most of these facts can be checked in an almanac. Circle the inaccurate information and write your corrections above the words.

William Jeffery Clinton became the 41st president of the United States on Jan. 20, 1993. At the age of 46, Clinton was the second youngest president to take office; John F. Kennedy was 44 when he was inaugurated in 1962. Clinton was sworn in about noon by U.S. Chief Justice William Renquist in front of the U.S. Capital. Then he turned and hugged his wife, Hillery, and his daughter, Chelsea. Just a few minutes earlier, 43-year-old Albert Gore was sworn in as vice president by Supreme Court Associate Justice Byron White as Gore's wife, Tipper, held the family Bible. The former Arizona governor is the first Democratic president in eight years.

As part of the inaugural ceremony, poet Maiya Angelou read a poem Clinton had requested her to write for the inauguration. The day ended with 11 inaugural balls featuring celebrities ranging from Barbara Streisand to Soul Asylum.

17-2. Libel quiz

Circle the correct answers.

1) The book has listed four defenses against libel (truth, Sullivan, privilege, fair comment and criticism). From a reporter's point of view, which is the strongest and why?
   A. Truth
   B. Sullivan
   C. Privilege
   D. Fair Comment & Criticism

2) With respect to libel law, what does "actual malice" mean?
   A. That the reporter was careless.
   B. That the reporter tried to be mean to the plaintiff.
   C. That the reporter was negligent.
   D. That the reporter made a false statement either knowing the information was wrong or with reckless disregard for whether it was wrong.

3) The "Actual Malice" standard comes into play in a libel suit
   A. With private figure plaintiffs who cannot prove negligence.
   B. With public figure or public official plaintiffs.
   C. Only when the newspaper refuses to print a correction.
   D. Only when the newspaper sues a public official for libel.

4) Which of the following is *not* a reason the Supreme Court established the "actual malice" test in Sullivan?
   A. To encourage robust debate on public issues.
   B. To encourage a free press to publish matters of public concern.
   C. In recognition that important public debate may include vehement, caustic and sharp attacks on public officials.
   D. In recognition that in a democracy, private figures, too, have to be ready for sharp or unpleasant attacks in the press.

5) With respect to libel law, "privilege" means
   A. You can report anything in a public place without worrying about checking facts.
   B. You can go on private property to gather information.
   C. You may print defamatory statements from a public proceeding or public record as long as you are being fair and accurate.
   D. You have the absolute privilege to report the news, guaranteed by the First Amendment.

6) As a news photographer, you use a telephoto lens to shoot pictures in your neighbor's back yard, some 300 feet from your location on a public sidewalk.

    A. You may be guilty of invasion of privacy under the intrusion category.

    B. You are protected from any action because you're a journalist.

    C. Your neighbor can sue you for libel if you print a topless picture of her.

    D. You are protected from an invasion of privacy – public disclosure of private facts action because you've taken the information from a public place, and that is the same as the public record.

7) Your advertising department wants to use a picture of the hometown baseball hero in an automobile dealer advertisement.

    A. Since he's a public figure, the ad people can simply clip a photo from the files and put it in without notifying the hometown hero.

    B. The ad people can use him because he is newsworthy.

    C. The ad people have to receive his permission and pay him if he requests it, since this is for commercial purposes.

    D. This could be considered an invasion of privacy under false light publicity.

8) You have been sued for Invasion of Privacy – Public Disclosure of Private Facts for publishing a person's less than flattering mental health history. You will likely win the suit if:

    A. You took the information from a public record.

    B. The person's physician said it was OK to use the information.

    C. You print a retraction.

    D. You obtained the document from an anonymous source.

9) With respect to accuracy, experienced journalists

    A. Don't worry about it too much since the Sullivan defense is there to protect them.

    B. Usually check the major facts, then "go with their gut."

    C. Check details, even little things, to see if a source or story "doesn't add up."

    D. Know the "corrections" column is there to back them up.

10) Showing your copy to sources before it is published

    A. Is never permitted.

    B. Is a sign that you doubt the truth of your story.

    C. Will lead to a lawsuit.

    D. Is a way that some journalists catch inaccuracies before publication.

Ethics 18

Journalists have to make difficult decisions in the course of doing their duty. It is not always possible to serve the public without causing harm to someone. Nor is it always possible to know you have made the right decision about what to report, write or display in a publication or broadcast. However, you can minimize harm if you use some moral reasoning guidelines to justify your actions. Using some of the principles in the textbook, consider the following cases. Make a snap judgment using your gut reaction. Then consider all the alternatives and the people who will be affected by your decision – including yourself, your organization, your readers or viewers and the sources in the story. Use some of the principles of philosophers to guide you. Then justify your final decision.

These cases are based on real dilemmas reporters, photographers and editors faced at *The Hartford Courant,* where Henry McNulty is the reader representative. It is his job to respond to readers' concerns and complaints. As an ombudsman for the newspaper, he often has to justify why the newspaper made some difficult decisions. And frequently, he is critical of his own newspaper. McNulty periodically writes a column in which he asks readers to play the role of editor and make a decision about dilemmas the journalists faced. He cautions readers that there are no right or wrong answers, and that editors often differ on how to handle each situation. Here are some cases McNulty presented to his readers. You be the editor; choose one of these options or devise an alternative to them and justify your decision.

18-1. Graveside photo

During the Persian Gulf war, your newspaper receives a wire photograph of the first Gulf-related funeral at Arlington National Cemetery. It shows a woman at graveside; her husband was killed in action. The anguish is evident from her expression. Her children are beside her and two are weeping.

❑ You don't print the photo because it is an invasion of the woman's privacy. She's gone through enough, losing her husband and facing the prospect of rearing her family alone. You don't want to add to her troubles by putting her face on your front page.

❑ You print the photo on Page 1. Her family's tears are the nation's tears, and the first Arlington funeral of the Gulf war needs to be shown.

18-2. The bad joke

Your reporter is covering a speech by a local politician. The politician makes a joke in the speech that offends several members of the audience, who stand up and walk out. The person covering the speech reports this, but in the story repeats the joke told by the politician. It has a sexual theme. In editing the story:

❑ You delete the joke because you consider it offensive and inappropriate for your newspaper.

❑ You let it stand on the grounds that otherwise your readers (or viewers) can't properly judge the actions of the politician and those people who walked out.

18-3. The telephone number

Your newspaper is about to publish a wire-service story about the "Overground Railroad," a network that would help women get abortions if *Roe v. Wade* were to be overturned. The story is neutral as to whether the right to an abortion should exist, but it includes, at the end, the toll-free number for the Overground Railroad headquarters. In editing the story:

❑ You let the phone number stand. You reason that it's simply a way to help interested readers, similar to printing the opening hours of an art exhibit. It's not free advertising, you argue, nor does it promote abortion.

❑ You delete the phone number. If the subject were non-controversial, you wouldn't object to providing this information. But the story deals with abortion, one of the most hotly debated issues of the day. And besides, other stories haven't had the phone number for groups like Operation Rescue.

18-4. Son of superintendent

A 20-year-old man in your city is arrested on morals charges involving a 17-year-old girl. Your reporter writes the story, and it includes the fact that the arrested person is the son of the superintendent of schools. In editing it:

❏ You leave in the mention of the father, because you believe this fact is important to readers. The father is well-known locally, and such unpleasant publicity is one of the prices of fame. Also, you don't want to be accused of covering up anything touching on a public official.

❏ You delete the reference to the father. He is in no way connected to the arrest, and you reason that to report the family connection would be unfair.

18-5. The synagogue letter

A synagogue is having trouble collecting dues from its members, so a stern letter is sent to all those who are delinquent. It threatens, among other things, to remove the children of delinquent members from religious school and to attach members' property if at least a portion of the dues isn't paid. The newspaper is made aware of the situation.

❏ You don't publish a story. The synagogue is a private body and its problems are its own. You also are sensitive to the concern that publishing this story might fuel anti-Semitic stereotypes.

❏ You do write about the synagogue's problems and recommend the story for Page 1. It's an economic story, showing how deeply the recession has affected all parts of society, even a community's religious life. And you argue that the newspaper frequently has stories about disputes involving religious groups.

Cases from *The Hartford* (Conn.) *Courant.* Reprinted with permission.

Multicultural Sensitivity 19

This chapter is designed to help you become sensitive to the concerns of people from many ethnic, racial and minority groups and to become aware of gender issues in the media. Although these exercises are intended to help you gain some awareness of multicultural needs, the best way to understand people who differ from you is to talk to them and ask them about their concerns as they relate to the media and to the way they are treated in society.

19-1. Media survey

If your instructor prefers, you may do this as a class project with each student assigned to a different organization.

Part 1: Conduct a survey of the media in your community and/or state (newspapers, magazines, television stations, advertising and public relations firms) to determine the number of minorities and women in various positions. How many minorities do these organizations employ in news/editorial positions? How many of these minorities or women are in management positions (as editors, for example)? How many minorities or women are in top management positions – managing editors, executive editors, news directors, publishers, and so on? How does this percentage or figure compare with the total number of minorities in the organization, and what types of jobs do the majority of minorities have?

Part 2: Interview top editors of these organizations and ask them if they have any official policies regarding recruiting and hiring of minorities and women and any policies regarding hiring minorities and women in management positions. Ask editors (or top officials) to explain any efforts they have taken to increase minority representation at their organizations. (If they say they are looking for qualified minorities and women, ask them to explain their definition of "qualified.")

19-2. Multicultural interview

The point of this assignment is to make you sensitive to the needs of people who may be considered in the minority, whether it is for racial, ethnic or social reasons, such as homosexuals. Interview a person from a minority group whose background is different from yours. If you are a member of a minority, choose someone from another minority group. You may write up your findings as a mini-profile or as a report, depending on your instructor's preference. If you are interviewing a person with a disability, ask for specifics about how the person is treated in society and how the person views media treatment of people with disabilities. Consider that many stories about people with disabilities feature them as extraordinary or as victims, "the pity party," as one media critic calls it.

Here are some questions you should ask, but you may add others that you think would be of help. Include basic information about the person, such as age, background, field of study if it is a student, why he or she chose this university or college, and so on:

How do you prefer to be addressed?

How do you think the media portrays people in your minority group? (Are the portrayals overly positive or negative? Give examples.)

Have you ever experienced insensitivity or prejudice because of your race, ethnic background, disability or special interests? Please specify.

Have you ever been interviewed by the media? Was your experience good or bad? Please specify.

What advice would you give to reporters about coverage of minorities such as yourself? [Ask for specifics – types of questions, how to be sensitive, how to address people, or pitfalls reporters may encounter when interviewing members of this minority group.]

19-3. Photo sensitivity

Analyze the photographs of minorities – particularly African-Americans, Hispanic-Americans, Asian-Americans or Native Americans – in your local newspaper or other newspapers for a week or more. Do they perpetuate stereotypes? (Make copies of some of the photographs you selected.) To understand the issue, read the following material before you do your analysis.

Many studies and articles criticize the media for using photographs that portray minorities in a negative light, such as photos portraying African-Americans in crime scenes. But criticism can take other forms, as well.

In 1993, *The University Daily Kansan* published two photographs of African-Americans dancing and singing as part of a three-day conference of the Black Student Government. Many African-American students complained. Ask yourself if you would have considered this photograph insensitive and if you would have handled the situation as the newspaper editor did in this column he wrote following the publication of the photographs:

Source: Daron J. Bennett, *The University Daily Kansan*

Newspapers have a responsibility to present the news in a way that portrays the reality of an event or issue.

At the *Kansan,* we take this responsibility very seriously.

But in regard to two photos used to illustrate the 16th annual Big Eight Conference on Black Student Government, our coverage was irresponsible.

On Page 3 of the Feb. 22 issue of the *Kansan,* we printed a story and two photos that were intended to summarize the events of the three-day conference.

To summarize a three-day conference in one story and two photos is nearly impossible, but sometimes space limitations force newspapers into tough situations. This fact is never a good excuse for representing an event inaccurately.

The conference brought about 750 university and high school students to the University of Kansas. The conference was scheduled to include about 45 hours of activities.

During most of that time, the students either participated in workshops that focused on issues that affected African Americans or listened to speakers such as Sonia Sanchez, poet and professor at Temple University, and Leonard Jeffries, professor of Black Studies at the City College of New York.

But the photos used by the *Kansan* to illustrate the event were not of the workshops or the speakers.

The photos we used were of the greek show and gospel extravaganza, events that lasted a total of four hours. These events were the evening entertainment for conference participants.

By including photos that represented only four hours of a three-day event, we misrepresented the conference.

But even worse, we perpetuated a stereotype.

The photos were of African Americans dancing and singing. On the sports page that same day, five African-American athletes were pictured. Those were the only photos of African Americans in that issue.

Dancing, singing and slam dunking: These are too often the only images of African Americans that newspapers provide to their readers

I or someone else in our newsroom should have realized before the photos were printed that we were perpetuating this stereotype of African Americans.

I am sure that many of our readers looked at the photos and did not perceive a problem. My goal for this column is to help our readers understand what we did and why we were wrong for doing it.

At the *Kansan,* we have learned from our mistake. We hope others will learn from it, too.

Greg Farmer, editor, *The University Daily Kansan.* Reprinted with permission.

19-4. Gender stereotypes

Analyze how men and women are portrayed in commercials on television. Be on the lookout for male bashing as much as for female stereotyping. Advertisements that may provide good examples include those for beer, automobiles, hygiene and household products. Write the name of the advertiser, a brief description and whether or not you believe the advertisement portrays men and women in stereotypical or sexist ways. If possible, watch the ads with a person of the opposite sex to compare your perceptions. Here are some qualities to look for:

Are women portrayed in commercials set in the kitchen more than men? Are men being portrayed as inferior to make women look strong, intelligent or superior?

Are women being used as sex symbols in commercials for products unrelated to physical appearance?

In commercials about physical appearance such as dieting, are more women featured than men?

What stereotypes do you think these commercials perpetuate?

You might also note how many of the commercials feature men and women of different races.

19-5. Loaded words

In 1992 when Bill Clinton was running for the presidency, the media was having a hard time dealing with "the Hillary Factor," as *Newsweek* magazine entitled its July 20 article in which Hillary Clinton was described as "dewy-eyed to buttoned-up." Stories about Hillary Clinton included her appearance, where she bought her clothes (off the rack in Little Rock, Ark.) and mostly about her "tough" style as a "serious" lawyer. Yet few articles ever discussed where Bill Clinton bought his clothes. In one case, a television teaser referred to her as "the blond bombshell." Hillary Clinton did not fit the stereotype of former presidential wives, and the media did not know how to handle it.

Stories about women, whether they are politicians, politicians' wives, or in other newsworthy roles, often abound with adjectives, while stories about men rarely describe them physically or emotionally. In the following passage, which is exaggerated with sexist terms and multicultural slurs, circle and discuss the words or phrases that you think might be considered as contributing to sexist stereotypes or multicultural insensitivity.

In 1993 Janet Reno became the first girl to be confirmed as attorney general of the United States. At 54, the well-preserved former Miami prosecutor, is a tough-talking woman who is often criticized for bluntness. Her 6-foot-2 frame gives her impressive stature to match her aggressive style in prosecuting cases like a barracuda, but she is not without compassion. Single and childless, she has little patience for those ghetto kids who break the law. Nor is she an Indian giver; when she makes a promise, she keeps it. Wearing a simply tailored, plaid dress the day she was nominated, she looked stunning and imposing at a press conference where she said she was honored to be considered for the office. Ever since she graduated from Harvard Law School in 1963, the statuesque woman established a reputation for herself as a serious lawyer. She has even been the subject of a rap song about forcing deadbeat dads to pay alimony, and she can be a real shrew in prosecuting them. One of her greatest losses when she was a prosecutor in Dade County, Fla. was a case against police officers who were acquitted in the beating of a Negro insurance agent, and the aftermath of the verdicts sparked violent riots in Miami. Although critics claimed she was nominated for her gender, she dismissed such concerns. This Amazon-like gal does not shy away from controversy. And she'll see plenty of it in her new job.

19-6. Age perceptions

Throughout this textbook you have been cautioned to avoid adjectives and, instead, favor concrete images of people in action or anecdotes that illustrate a point. This is particularly true when you are trying to be sensitive to multicultural issues. However, for this exercise you will be asked to consider the use of some adjectives just to test your perceptions about age. Make sure you list your own age. Then you can compare the results to those of other students. Or you can give this exercise to someone much older or much younger than you and see if the results differ. Discuss whether age perceptions vary and why.

Place the number for an age group next to the following nouns or adjectives. You may use one age group more than once.

Noun/Adjective	Age
_____Baby	(1) Less than 1
_____Infant	(2) 1 to 2
_____Toddler	(3) 2+ to 3
_____Child	(4) 3+ to 4
_____Youth	(5) 4+ to 5
_____Kid	(6) 5+ to 6
_____Teenager	(7) 6+ to 10
_____Young	(8) 10+ to 12
_____Middle Age	(9) 13 to 19
_____Old	(10) 20 to 25
_____Baby boomers	(11) 25 to 29
_____Elderly	(12) 30 to 39
_____Senior citizen	(13) 40 to 49
_____Woman	(14) 50 to 59
_____Man	(15) 60 to 69
_____Girl	(16) 70 to 79
_____Boy	(17) 80 to 89
_____Octogenarian	(18) 90 to 100
	(19) Over 100

Your age_____   Your sex: Male(_____)   Female(_____)

Obituaries 20

These exercises will give you practice writing standard-form obituaries and feature obituaries in the style suggested by Jim Nicholson, of the *Philadelphia Daily News*. Use the form in your textbook for basic obituaries. Include the cause of death and courtesy titles, even though many newspapers may not require either. Use Associated Press style, not the style in the paid death notices. Write the obituaries as directed.

20-1. Basic obituaries

a. Your editor asks you to check the death notices (paid announcements of funerals or other services) and write obituaries from them. Write this obituary in standard form with courtesy titles for the person who died, male or female. This information is taken from an obituary published in *The Oregonian,* but the name of the deceased has been changed. Here is the paid notice.

Samuel Morris Burnside, beloved father of Harold G. of Salem and Dr. Robert M. of Springfield; devoted grandfather of 10 grandchildren, eight great-grandchildren; and two great-great-grandchildren, passed away Monday. He was a retired real estate broker and past president and lieutenant governor of Division 64 of Kiwanis Pacific Northwest District. Funeral services, 1 p.m. Friday in the chapel of Young's Funeral Home in Tigard. Burial in Crescent Grove Cemetery. The family suggests remembrances be contributions to Southwest Hills Kiwanis Club.

You call the funeral home and the family and get this additional information:

He was born April 29, 1900. The family says the cause of death is age-related. He died in the Portland Care Center in Southwest Portland where he had resided for the last 10 years.

He was born in Weber, Utah and grew up on a farm near Grant, Idaho. He moved to Portland from Jerome, Idaho in 1942. He attended the University of Idaho and

Albin State Normal School. He retired many years ago but had worked as a real estate broker in the Southwest Portland area for many years.

He was past president and lieutenant governor of Division 64 of Kiwanis Pacific Northwest District. Survivors include his sons, Harold G. of Salem and Dr. Robert M. of Springfield;10 grandchildren, eight great-grandchildren; and two great-great-grandchildren.

Based on an obituary from *The Oregonian*. Used with permission.

b. Your editor wants you to start this obituary with the funeral arrangements because the person died five days earlier. Use courtesy titles for the deceased and cause of death. Be sure to follow Associated Press style, not the style that appears in the following information from a paid death notice.

Sandra K. Sullivan, beloved daughter of Zoe Margolis, loving mother of sons, Christopher Jr., and Vernon of [your town] and Archie of Lansing, MI.; and daughter Mattie Hills of San Francisco, CA., died Saturday. Leaves numerous nieces and nephews. She was born June 12, 1950. A native of (your town) and lifelong resident, she devoted herself to helping others. Friends are welcome for Visitation Friday from 9 A.M. to 9 P.M. and are respectfully invited to attend Funeral Services Saturday at 10 A.M. in the St. Paul's Baptist Church, 9030 Addison Place, [Your town]. Private interment. Remembrances may be made to the Sandra K. Sullivan musical scholarships at the church.

You call the family and funeral home. You notice that Sandra Sullivan is survived by her mother and children, but there is no mention of a husband in the paid notice. You ask how she would prefer to be addressed, and her family tells you to use "Ms." Other information from the family and funeral home includes:

Cause of death – cancer. She died in her home.

Occupation: She was director of the private Foundation for Independent Living in your town, an organization that helps disabled people. She worked for the organization for 25 years and was director for the past 10 years. She was also an accomplished pianist and choir musical director for St. Paul's Baptist Church. She graduated from the high school in your town and earned a bachelor's degree in social work from Michigan State University and a master's degree in social work from New York University.

She was divorced in 1970 from Harry G. Sullivan, but her family says they do not want that mentioned in the obituary.

c. This information is also from a paid death notice. You supplement it with interviews from the family. Use courtesy titles and cause of death.

Brett Stephen Huff entered into rest Monday. Beloved son of Martha and Edward Huff [of your town], and beloved brother of John of Ames, IA.; James of Scarsdale, N.Y., and Joseph of Dallas, TX.; dearly beloved grandson of Mary Margaret Huff, and nephew of Linda May Love of Detroit, MI. He was born [in your town] in 1960 and graduated from [your town's high school]. He earned a bachelor's degree in art from the University of Missouri in Columbia, MO. He owned his own graphics design firm [in your city] and had designed many brochures for area firms. A Mass of Christian Burial will be said at 10:30 A.M. [use tomorrow's day] at Our Savior Church, 2020 Marysville Ave. Burial will be in Greenlawn Cemetery, 30 Main Street, [your town]. Contributions may be made to the AIDS Research Fund, Fernwood Hospital, 373 Paloma Street, [your town].

You suspect the cause of death is related to AIDS, and you call the family for information. Huff's mother confirms that he had AIDS. She says he died at her home [in your town]. She tells you that in the past year that he had spoken to school students in many area high schools to educate them about the disease. He was diagnosed with AIDS in 1991 when he was living in Los Angeles. He had worked for the Tucker Design Group in that city, but in 1992 he moved your city to be near his family, and he started his own firm, Huff Designs. "He wanted to alert people to ways of preventing AIDS," his mother says. "He tried to make people more sensitive to people who have the disease."

20-2. Feature obituary

This material is from an obituary written by Jim Nicholson of the *Philadelphia Daily News*, and it includes most of his techniques discussed in the textbook. Write it as a profile, including dialogue and anecdotes as well as the standard obituary information. The cause of death is not listed because the newspaper does not use it. Some of these sentences were taken directly from the obituary, and you may use them as written if you wish.

Basic obituary information: Francis J. McBride died Monday at the age of 78. He lived in the Grays Ferry section of Philadelphia. He was a member of the Men of Malvern, Veteran of Foreign Wars and the American Legion. He is survived by his son, Francis J. Jr., two granddaughters, Mary Kate and Kathleen and a sister, Catherine Vetrone. Mass of Christian Burial will be celebrated at 9:30 a.m. tomorrow at St. Gabriel's Church, 29th and Dickinson streets. Friends may call between 7 and 9 tonight at the Shea Funeral Home, 29th and Dickinson streets. Burial will be in Ss. Peter and Paul Cemetery, Sproul and Crum Creek roads, Marple Township, Delaware County. Contributions may be made to the church memorial fund.

From interviews with his son and friends.
    Favorites: the Phillies (baseball team), kids, Ortliebs beer, Pall Mall cigarettes, his church, hard work, taprooms and most of all, his wife, Kate.
    Occupation: He worked at Midvale-Heppenstall Steel Co. at Roberts and Wissahickon avenues for 41 years. He ran the furnace in the heat-treating department. In March 1976, the company gave him a pink slip when it folded. It closed six months short of his 62nd birthday and he lost his pension. President Jimmy Carter had given the steel industry a three-month moratorium on vesting pensions, and a lot of officials grabbed the money. Oakie was part of a class action suit that went nowhere.
    After the steel plant closed, he got a job driving a cab. Then he went to work as a janitor for SEPTA (Southeastern Pennsylvania Transportation Company) until he retired four years ago. He also worked part time in the kitchen at the Barrett-Nabuurs Community Center.
    Until recently, when his health failed, he took the collection at St. Gabriel's Church.
    Characteristics: He was known for telling stories that kept people laughing. He loved the Phillies and could not be consoled when they lost the National League pennant in 1964 with a losing streak in the last dozen games. But he remained faithful. He never went to a game alone. He would round up neighborhood kids or friends and take them to the game.
    Education: His formal education ended at eighth grade.
    Historical information: As a kid, he and other boys used to hop the freight trains and throw coal over the side, jump off the train and walk back to gather up the

coal, which they would then sell for food.

Information from an interview with his son, Francis (he prefers to be called Frank) **J. "Bear" Jr.:** His father's nickname was "Oakie." He said his father got the nickname when he was Seaman McBride in the Navy and was shipped out overseas during World War II and sent straight to Okinawa. His father's bunkmate was film actor Caesar Romero and he even had a snapshot of himself with the dapper Romero. "I taught him how to dress," Oakie would say matter-of-factly.

He said his father was a "super" dad. He said his father adored his mother, who died two years ago, shortly after they had celebrated their 50th wedding anniversary. He said a part of his father's heart went with her. He (Oakie) would later say that he wanted to be with her again.

He said his father and mother used to dress up for Halloween. One Halloween she dressed him like a woman and even painted his nails bright red. The next day, after finishing his shift at Midvale, Oakie went into the company shower before he realized he hadn't taken the polish off his toenails. What the guys said next is unprintable.

He said his father loved the Phillies so much, and someone gave him a baseball that had been hit foul at a Phillies game. The baseball will be placed in Oakie's casket. Oakie would have been as proud of it as one hit out of the park.

One time at an in-law's house after a big family get-together, Oakie walked out the front door, not realizing the porch rail was down for repairs. He fell six feet into the azaleas, rolled down a hill into the driveway and under the front of a Volkswagen. Family members rushed to get him, and when they pulled him out, his first words were "You need shocks."

The son said his father loved dogs. "We were never without a dog. We had a dog named T-Bone he'd take out drinking with him all the time. He'd drink out of a round metal tray. They'd pour the beers in there. My mother said she never knew who came in drunker."

One night, though, Oakie indisputably drank T-Bone under the table.

After a long evening at Magnan's Bar at 28th and Dickinson streets, Oakie closed the place and went home. He forgot T-Bone, who had lapped himself into a stupor and passed out under the table. In the wee hours of the morning, T-Bone awoke, dazed and confused. He began howling and barking. This awakened owner Bill Magnan sleeping upstairs. He got T-Bone and walked him home.

Then there was the time the beer man came to brink in a fresh case and get the empty in the cellar.

After about 45 minutes, Oakie looked at Kate and said, "What happened to the beer man?"

They went downstairs and saw the beer man cowering in the corner, still holding a case of beer, held at bay by another dog, Nellie. The beer man said every time he opened his mouth to call out, the dog growled.

But not all of Oakie's dogs were drunks or brawlers. Every day in the summer, a dog named Whitey would trot through the neighborhood until he found the ice-cream truck and then follow it to the McBride house where Oakie would buy Whitey a milkshake.

From an interview with Joe Markey: a nephew and well-known character in the neighborhood. His nickname is "Lord of Tasker" for Tasker Street.

Markey said Oakie would always take kids to the games with him and the neighborhood kids would fight to see who could sit in his uncle's rumble seat for the drive to Shibe Park.

Markey said there were other rides he'll never forget. "He must of got 10 guys jobs at Midvale Steel, including me," said Markey. "A few of us would go to work with him in his little Corvair up the expressway. He had a cigarette cough. You could pick him out of a crowd. He would light up in the car and start coughing and the car's all over the expressway. Our hearts are palpitating. By the time we get to work we're soaking wet and ready to go back home again."

Markey said that after the plant closed, his brother (Markey's brother), Monk, got his uncle a job driving a cab. The first night out, at 24th and Pine streets, a guy pulled a gun and held up Oakie. "He called up Monk and gave him hell. He says 'Waddya tryin' to do, get me killed you sonuvabitch?!' "

Based on an obituary by Jim Nicholson, *Philadelphia Daily News.* Used with permission.

20-3. Style quiz

Correct the errors in the following sentences:

1. He is survived by his sons in Lansing, MI. and a daughter in Dallas, TX.

2. Jim Henson began appearing on television with the Muppets in the 1960's.

3. Funeral services will be held at 1 P.M. Friday.

4. A mass of Christian burial will be held at 10:30 a.m. Thursday.

5. She passed away on September 9, 1992.

6. Father James Flanagan is the priest at that roman catholic church.

7. She received her masters degree from Florida State University.

8. Survivors include fifteen grandchildren and six great grandchildren.

9. Interment will be in the Greenlawn Cemetary.

10. She lived at 1,200 Westside Rd.

21

Speeches, Press Conferences and Meetings

This chapter will give you practice writing the kinds of stories reporters cover frequently. You can choose hard-news or soft approaches, depending on the material. Use your judgment.

21-1. Burl Osborne speech

These are excerpts from a speech by Burl Osborne, editor and publisher of *The Dallas Morning News*. He made this speech in 1991 at a convention of the American Society of Newspaper Editors when he was president of the organization. Write a news story based on this speech as though Osborne gave it at your journalism school to an audience of 100 journalism students and teachers. Write it for tomorrow's campus newspaper, using yesterday (use the day of the week) as your time frame. Tailor your angle to your campus audience.

This is the bicentennial of the Bill of Rights, a time to celebrate freedoms articulated in those initial constitutional amendments, especially the First Amendment. This is a year in which freedom of the press began to blossom in the former Communist countries of East and Central Europe, where it had been smothered for up to 70 years; a year in which democracy pushed toward the surface in China; a year in which Nelson Mandela was free to speak in South Africa.

It is ironic that during a year that should be a milestone for free expression, we are losing ground. All around us there are opportunities to validate free speech and a free press. Yet there is an increasingly restrictive atmosphere on college campuses.

On college campuses all across the country there are growing restraints on free speech and academic freedom.

It is troubling that the attacks are coming from those who once defended the right to free expression – and who achieved their own status by exercising it.

It was troubling to hear President Derek Bok of Harvard, a great defender of free expression, take the view that this really doesn't rank very high on the list of problems at the country's universities. I would like to be wrong, but I share the view of Professor Alan Dershowitz that this is a serious problem.

Trying to squelch unpopular speech isn't a new idea, of course. In the era of Sen. Joseph McCarthy in the 1950s, supposed Communists and their sympathizers were the targets and the security of the United States was the excuse.

More recently, proposed laws would have imprisoned those who burn the American flag as a form of political protest. Congress made such a law, which the Supreme Court struck down. There was talk of a constitutional amendment but that also was beaten back – at least

123

for the moment.

Most people don't want to endanger democracy or burn the flag. But it is just plain wrong to try to protect democracy by denying its principles, or to try to protect the flag by denying the rights that it stands for.

In these, and most, cases, the urge to censor is the reaction of well-intentioned people to the expression of views they find repugnant.

Censors are always certain they are acting for the common good. The current wave of censorship has all these characteristics. The common good for which the censors would supersede the constitution is protection from being offended, insulted or ridiculed.

The goal is to eliminate prejudice, particularly that based on race, gender or sexual orientation. That is an admirable goal. Using censorship as a tool to achieve that goal is not an admirable strategy. Yet censorship has become the strategy of choice.

A growing number of campuses now forbid offensive speech or expression, with penalties ranging from censure to expulsion to thought-remedial visits to a psychologist. Behavior that complies with what is deemed to be proper is politically correct. Censorship is the discipline imposed on the politically incorrect.

The core activities of a university, the competition of ideas and the pursuit of academic inquiry, can flourish only with the right to express any opinion or ask any questions without regard to the correctness of the premise. It is one thing to disagree with an opinion and defeat it with logic. To deny the mere expression of a bad idea is quite another. We find ourselves accepting intolerance of disagreeable or offensive speech in order to fight intolerance of other kinds.

Here are some examples culled from journals and magazines during the last several months. I disagree with many of the views that are expressed, but I disagree more with the notion that one shouldn't be permitted to express them at all.

At the University of California at Berkeley, a professor wrote in a magazine that he believed the school's affirmative action program discriminated against white and Asian applicants. Students who disagreed disrupted his class and the university gave him to wonder whether or not he would be permitted to continue teaching.

In the New York University law school, the moot court board assigned a case concerning the custody rights of a lesbian mother. Students temporarily forced withdrawal of the case on grounds that arguments against the mother would be hurtful to a particular group.

The University of Connecticut prohibited "inappropriately directed laughter" and "conspicuous exclusion of students from conversations." A woman student was banned from campus for posting a sign on her dormitory door that was judged to be offensive and thus in violation of the student code.

The student senate at the University of Wisconsin in Madison protested an "All-American Halloween Ball," on the grounds that masked students might anonymously insult others.

At San Francisco State University, 30 students disrupted a class in black politics. They were not protesting anything the professor said; they objected because the course was listed in the catalog under Political Science rather than Black Studies.

A University of Michigan student read a limerick containing joking references to homosexuality. He was required to publish a written self-criticism, "Learned My Lesson," in the student newspaper.

At the University of Minnesota, an entire department, including one woman, was charged with sexual harassment. One charge was based on a professor's negative comment about a woman student's paper; another was that a professor failed to return a greeting before class.

At Harvard, a student displayed a Confederate flag to demonstrate what she described as a surge of Southern pride stimulated by the war in the Persian Gulf. An African-American student was offended and displayed a swastika to demonstrate his view that the Confederate flag is a hateful sign. Jewish students were offended because of the swastika's Nazi symbolism. The first student was offended because the Confederate flag didn't mean to others what it means to her.

President Derek Bok did not follow the lead of many of his peers at other universities when he responded. Bok said that while the actions of the students were insensitive and unwise, they were protected by the First Amendment. But the fact that it is protected, he said, does not mean it is right, proper or civil.

At Smith College, students were given a list of terms of oppression, including, with appropriate references to racism and sexism, some others that required new words because the victims, as the handbook took note, may not yet know they are oppressed.

Ableism, for example, is defined as the oppression of the differently abled by the temporarily abled. Classism is the oppression of the working class and non-propertied by the upper and middle classes. Lookism, is, in part, the construction of a standard for beauty or attractiveness.

In the course of collecting written material on this subject, I ran across a tongue-in-cheek forecast of particular interest to me. It predicted that the next ism might be heightism, whose victims would no longer be called short, but instead would be known as the vertically challenged.

Gotcha. Some of you were guilty of inappropriately directed laughter. Even though the story didn't offend me, it might offend someone. For the benefit of the thought police, I need to point out that I was trying not to poke fun at their good intentions but to point out the complexity of deciding exactly what speech is permissible and what isn't.

I take the entire subject very seriously. But I have to say that if we hope to make good on this country's promises of freedom to speak one's mind, then we are not going about it in a very productive way.

What we should be doing is defending and promoting the right of free speech; that is the best way to persuade each other of the moral validity of the civil treatment of everyone.

These concerns are especially important to journalists because censorship on the campus today will be censorship in the newsroom tomorrow. Campus newspapers are speaking out on this subject in places like the University of Colorado in Boulder. In others, I suspect the fear of offending has kept them quiet; they need First Amendment protection, too.

I am pleased that the ASNE, under the direction of David Lawrence, our incoming president, will intensify efforts to strengthen First Amendment values.

I hope that ASNE will study what is happening on the campuses. We need to know whether what we are seeing is a fad or a permanent change on the university scene.

Last night several editors met for dinner at the Cafe Budapest. The group was met by an elegant, silver-haired woman in a flowing white gown. She was the owner of the restaurant, Dr. Livia Hedda Rev-Kury. As she welcomed the party, Dr. Rev-Kury asked about the "Celebrate the First" button that editor Frank Sutherland was wearing.

"It celebrates the First Amendment," he said. "Would you like to have it?" he asked. "Oh, yes," she responded.

As she took the button, she said, "I know a little about the First Amendment," and she paused.

"You know, I love America more than you do."

"Why is that," the editor asked.

She rolled up her sleeve and extended her arm. "You see, I have these numbers...."

That was one more First Amendment minute given to us by a survivor of Dachau and Auschwitz and citizen of the United States. The tattoo she carries is a permanent reminder of the value of the First Amendment. We need to somehow tattoo that value on our souls. We need to figure out how to reduce prejudice without sacrificing individual liberties and freedom of thought and expression.

If we fail, this bicentennial celebration of the Bill of Rights will have a hollow ring. If we succeed, we can start now to celebrate the next hundred years of freedom.

Burl Osborne. Reprinted with permission.

21-2. Clinton inaugural address

This exercise will test your ability to summarize the main points and choose the best quotes. On Jan. 20, 1993 William Jefferson Clinton was inaugurated as the 42nd president of the United States. The address lasted 14 minutes and was delivered on the west side of the Capitol in Washington, D.C., after he took the oath of office at 12:01 p.m. from Chief Justice William Rehnquist. To help you decide which quotes are worth using in your story, underline the quotes that you think are strong enough to use as pull quotes. Write this as a speech story as though the event happened yesterday. Here is his address:

My fellow citizens:

Today, we celebrate the mystery of American renewal.

This ceremony is held in the depth of winter. But, by the words we speak and the faces we show the world, we force the spring.

A spring reborn in the world's oldest democracy, that brings forth the vision and courage to reinvent America.

When our founders boldly declared America's independence to the world and our purposes to the Almighty, they knew that America, to endure, would have to change.

Not change for change's sake, but change to preserve America's ideals — life, liberty, the pursuit of happiness. Though we march to the music of our time, our mission is timeless.

Each generation of Americans must define what it means to be an American.

On behalf of our nation, I salute my predecessor President Bush for his half-century of service to America, and I thank the millions of men and women whose steadfastness and sacrifice triumphed over depression, fascism and communism.

Today, a generation raised in the shadows of the Cold War assumed new responsibilities in a world warmed by the sunshine of freedom but threatened still by ancient hatreds and new plagues.

Raised in unrivaled prosperity, we inherit an economy that is still the world's strongest, but is weakened by business failures, stagnant wages, increasing inequality, and deep divisions among our own people.

When George Washington first took the oath I have just sworn to uphold, news traveled slowly across the land by horseback and across the ocean by boat. Now, the sights and sounds of this ceremony are broadcast instantaneously to billions around the world.

Communications and commerce are global; investment is mobile; technology is almost magical; and ambition for a better life is now universal. We earn our livelihood in America today in our peaceful competition with people all across the earth.

Profound and powerful forces are shaking and remaking our world, and the urgent question of our time is whether we can change our friend and not our enemy.

This new world has already enriched the lives of millions of Americans who are able to compete and win in it. But when most people are working harder for less, when others cannot work at all, when the cost of health care devastates families and threatens to bankrupt our enterprises, great and small, when fear of crime robs law-abiding citizens of their freedom and when millions of poor children cannot even imagine the lives we are calling them to lead — we have not made change our friend.

We know we have to face hard truths and take strong steps. But we have not done so. Instead, we have drifted, and that drifting has eroded our resources, fractured our economy and shaken our confidence.

Though our challenges are fearsome, so are our strengths. Americans have ever been a restless, questing, hopeful people. And we must bring to our task today the vision and will of those who came before us.

From our revolution to the Civil War, to the Great Depression to the civil rights movement, our people have always mustered the determination to construct from these crises the pillars of our history.

Thomas Jefferson believed that to preserve the very foundations of our nation, we would need dramatic change from time to time. Well, my fellow Americans, this is our time. Let us embrace it.

Our democracy must be not only the envy of the world but the engine or our own renewal. There is nothing wrong with America that cannot be cured by what is right with America.

So today, we pledge an end to the era of deadlock and drift — and a new season of American renewal has begun.

To renew America, we must be bold.

We must do what no generation has had to do before. We must invest more in our own people, in their jobs and in their future, and at the same time cut our massive debt. And we must do so in a world in which we must compete for every opportunity.

It will not be easy; it will require sacrifice. But it can be done, and done fairly, not choosing sacrifice for its own sake. We must provide for our nation the way a family provides for its children.

Our founders saw themselves in the light of posterity. We can do no less. Anyone who has ever watched a child's eyes wander into sleep knows what posterity is. Posterity is the world to come – the world for whom we hold our ideals, from whom we have borrowed our planet, and to whom we bear sacred responsibility.

We must do what America does best: offer more opportunity to all and demand more responsibility from all.

It is time to break the bad habit of expecting something for nothing, from our government or from each other. Let us all take more responsibility, not only for ourselves and our families but for our communities and our country.

To renew America, we must revitalize our democracy.

This beautiful capital, like every capital since the dawn of civilization, is often a place of intrigue and calculation. Powerful people maneuver for position and worry endlessly about who is in and who is out, who is up and who is down, forgetting those people whose toil and sweat sends us here and pays our way.

Americans deserve better. And in this city today, there are people who want to do better. So I say to all of you here, let us resolve to reform our politics, so that power and privilege no longer shout down the voice of the people. Let us put aside personal advantage so that we can feel the pain and see the promise of America.

Let us resolve to make our government a place for what Franklin Roosevelt called "bold, persistent experimentation," a government for our tomorrows, not our yesterdays.

Let us give this capital back to the people to whom it belongs.

To renew America, we must meet challenges abroad as well as at home. There is no longer clear division between what is foreign and what is domestic – the world economy, the world environment, the worlds AIDS crisis, the world

arms race – they affect us all.

Today, as an old order passes, the new world is more free but less stable. Communism's collapse has called forth old animosities and new dangers. Clearly America must continue to lead the world we did so much to make.

While America rebuilds at home, we will not shrink from the challenges, nor fail to seize the opportunities, of this new world. Together with our friends and allies, we will work to shape change, lest it engulf us.

When our vital interests are challenged, or the will and conscience of the international community is defied, we will act – with peaceful diplomacy whenever possible, with force when necessary. The brave Americans serving our nation today in the Persian Gulf, in Somalia, and wherever else they stand are testament to our resolve.

But our greatest strength is the power of our ideas, which are still new in many lands. Across the world, we see them embraced – and we rejoice. Our hopes, our hearts, our hands, are with those on every continent who are building democracy and freedom. Their cause is America's cause.

The American people have summoned the change we celebrate today. You have raised your voices in an unmistakable chorus. You have cast your votes in historic numbers. And you have changed the face of the Congress, the presidency, and the political process itself.

Yes, you, my fellow Americans have forced the spring.

Now, we must do the work the season demands.

To that work I now turn, with all the authority of my office. I ask the Congress to join with me. But no president, no Congress, no government, can undertake this mission alone.

My fellow Americans, you, too, must play your part in our renewal.

I challenge a new generation of young Americans to a season of service – to act on your idealism by helping troubled children, keeping company with those in need,

reconnecting our torn communities. There is so much to be done – enough, indeed, for millions of others who are still young in spirit to give of themselves in service, too.

In serving, we recognize a simple but powerful truth: We need each other. And we must care for one another.

Today, we do more than celebrate America; we rededicate ourselves to the very idea of America.

An idea born in revolution and renewed through two centuries of challenge; an idea tempered by the knowledge that, but for fate we – the fortunate and the unfortunate,– might have been each other; an idea ennobled by the faith that our nation can summon from its myriad diversities the deepest measure of unity; an idea infused with the conviction that America's long heroic journey must go forever upward.

And so my fellow Americans, as we stand at the edge of the 21st century, let us begin with energy and hope, with faith and discipline, and let us work until our work is done. The Scripture says, "And let us not be weary in well-doing, for in due season, we shall reap, if we faint not."

From this joyful mountaintop of celebration, we hear a call to service in the valley.

We have heard the trumpets. We have changed the guard. And now – each in our own way, and with God's help – we must answer the call.

21-3. Anita Hill testimony

In your textbook you have an exercise to cover the testimony of Clarence Thomas at his Senate confirmation hearings for Supreme Court Justice. Here is the testimony of Anita Hill, the woman who accused Thomas of sexual harassment. Although this is not a speech in the traditional sense, her statement before the Senate Judiciary Committee is similar to a speech. Her statement contains very graphic sexual detail, the kind that most newspapers usually do not print. However, because it was a key factor in her testimony, the sexual references could be considered crucial to the story. You decide if you think that information is needed.

Background: Anita Hill, a professor of law at the University of Oklahoma, worked for Clarence Thomas when he was an assistant secretary in the Department of Education's Office of Civil Rights in 1981 and a year later when he chairman of the Equal Employment Opportunities Commission. She accused Thomas of sexual harassment in 1991 when she was interviewed by the FBI as part of background checks the agency was conducting into Thomas. Her testimony before the Senate Judiciary Committee was given on Oct. 11, 1991, but for purposes of this assignment, assume that you are covering it for tomorrow's newspaper and that it occurred today.

Here is her opening statement to the committee:

Mr. Chairman, Senator Thurmond, members of the committee, my name is Anita F. Hill, and I am a professor of law at the University of Oklahoma. I was born on a farm in Okmulgee County, Oklahoma, in 1956. I am the youngest of 13 children. I had an early education in Okmulgee County. My father, Albert Hill, is a farmer in that area. My mother's name is Irma Hill. She also is a farmer and a housewife.

My childhood was one of a lot of hard work and not much money, but it was one of solid family affection, as represented by my parents. I was reared in a religious atmosphere in the Baptist faith, and I have been a member of Antioch Baptist Church in Tulsa, Oklahoma, since 1983. It is a very warm part of my life at the present time.

For my undergraduate work, I went to Oklahoma State University and graduated from there in 1977. . . .

I graduated from the university with academic honors and proceeded to the Yale Law School, where I received my J.D. degree in 1980. Upon graduation from law school, I became a practicing lawyer with the Washington, D.C. firm of Ward, Hardraker and Ross.

In 1981 I was introduced to now Judge Thomas by a mutual friend. Judge Thomas told me that he was anticipating a political appointment, and he asked if I would be interested in working with him. He was, in fact, appointed as assistant secretary of education for civil rights. After he had taken that post, he asked if I would become his assistant, and I accepted that position.

In my early period there, I had two major projects. The first was an article I wrote for Judge Thomas's signature on the education of minority students. The second was the organization of a seminar on high-risk students which was abandoned because Judge Thomas was transferred to the EEOC where he became chairman of that office.

During this period at the Department of Education, my working relationship with Judge Thomas was positive. I had a good deal of responsibility and independence. I thought he respected my work and that he trusted by judgment. After approximately three months of working there, he asked me to go out socially with him.

What happened next and telling the world about it are the two most difficult things – experiences of my life. It is only after a great deal of agonizing consideration and sleepless number – a great deal of sleepless nights that I am able to talk of these unpleasant matters to anyone but my close friends.

I declined the invitation to go out socially with him and explained to him that I thought it would jeopardize what at the time I considered to be a very good working relationship. I had a normal social life with other men outside of the office. I believed then, as now, that having a social relationship with a person who was supervising my work would be ill-advised. I was very uncomfortable with the idea and told him so.

I thought that by saying no and explaining my reasons my employer would abandon his social suggestions. However, to my regret, in the following few weeks, he continued to ask me out on several occasions. He pressed me to justify my reasons for saying no to him. These incidents took place in his office or mine. They were in the form of private conversations which would not have been overheard by anyone else.

My working relationship became even more strained when Judge Thomas began to use work situations to discuss sex. On these occasions, he would call me into his office for reports on education issues and projects, or he might suggest that, because of time pressures of his schedule, we go to lunch to a government cafeteria.

After a brief discussion of work, he would turn the conversation to a discussion of sexual matters.

His conversations were very vivid. He spoke about acts that he had seen in pornographic films involving such matters as women having sex with animals and films showing group sex or rape scenes.

He talked about pornographic materials depicting individuals with large penises or large breasts involved in various sex acts. On several occasions, Thomas told me graphically of his own sexual prowess.

Because I was extremely uncomfortable talking about sex with him at all and particularly in such a graphic way, I told him that I did not want to talk about these subjects. I would also try to change the subject to education matters or to non-sexual personal matters such as his background or his beliefs. My efforts to change the subject were rarely successful.

Throughout the period of these conversations, he also from time to time asked me for social engagements. My reaction to these conversations was to avoid them by eliminating opportunities for us to engage in extended conversations. This was difficult because at the time I was his only assistant at the Office of Education – or Office for Civil Rights.

During the latter part of my time at the Department of Education, the social pressures and an conversation of his offensive behavior ended. I began both to believe and hope that our working relationship could be a proper, cordial and professional one.

When Judge Thomas was made chair of the EEOC, I needed to face the question of whether to go with him. I was asked to do so, and I did. The work itself was interesting, and at that time it appeared that the sexual overtures which had so troubled me had ended. I also faced the realistic fact that I had no alternative job. While I might have gone back to private practice, perhaps in my old firm or at another, I was dedicated to civil rights work, and my first choice was to be in that field. Moreover, the Department of Education itself was a dubious venture. President Reagan was seeking to abolish the entire department.

For my first months at the EEOC, where I continued to be an assistant to Judge Thomas, there were no sexual conversations or overtures. However, during the fall and winter of 1982, these began again. The comments were random and ranged from pressing me about why I didn't go out with him to remarks about my personal appearance. I remember his saying that some day I would have to tell him the real reason that I wouldn't go out with him.

He began to show displeasure in his tone and voice and his demeanor and his continued pressure for an explanation. He commented on what I was wearing in terms of whether it made me more or less sexually attractive. The incidents occurred in his inner office at the EEOC.

One of the oddest episodes I remember was an occasion in which Thomas was drinking a Coke in his office. He got up form the table at which we were working, went over to his desk to get the Coke, looked at the can, and asked, 'Who has put pubic hair on my Coke?" On other occasions, he referred to the size of his own penis as being larger than normal, and he also spoke on some occasions of the pleasures he had given to women with oral sex.

At this point, late 1982, I began to feel severe stress on the job. I began to be concerned that Clarence Thomas might take out his anger with me by degrading me or not giving me important assignments. I also though that he might find an excuse for dismissing me.

In January of 1983, I began looking for another job. I was handicapped because I feared that, if he found out, he might make it difficult for me to find other employment and I might be dismissed from the job I had. Another factor that made my search more difficult was that there was a period – this was during a period of a hiring freeze in the government. In February of 1983, I was hospitalized for five days on an emergency basis for acute stomach pain, which I attributed to stress on the job.

Once out of the hospital, I became more committed to find other employment and sought further to minimize my contact with Thomas. This became easier when Alison Duncan became office director, because most of my work was then funneled through her and I had contact with Clarence Thomas mostly in staff meetings.

In the spring of 1983, an opportunity to teach at Oral Roberts University opened up. I participated in a seminar – taught an afternoon session . . . . The dean of the university saw me teaching and inquired as to whether I would be interested in furthering – pursuing a career in teaching, beginning at Oral Roberts University. I agreed to take the job in large part because of my desire to escape the pressures I felt at the EEOC due to Judge Thomas.

When I informed him that I was leaving in July, I recall that his response was that now I would no longer have an excuse for not going out with him. I told him that I still preferred not to do so.

At some time after that meeting, he asked if he could take me to dinner at the end of the term. When I declined, he assured me that the dinner was a professional courtesy only and not a social invitation. I reluctantly agreed to accept that invitation, but only if it was at the very end of a working day.

On, as I recall, the last day of my employment at the EEOC in the summer of 1983, I did have dinner with Clarence Thomas. We went directly from work to a restaurant near the office. We talked about he work I had done, both at Education and at the EEOC. He told me that he was pleased with all of it except for an article and speech that I had done for him while we were at the Office for Civil Rights. Finally, he made a comment that I vividly remember.

He said that if I ever told anyone of his behavior that it would ruin his career. This was not an apology, nor was it an explanation. That was the last remark about the possibility of our going out or reference to his behavior. . . .

It is only after a great deal of agonizing consideration that I am able to talk of these unpleasant matters to anyone except my closest friends. As I've said before these last few days have been very trying and very hard for me and it hasn't just been the last few days this week. It has actually been over a month now that I have been under the strain of this issue.

Telling the world is the most difficult experience of my life, but it is very close to having to live through the experience that occasioned this meeting. I may have used poor judgment early on in my relationship with this issue. I was aware, however, that telling at any point in my career would adversely affect my future career. And I did not want early on to burn all the bridges to the EEOC.

As I said, I may have used poor judgment. Perhaps I should have taken angry or even militant steps, both when I was in the agency or after I left it. But I must confess to the world that the course that I took seemed the better as well as the easier approach.

I declined any comment to newspapers, but later when Senate staff asked me about these matters I felt I had a duty to report. I have no personal vendetta against Clarence Thomas. I seek only to provide the committee with information which it may regard as relevant.

It would have been more comfortable to remain silent. I took no initiative to inform anyone. But when I was asked by a representative of this committee to report my experience, I felt that I had to tell the truth. I could not keep silent.

21-4. Press conference

Terry Anderson, the chief correspondent in the Middle East for The Associated Press, was abducted on March 16, 1985 by the Islamic Jihad faction of the Iranian-backed Lebanese Shiite Muslims. He was held in captivity for 6 1/2 years, the longest held captive of any of the hostages in Lebanon. On Dec. 4, 1991 he was freed, and he conducted a news conference at the Syrian Foreign Ministry in Damascus, Syria. He was 44 at the time. He wore a white shirt and a dark cardigan he had received from his captors the day before. He was scheduled to be released earlier but was delayed by a snowstorm, officials said. Write this story as though he had just been released and you are writing for tomorrow's newspaper.

Background: Anderson was abducted in West Beirut after he finished playing a tennis game with an AP photographer, who was held at gunpoint while Anderson was whisked away by his captors. The terrorists had claimed they were taking hostages as an attempt to force Israel to release Palestinian prisoners.

Anderson, who was separated from his first wife, had been living with Madeleine Bassil, a Lebanese woman who was pregnant at the time of his capture. She gave birth to his daughter, Sulome, three months after he was captured. When he was freed, he saw his 6-year-old daughter for the first time. Bassil was his fiance. Throughout his captivity, his sister, Peggy Say, continued to press officials for his release.

Prior to Anderson's release, two other American hostages – Alann Steen and Joseph Cicippio – were freed earlier in the week. British envoy Terry Waite and Thomas Sutherland, an American who was a professor at American University, also were held captive with Anderson and were freed earlier.

Here is his press conference; reporters' questions and comments are in boldface type:

I'm going to try to shake as many people's hands as I can after we get finished here. I mean you're all my friends, but I can't get to you all.

You can't imagine how glad I am to see you. I've thought about this moment for a long time. And now it's here, and I'm scared to death. I don't know what to say.

I have, of course, to thank the Syrian, Lebanese and Iranian governments for their cooperation and other work in helping to free so many hostages recently. I feel the deepest gratitude to Mr. (Giandomenica) Picco and the (U.N.) Secretary General (Javier Perez de Cuellar). I don't know how to express it. I mean thanks just doesn't cover it.

Your support, all my colleagues, journalists, has been very important. I've heard so many things over the years – on the radio, in the few magazines and newspapers we've gotten – about your work for me. Again, I just can't say how grateful I am.

Also, for thousands and thousands of people, whom I don't know, never met, who don't know me, who I know have been working and praying for us all, all the hostages, your support, your prayers were important. They made a big difference, they made a difference for us in some very dark times.

My family, of course, my incredible sister, Peg, I will be thanking shortly myself and personally.

There are a couple of you I'd like to mention individually, obviously. Where's the BBC man? Here some place?

(Reporter: He's not here.)

Couldn't make it, huh? Well after all the wonderful things that Tom (Sutherland) and Terry (Waite) said about the BBC, I suppose I should be a little critical and niggly here and there, but I haven't got the heart for it. I've spent a lot of time listening to the radio recently, most of the time to the BBC. Your news coverage always has been superb. My special thanks to the"outlook" team. . . for the many times and much effort they spent to bring me messages from my family and my friends, and often their voices, and that was very, very important.

And I'd like to thank my Lebanese colleagues in the television and newspapers both, because each year they brought a message to me from my family on my birthday, on Christmas and sometimes elsewhere. And they did this in midst of their own terrible troubles. And that shows a depth of concern and support that again, I just keep saying, I'm very grateful for.

I'm grateful to you all, to everyone. Oh, we'll niggle a little bit. I was never a Marine captain. I was a Marine sergeant. And I'm very proud to have been that, by the way.

I spent the afternoon, interestingly enough, playing solitaire by candlelight and listening to the BBC reporting on my progress toward Damascus. Well, it was kind of like listening to your own obituary. You were very nice to me, thank you.

I'll try to answer a few questions. Although you'll understand I have a date with a couple of beautiful ladies, and I'm already late.

Can you tell about your journey here and when you were actually freed?

Yesterday afternoon, my captors came in, brought some new clothes, new shoes — my first in seven years, and they hurt my feet, by the way — and they said that I would be going home today. They asked me to read a statement from them to the world about this kidnapping episode. And I did so on a videotape, which they said they took to the AP today.

We got it!

OK, making very clear that it was their statement, not mine, but I felt it was worthwhile to listen to what they had to say. Spent the night awake mostly. Today, I spent the day pacing the room and playing solitaire and waiting. I think this last 24 hours has been longer than the whole 6 1/2 years beforehand. I was taken from my cell about 6:20 or 6:30, and driven to a nearby place, turned over to Syrian officers, and brought, with a couple of brief stops, here and to face you. I almost walked in on you when I came in the door, except I heard a low growl go up and I figured I better go the other way.

Tell us something more about what it's been like in captivity.

Oh Lord. Um. It would take a book. That's an idea, by the way.

How do you feel about your title of longest-held hostage?

It's an honor I would gladly have given up a long time ago.

What about the German hostages, you mentioned something about them. Did they mention anything about them?

I wish I had some news about them. I don't. I hope for their release. I hope for the release of all the Lebanese very very soon and I know with fine men like Mr. Picco and Mr. de Cuellar working on it that there's a good chance it will happen. I don't have any news. My captors always denied having any control of information or business to do with other hostages other than the ones that we knew about, the ones that were kept together with me.

What kept you going?

Well, my companions. I was lucky enough to have other people with me most of the time. My faith. My stubbornness, I guess. You just do what you have to do. You wake up every day, and you summon up the energy from somewhere, even when you think you haven't got it and you get through the day. And you do it day after day after day.

How did you occupy yourself after you were the last one left?

Paced back and forth. I had a couple of plastic bottles that I filled up with water and used as dumbbells. Played a lot of solitaire — I had a deck of cards — and listened to the radio, mostly to the BBC.

What were your last words to the kidnappers?

Goodbye.

21-5. Meeting advance

The story you write before the meeting about issues the governmental body will discuss is often more important than the actual meeting story. The meeting advance informs readers so they have a chance to express their views at the meeting. You should get a copy of the meeting agenda a few days before the meeting. Write a meeting advance based on the following information:

You have received an agenda of the city commission meeting in your community. (Substitute commission for council or whatever your local city government body is called.) Read the following agenda and decide what item or items you think are worthy of an advance story. Here are some of the items on the agenda:

A. Consent agenda: All matters listed on the consent agenda are considered under one motion and will be enacted by one motion. There will be no separate discussion of those items. If discussion is desired, that item will be removed from the consent agenda and considered separately.
1. Review and approve minutes of various boards and commissions:
   City Commission meeting of previous week.
   Aviation Advisory Board meeting of previous week.
2. Approve renewal of the following licenses:
   a. Drinking establishments: Benchwarmers, Inc., 1601 W. 23rd; Don's Steak House, 2176 East 23rd.
3. Bid item:
   a. Set bid date of Jan. 5 for annual lubricants contract (Public Works)
4. Approve on second and final reading, the following ordinances
   a. Ordinance No. 6354 annexing a 28.5 acre tract of land generally located south of Sixth Street and west of Wakarusa Drive.
5. Ordinance No. 6395 authorizing the issuance of $6,000,000 multi-family housing development revenue refunding bonds for Brandon Woods nursing home, 15th and Inverness Drive. (Approved by the commission on [date specified].
B. Consider the following regular agenda items:
1. Conduct a public hearing and consider adopting Resolution No. 5501 declaring house at 1222 Summit St. blighted.
   Action: Adopt Resolution No. 5501 if appropriate.
2. Consider proposed request for proposals for architectural consultant services related to proposed renovation and expansion of city art center.
   Action: Authorize request for proposals.
3. Receive feasibility update report from consulting team about building a public golf course.
   Action: Receive and discuss study
4. Receive staff report and draft ordinance prohibiting nudity in establishments selling intoxicating liquors.
   Action: Receive staff report, direct placement of ordinance on next agenda.
5. Consider approval of contract with Hamm Quarry Inc. for landfill services.
6. Consider appointments to various boards.

You have reviewed the agenda and have decided to focus on the proposed ordinance banning nudity or the consultants' report on the proposed city golf course. You call some of the commissioners (there are five) and find out they are really concerned about nudity in the local bars. City Manager Mike Wildgen tells you the concern was fostered because they received a proposal from a man who wants to start a bar featuring topless female dancers. The manager and commissioners don't tell you who he is, but they say they want to create an ordinance preventing nudity in bars or other establishments that serve liquor just to prevent someone from setting up such a place. Currently no bars in your city feature nude dancers.

Background:

The proposed ordinance would affect only businesses licensed to sell alcohol. It would not affect other "adult entertainment" establishments such as X-rated movies theaters. The proposed ordinance says: "Alcohol-licensed establishments that offer nude dancing foster and promote incidents of criminal activity, can and do adversely affect property values, can and do contribute to neighborhood decay and blight, and do create direct exposures to health risks and potential health hazards."

Johnson County, a neighboring county, is being sued by a club and several nude dancers who say that the county's ban on nude dancing is unconstitutional.

Here are some of the commissioners' comments:

Commissioner Bob Walters: "I'm not a prude. But I don't think that nude entertainment in any form should be allowed in any business with access to the public. Sometimes I don't understand why we can't do what we think is in the best interests of the community."

Commissioner Bob Schumm: "We just don't need it (nudity). We're doing fine without it. This is a wholesome city, a good place to raise a family and we don't need all the problems that go along with (adult entertainment)."

Commissioner Shirley Martin-Smith: "I am not into banning free speech or banning anything, but I am into putting some controls on entertainment that is not a benefit to the community. People are just amazed that this even needs to be an issue. I think the point of the ordinance is to eliminate the possibility of nudity as entertainment in the city. I think we just have to pursue it and see where it takes us, which is what we do on a lot of issues."

County Chief Deputy Counselor, LeeAnne Gillaspie: The legal basis for restricting behavior in such clubs was firmly stated in the 21st Amendment to the Constitution, which outlawed Prohibition and gave states the power to restrict alcohol consumption. She said once the law moves away from alcohol (such as regulating juice bars, for example), the issue moves into the First Amendment and freedom of expression guarantees.

The meeting will be conducted at 6:30 p.m. Monday in your city hall (give the address) or use Sixth and Massachusetts streets.

Based on a story from the *Lawrence* (Kan.) *Daily Journal-World.* Used with permission.

21-6. Meeting story

Write a story based on the following information from a city council meeting:

The City Council (five members including the mayor and vice mayor) in your town is conducting its regular weekly meeting. Several items are on the agenda. They include:

Consent agenda:
Approve minutes of the last meeting.
Consider spending $44,000 for two vans and a four-wheel drive pickup for use by the city's maintenance personnel.
Receive an annual audit report from the accounting firm of Schehrer, Harrod and Bennett.

Other items:
Consider cutting five positions from the Police Department and consolidating some police support services with the county for a savings of $762,301.
Consider a recommendation from the Planning Commission to rezone 34 acres of agricultural land in the western part of the city to residential use.
Consider revising an ordinance prohibiting potbellied pigs.

The meeting was called to order at 8 a.m. A motion was made to approve the consent agenda. It was unanimously approved.

Vice Mayor Charles Shorter moved to cut five positions from the police department. Police Chief Samuel Safety strenuously objected. He said the cuts would hamper his department's ability to patrol the streets. He said the loss of police officers is coming at a time when the crime rate is increasing. Shorter said the city had to reduce spending somewhere, and by consolidating some other services with the county, the Police Department could cut the positions from its administrative and clerical staff. "I am not recommending that the reductions be made to the police force," Shorter said. The motion was approved unanimously.

Commissioner Shirley Wise moved to accept the recommendation of the Planning Commission. The motion was unanimously approved.

Shorter moved to reconsider an ordinance the council passed last week outlawing swine in city limits. He said a pig owner had caused him to reconsider.

Mayor David Fischer asked if any members of the public wished to speak to the issue.

Janie Finck, the owner of a Vietnamese potbellied pig, requested to speak. She brought her pet with her. She said her pig is named Bo Jackswine, in honor of athlete Bo Jackson. Finck was wearing pig emblem earrings as she showed her 42-pound pig to the council members. Finck had the pig sit up for a treat. After seeing the pig, several council members expressed their support and engaged in pig puns.

The pig wore a red bow around his neck. He swished his tail constantly and walked to the end of his leash to sniff people curiously.

Councilman Robert Stewart said: "Let me mention that Bo Jackswine has been a constituent of mine for over a year and there have been no complaints. He's a perfect neighbor."

Shorter said he was so impressed by the pig that he might consider getting one himself.

"Talk about rolling over," Fischer quipped. "All right, let's have a swine call."

The council voted unanimously to ask the city attorney to rework city laws to reclassify Vietnamese potbellied pigs as domestic animals. That would make it legal to keep them within city limits.

Finck told council members: "Thank you very much. Bo thanks you very much. I am very happy. And Bo did excellent. He was definitely a ham."

After the vote you get these reactions from the people who came to urge council to change the ordinance so they could keep their potbellied pigs.

From John Hood, who owns a white Vietnamese potbellied pig named Gidget: He said his pig means the world to him. "It was either they pass it or I'd have moved out. You can steal my truck or anything else, but you better leave my pig alone."

From Kris Guidice, owner of Popeye and Ryne, two Vietnamese potbellied pigs: "I took off work. I haven't slept in two days because I've been so worried about it."

The council will conduct a public hearing and consider final approval of the revised ordinance at 8 a.m. on May 7 at City Hall.

The pig ordinance information is from a story in the *St. Petersburg* (Fla.) *Times.* Used with permission.

21-7. School board meeting

Read the following script of a school board meeting and write a story, choosing the most interesting item for your focus.

The Rockville School Board is conducting its weekly meeting at 7 p.m. in the school administration building, at 2500 Addison Place. (You may substitute the name of the school board in your town for this exercise.) Write a story based on the scenario that follows.

School board members are as follows: Alfred C. Robertson (president) William Harold, Maria Santana, Peter Bodine (Board secretary), Denise Davis. The meeting begins with a motion to approve the minutes of the last meeting, and the board unanimously approves.

Robertson: Next item on the agenda is to receive bids for three new school buses.

Bodine: We've got kind of a deal here. One bus company, Sierra Busing, has entered a bid of $23,520. Now that's for a normal bus that can hold 84 students. Another company, Buses Unlimited, offers an 84-seater that runs on diesel for $24,000 even. The Springfield Valley Unified School District has offered one of their used buses for $12,000. Again it holds 84 people, but it's got 80,000 miles on it and is a '78 model.

Davis: Is 80,000 too many?

Bodine: No, I don't think so. I'd recommend that bus.

Santana: Why are they selling it?

Bodine: The district is growing smaller and they don't need it. And they're in a budget crunch.

Davis: But why this particular one? Something wrong with it?

Bodine: No. Our district's mechanic checked it out and said it's fine. Purrs like a kitten were his exact, if unoriginal, words.

Davis: I move we accept the bid of $12,000 from the Springfield Valley Unified School District for the offered bus.

Robertson: Do I hear a second.

Harold: Second.

Robertson: All in favor say aye.

(Board unanimously approves.)

Robertson: Next item on the agenda is the appropriation of funds to put the basketball team up in a hotel for three days. The high school's team won the division tournament and is going to the state finals in Phoenix. If they continue their winning ways, they will have to stay up there at least three days. The appropriation requests $125 per night so the basketball team can compete in state playoffs for a s long as they need to stay in Phoenix.

(The motion is seconded, and the board unanimously approves.)

Robertson: The next request is from the high school librarian for money. Mr. Secretary, will you please read the request?

Bodine: I have a request here from Mrs. Phyllis Laird, head librarian. It reads: "In order to keep our library in tune with modern times, update reference materials, replace damaged and lost books, and add new magazines to our subscription list, we are asking for $543 before the next school year. A well-stocked library is a necessary part of a student's education, and so I hope you will grant our request." Mrs. Laird goes on to list how the money would be spent. . . .

Robertson: For a set of new encyclopedias to replace our 1975 versions, a new set of science-oriented encyclopedias, magazine subscriptions to *Time, Newsweek, Sports Illustrated, Boys Life* and something called *Dragon*. I don't know what that is for sure. Then she's got an almanac and other reference materials and about 200 books. You all have read the lists, right?

All: Nod and mumble in the affirmative.

Robertson: What do you think of Mrs. Laird's choices?

Harold: I have no problems with the request and I move we vote to authorize the appropriation for $543 for the school library.

Robertson: Well, before we take a second on your motion, I think we ought to discuss these books and magazines a little.

Harold: What's to discuss? They're all fine books.

Bodine: I'm not so sure I want to agree to this authorization. Some of these books, I think, are questionable. I have no objections to Shakespeare or even books like *Megatrends* or Lee Iacocca's autobiography. But some of these bother me. As an example I give this one – Kurt Vonnegut's book, *Slaughterhouse Five.* There are some sections in here that deal with sex, others put down the United States. It's strange fare and I'm not so sure Rockville kids need to read stuff like that.

Robertson: Well, I had some reservations on some of these myself, Mr. Bodine. I've heard that this *Catcher in the Rye* by J.D. Salinger, down near the bottom of the list, is about homosexuality. I don't think our students ought to be educated about such topics.

Harold: Mr. President, am I to assume you don't want to approve the request for money because of some of the books on the list?

Robertson: No, Mr. Harold. I'm willing to approve the request, just minus some of the books and magazines.

Harold: That sounds like censorship to me.

Bodine: I think it's censorship, Bill, but it's good censorship. We're concerned for these children, and I think that some of these books can only hinder a student's development. We should be careful here. Would you want students to read a book that perpetuates racial stereotypes? Have you ever read *Huckleberry Finn?* That novel just reeks with the degradation of blacks.

Robertson: I don't even think we need to look at some of them. Students don't need to read trash. Though, I wonder what you've got against Huck Finn. I read it as a boy, and I think it's a fine novel.

Santana: I think I agree with Mr. Bodine. I try to watch my kids. I've read reports in newspapers about kids who read comic books or those sword and sorcery books and then go out and play Dungeons and Dragons and then end up committing suicide. Maybe we should look at these things.

Harold: Maria, do you monitor what your kids watch on TV?

Santana: No, not really.

Harold: So you let your kids watch something where people run around shooting 1,000 rounds of ammunition per show. Now, do your kids run out and grab machine guns and start shooting each other? No, so why would books have that effect?

Bodine: I think it's the potential for that effect. A student who is violent or depressed may be pushed over the edge.

Harold: You can't protect them from everything. And in the meantime, they could lose something valuable. It's important that a child reads, and I don't care if the kid reads cigarette packages or *War and Peace*. The important thing is that they are learning how words work and how to communicate.

Bodine: OK, then, why don't we put *Playboy* in the library? So long as reading is the only thing that's important.

Harold: Get serious, Peter. You know I'm not advocating that.

Bodine: So you will censor, just to a different degree.

Davis: I've been sitting here watching you debate. Twenty-five years ago we had this same type of discussion. But back then we were talking about John Steinbeck. A number of parents were concerned that the subject matter in *The Grapes of Wrath* would be too shocking to students. They believed it portrayed a world and an attitude of negativism and pessimism. A book is neither good or bad. It all depends on how it is used and read. I would give students the option. Open up our library to different books and let them decide. I don't believe it is our place to dictate what a student can and cannot read.

Santana: Well, are we going to vote on something? Maybe we should have a new motion.

Bodine: I move we set a public hearing two weeks from today to get parents' reactions to these books.

Santana: I second the motion.

Harold: Mr. President, I wonder exactly what that will accomplish. We have over 200 books on this list. I doubt that the public has read all of them. I doubt we've read all of them. You're still talking as if you intend to censor if parents say it's all right with them. Are we each going to vote on 200 books? Where do you start and stop?

140

Davis: I agree with Bill. Even if we decide that the board has the power to censor, I believe it would be too difficult to decide what should be censored. And that is the strongest argument for not censoring. The world is out there, good and bad. We can't stop it from touching the children. Teach them what's good and bad and use those books as examples. But don't close their minds.

Robertson: We have a motion on the floor to schedule a public hearing regarding the book list Mrs. Laird has submitted. I'd like a roll call vote. How do you vote?

Davis: No.

Harold: No.

Santana: Yes.

Bodine: Yes.

Robertson: Aye. The ayes have it. By a vote of 3-2 a public hearing will be scheduled for Friday, April 18, at 7 p.m. here to discuss the book list and appropriation request.

Member of the audience: You're all nuts. I'll be back here in two weeks to tell you that. I can't believe you're so damn foolish.

Harold: (addressing the audience member) I believe they're that foolish. I'll vote against every stupid goddam thing you propose.

Robertson: Do we have a motion to close this meeting?

Santana: So moved.

The board seconded and approved the motion, and the meeting was adjourned.

This script was adapted from one written by journalism students at the University of Arizona.

21-8. Style quiz

Correct the spelling and style errors in the following sentences.

1. Clarence Thomas angrily denied sexual harrassment charges a former aid made against him.

2. The Lawrence city commission will discuss an ordinance to bann nudity from bars or restaurants that serve alchohol.

3. Mike Wildgen, City Manager, said the proposed law would only effect busineses that serve liquor.

4. The first amendment to the constitution guaranties the right to freedom of expression so the proposed ordinence can not be applied to places that don't serve alcohol, said the county's Chief deputy counselor.

5. Vice mayor Charles Shorter was so impressed by the pig that he said he might consider getting one himself.

6. The issue of banning pigs was discussed by the St. Petersburg city council.

7. One woman brought her potbellied pig to city hall when the council debated the ordinence.

8. Earvin Magic Johnson had a garanteed contract for $3,100,000 dollars.

9. Anita Hill said Clarence Thomas had made sexual advances toward her and discussed lude subjects when she worked for him in the 1980's.

10. William Jefferson Clinton became the 42 President of the U.S. on January 20, 1993.

Bureaucratic Stories 22

This chapter will give you practice writing anecdotal and hard-news leads, particularly impact leads, to stories about bureaucracy. It will also emphasize how to use graphics in stories. Many stories about bureaucracy lend themselves to impact leads or impact paragraphs so they can help the reader see how the stories affect them. If you were covering these stories, you should seek anecdotes and reactions from people affected by a governmental action so they can humanize these stories.

22-1. Anecdotal approach to legislative story

You are writing this story for a Colorado newspaper. For a human-interest approach, write an anecdotal lead. Here is your information:

There was a meeting yesterday [use day of the week] of the House Judiciary Committee in Colorado. The committee was considering a bill that would provide the death penalty for certain child-abuse crimes. The committee heard testimony from several witnesses. After the testimony the committee passed the bill. Under provisions of the bill, intentional child abuse that results in the death of the child would be punishable by the death penalty. Child abuse that results in injuries would be a felony.

Jeff Shoemaker, R-Denver, sponsored the bill. He said: "It sends a message. It is wrong to say, 'If you commit murder that's one thing. If you shake a child intentionally and that child dies from it, it's another."

Steve Erkenbrack, district attorney for Grand Junction, testified in favor of the bill. He said as the law now stands, a person convicted of torturing and killing a child in Colorado could be out of prison in as little as eight years.

Jacque Gomez, a Colorado woman, testified before the committee. Her voice was shaking as she testified in favor of the bill. She recalled her daughter's death. She said her 6-month-old baby was shaken so severely by her baby sitter that the baby was left paralyzed and blind for six years before she died in May from a seizure. The baby sitter received 90 days in jail and four years of probation. Gomez said she was testifying in hopes of protecting the next child.

Based on a story from the *Rocky Mountain* (Colo.) *News.* Used with permission.

22-2. Human interest approach

Here is another story about a legislative committee hearing that lends itself to a human-interest approach. Use an anecdotal lead.

The House Judiciary Committee in the Colorado Legislature is conducting hearings on a "right-to-die" bill. The measure has already been approved by the Senate in Colorado. It would allow patients or their proxies to make life-and-death medical decisions. That would include rejection of artificial nourishment. Patients or their proxies also could refuse to have the patient receive cardiopulmonary resuscitation. Several people, including legal experts, physicians and a Denver probate judge, testified in favor of the bill. A few testified against it. The committee will continue the hearing on the bill tomorrow [use the day of the week].

Dr. Carla Murphy, an emergency medical specialist is president of the Colorado Chapter of the American College of Emergency Physicians. She testified in favor of the bill. She said: "Almost all of us have performed CPR on patients who did not want it. Many of us have had to break ribs of older people, put tubes in their throats, resuscitating them when they did not want us to."

Mildred Stanley is a Colorado resident who uses a wheelchair and has a large oxygen tank that is always at her side. She also urged lawmakers to pass the bill. She said she has signed a living will. She has given power of attorney to friends and has made it clear to her doctor that she wants no heroics. She said she hates becoming more dependent on others every day. She said that last June she had trouble breathing and she called 911 just wanting oxygen. "I was resuscitated in the ambulance against my will. When the paramedics were going to put a tube down my throat, I said, 'No! No! No!' " She began to shout. "To me it will mean freedom! Freedom from that fear of being resuscitated again! The glorious state of Colorado will have given me the freedom for my right to die." She is 81.

Dr. Walt Oppenheim is past president of the Clear Creek County Medical Society. He testified against the bill. He said: "I certainly agree with the need for compassion and not having extraordinary means. But what does God want? . . . We are here to comfort the sick, relieve pain and cure the ill. Not to determine the beginning and ending of life."

Stanley shouted from the audience: "And prolong the death process!"

Nicolas Cordova , who has a terminal illness, testified in favor of the bill. He did not want to specify the nature of his terminal illness. He said as his condition deteriorates, he doesn't want doctors to prolong his misery or waste money keeping him alive. "I have a terminal illness. Suicide is a comfortable alternative. But I choose to live. . . . I want to die with dignity."

Based on a story from the *Rocky Mountain News*. Used with permission.

22-3. Statistics – crime rates

Assume that these are the annual crime rate statistics for your state, released by your state Bureau of Investigation. Read the statistics in this chart and decide which are the most dramatic findings to report. Using the statistics and information from sources, write a news story. Do not flood your lead with statistics. Analyze the most interesting information and write a summary lead based on that. Your story will be accompanied by the following chart and a graphic comparing murder rates for 10 years. You don't need all the statistics in your story, but you should include the most important ones.

Type	1991	1992	Percent change
Murder	138	204	+47.8
Forcible rape	1,518	1,584	+4.3
Robbery	2,982	3,637	+21.6
Aggravated assault	12,673	13,429	+6.0
Burglary	39,626	38,869	-1.9
Larceny/theft	127,336	131,305	+3.1
Motor vehicle theft	14,094	14,346	+1.8
Total:	198,367	203,364	+2.5

Source: [Your state] Bureau of Investigation

Murder rates – 10-year comparison

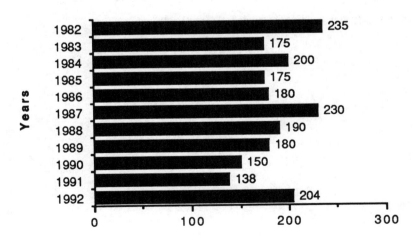

145

Other statistics from your State Bureau of Investigation:

Based on statistics for the current year, bureau officials say that in your state:

- ☛ Someone becomes a victim of violent crime every 30 minutes.
- ☛ An assault is committed (in your state) every 41 minutes.
- ☛ A rape is committed every 5 hours and 46 minutes.
- ☛ A murder is committed every 63 hours.

Comments from sources:

You have interviewed the following people and asked them about the increase in violent crime. You may use their comments wherever you think they are most appropriate in the story, not necessarily all in one block for each source.

From Mike Stiers, division chief of the bureau: "The increase in violence is what really concerns us. They're either bashing them in the head or shooting them when it's not necessary. The increase in volent crime reflects a greater social problem that can't be solved by police alone. We're losing the battle here. People need to realize this. They need to demand of their legislators, both state and municipal that they don't want to live like this."

From Julie Reaman, a therapist with Ending the Violence Effectively, a counseling group for victims: Increased publicity about sexual assault and incest may have boosted the reporting rate.

From Anne Byrne of the Rape Awareness and Assistance Program : "I don't think it's a huge increase in the amount of reports. I think more sexual assaults are going on. I don't know why; it's alarming."

From Bob Allen, county undersheriff: "I think it has to do with a general downward trend in morality, a breakdown in family. That's a community function, everybody pulling together and starting to work together. Many murders are committed by family or acquaintances. I personally feel that people who do it are people who know each other. That's typical of homicide. You always hurt the one you love."

Based on a story from the *Rocky Mountain News.* Used with permission.

22-4. Weather statistics

Was it the hottest or coldest season, the wettest or driest? People like to read about weather. So reporters periodically have to write weather stories summarizing the statistics for the month, the season or the year. Here are some annual statistics – minus December – for three counties in South Florida, where weather is important news. Compare the statistics and find an angle for your story.

The following statistics compare rainfall levels (in inches) for the months with normal rainfall. Months are divided into the normally wet and dry seasons for Broward, Palm Beach, and Dade counties. You are writing this story in November for a newspaper that serves these three counties, but the major circulation is in Broward and Palm Beach. For perspective, you should know that Hurricane Andrew, which devastated parts of Dade County, occurred in August. Assume you are writing this for the current year. This chart will run with your story. The only comment you have is from Geoff Shaughnessy, meteorologist for the South Florida Water Management District, who said the rain in November came from moisture-laden weather fronts that stalled over South Florida, a phenomenon that is more typical for October. Write a very brief story, approximately six to eight inches, or about a page and a half of typed copy. Assume that you have a weather forecast of a new front coming through that is expected to bring more rain.

Dry	Broward	Palm Beach	Dade	Norm
Jan.	2.88	1.89	2.15	2.41
Feb.	2.49	3.86	1.64	2.19
March	1.97	2.00	3.01	2.70
April	3.63	3.05	2.75	3.43
Wet				
May	0.94	1.10	0.81	5.87
June	16.84	16.45	20.95	8.10
July	3.35	2.91	3.50	6.41
Aug.	8.40	8.38	11.41	6.83
Sept.	3.81	6.81	4.07	8.52
Oct.	1.88	1.27	1.63	7.84
Dry				
Nov.	6.91	11.14	6.41	2.84
Dec.	——	——	——	2.02
Total	53.09	58.86	58.33	59.16

22-5. College budget story

Assume that this is the proposed budget for your university or that you are covering this story for a Louisville, Ky., newspaper. Write an impact lead and consider using the list technique.

Western Kentucky University has a 12-member committee that developed 68 recommendations for cutting the university's budget to cope with a $6.1 million budget shortfall. The committee, headed by the university President Thomas Meredith, gave its recommendations to the Board of Regents yesterday.

The university's shortfall is the result of both a $44 million cut in state funding and a need to find $1.5 million to cover some fixed rising costs and to make some improvements.

The main recommendations included suspending the school's football program, raising tuition and some student fees and eliminating a variety of staff positions and some administrative offices. The list of recommendations was mailed to the regents last night. The regents are supposed to act on the proposals April 30.

The committee recommended that student fees be increased 6 percent to 7 percent for Kentucky residents, to $720 per semester for undergraduates and $790 per semester for graduates. Tuition for out-of-state residents would increase roughly 4 percent, to $2,020 per semester for undergraduates and $2,230 for graduates.

Student fees would increase from $70 per semester to $103.

The football program had a budget of $525,479 this year, in addition to roughly $300,000 in scholarships.

Meredith's letter noted that "except for letters from parents of players, current players, and former players and coaches, there has been very little support demonstrated for the program."

Some of the other recommendations of the committee included closing the Sponsored Programs office, which helps find grants to faculty research and other programs. The committee also recommended closing the Office of the Graduate College Dean and moving the responsibilities to other administrators.

In addition, the committee recommended closing the in-house university attorney's office and contracting with a law firm for legal work. The committee also recommended eliminating at least 15 positions, possibly through layoffs, and dozens more with a hiring freeze that includes vacancies now open.

In his letter to the regents, Meredith wrote that the decision about what to do with the football program is "probably one of the most emotional" decisions the regents will have to make. But he offered hope that the program might continue this fall.

His letter said the question before the regents is: "Should the board suspend football, keep the program as is, reduce the program by some degree or move to a non-scholarship and reduced number of coaches status?

"If a plan can be put together for 1992-93 that would require no additional institutional funds beyond those recommended by the budget committee, then consideration will be given to having a football program for the 1992 season. This would require a much reduced program and possibly increased private funding. I believe this could be accomplished."

The committee also proposed that all faculty be given full-time teaching loads, that the time allotted to them for research and special projects be dramatically cut, and that all administrators with faculty rank teach at least one class.

Based on a story from *The* (Louisville) *Courier-Journal.* Used with permission.

22-6. City budget story

Your City Commission (or whatever your local governing body is called) is considering a proposed budget for 1993. The budget was presented to the commission yesterday by the city manager. Read the following budget information and analyze where expenditures increased or decreased the most. Decide what kinds of questions you might ask the city manager. Look at the tax rate (the mill levy) and decide if it has increased, decreased or stayed the same. Then, using the chart on how to figure your taxes, explain in your story what that rate will mean for the owner of a home assessed at $15,000, an average assessment in your community. The city assesses homes at 15% of market value, so a home worth $100,000 would be assessed at $15,000 for tax purposes. Use an impact lead telling readers what this budget means to them and explaining how their money will be spent. Comments from the manager follow.

General operating budget – summary of expenditures

Item	1991 $	1992 $	1993 Proposed $
Public works	573,089	784,700	864,000
Water/sewage	9,117,586	10,359,758	10,977,027
Parks/recreation	634,945	697,400	810,800
Business improvement	0	0	83,689
Employee benefits	3,102,708	3,446,800	3,380,450
Bonds/interest	3,643,654	3,125,413	4,252,000
Sanitation	2,241,201	2,641,200	2,949,540
Police	2,881,738	3,101,800	3,197,350
Fire	2,014,616	2,191,750	2,343,050
Animal control	132,722	128,550	130,120
Library	581,390	662,180	723,913
General operations	6,554,490	7,227,339	6,927,180
Total	31,478,139	34,366,890	36,639,119
Mill levy	42.2	42.10	42.20

Revenues: About 57% of revenues come from property taxes. Other sources include $15,805,749 from various taxes such as:

Property tax	$ 20,833,370
Gas taxes	$ 1,089,440
Alcohol	$ 230,133
Guest tax	$ 185,000
Water/sewer	$ 10,977,027
Sanitation	$ 2,949,540
Fed. revenue sharing	$ 25,000
Parking meters	$ 265,920
Business improvements	$ 83,689
Total	**$36,639,119**

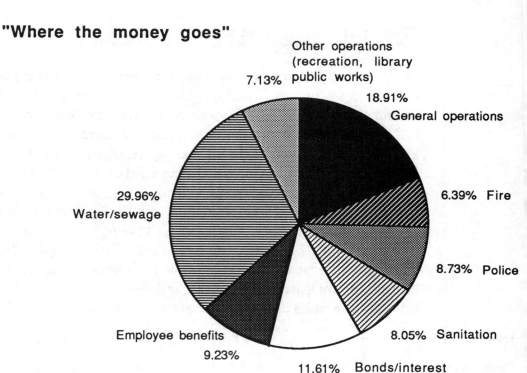

"Where the money goes"

- Other operations (recreation, library public works) 7.13%
- 18.91% General operations
- 6.39% Fire
- 8.73% Police
- 8.05% Sanitation
- 11.61% Bonds/interest
- Employee benefits 9.23%
- 29.96% Water/sewage

How to figure your property tax

1. Write the assessed value of your property in Box A. This is the amount your property is appraised for tax purposes, not the amount of money it would sell for on the market. For example, if you have a house worth $100,000 and the city assesses it at 15% of its value for taxes, your assessed value is $15,000.

2. Divide the figure in Box A by 1,000 because a mill is $1 tax on every $1,000 of assessed value. Write the result in Box B.

3. Write the mill levy in Box C. For this city, the levy proposed is 42.2 mills.

4. Multiply the figures in Boxes B and C. Write the result in Box D. This is the amount of taxes you will owe to the city.

Calculate your tax rate

Assessed value:	**A**
Divided by 1,000:	**B**
Mill levy:	**C**
Multiply B X C =Taxes:	**D**

When City Manager Michael A. Thrifty presented the budget to City Council, he included these remarks:

I am hereby submitting the recommended budget for the fiscal year commencing January 1, 1993. The 1993 budget is presented as a working document for your consideration. (City commissioners must conduct public hearings before they can adopt it. Public hearings will be scheduled at the end of the month.) The proposed budget totals $36,639,119 as compared to the 1992 budget of $34,366,890. The proposed budget will require a mill levy of 42.20 mills or $42.20 per $1,000 of assessed valuation. We have estimated the assessed valuation at the time of budget preparation to be $493,681,760. The real estate valuation has grown $5,100,000 in the past year, which will provide us with more revenue from property taxes without raising taxes. The 1993 budget is presented to you with essentially the same rate of 42.20 mills. The budget concentrates on providing current staff levels. However, the growth we are experiencing places pressure on current staffing levels in public safety, public works and parks maintenance.

Our bond indebtedness continues to increase. Part of that is due to a $1 million bond issue voters approved in the last election to fund a new recreation center.

Providing water and sewage treatment for our growing population continues to be a significant portion of our budget.

Specific recommendations in this budget are as follows:

■ A 3% salary increase for all employees

■ The amount of refuse collected, number of customers added and size of area serviced for the Sanitation Department has significantly increased in the past five years.   I am recommending addition of one residential crew supervisor, one commercial crew supervisor, two commercial drivers, and two commercial loaders. In 1990 city crews collected 34,018 tons of refuse; in 1991, 41,357 tons and to date the rate will result in 44,734 tons.

■ Two of the downtown parking lots will be overlaid with asphalt this summer, and I am recommending $25,000 be allocated in the parking meter fund to continue the maintenance program.

■ The Business Improvement District is included for the first time. The income from this district with a 1 percent tax for improvement of the downtown business area will be the revenue source.

Respectfully submitted,
City Manager Michael A. Thrifty

(In addition to city taxes, residents pay county and school taxes, but those taxes are levied in separate budgets by the school district and the county. The total tax rate last year for city, county and school taxes was 127 mills.)

22-7. Style quiz

1. Jeff Shoemaker, Republican from Denver, said the bill seeking the death penalty for intentional child abuse that results in death was nesessary.

2. Crime rose 2 and a half % and robberies increased 21.6 percent.

3. Broward County's 6.91 in. of Nov. rain was more than 2 times the normal amount.

4. A 12 member commitee headed by Thomas Meredith, President of Western Kentucky University, proposed that all faculty be given full time teaching loads.

5. Taxpayers will pay $42.20 for every $1000 of asessed value on there property.

6. The budget was recommended by city manager Michael A. Thrifty.

7. A mill is equal to $100 for every one thousand dollars of assessed property value.

8. The Colorado legislature was debating a right to die bill.

9. The weather forcast calls for more rain in Palm Beach county.

10. The bill being debated by the Colorado house judiciary committee is similar to ones proposed in Legislatures in other states.

Crime and Punishment 23

This chapter will give you practice writing crime and court stories. You must be careful to attribute all accusatory information. The stories are geared to a variety of writing techniques, but you should exercise good judgment before writing a soft lead or using a lighthearted tone.

23-1 a–c. Police reports

Assume that you are a police reporter and you check the police reports every day. You conduct interviews for major crime stories and write briefs from the reports for all accidents and other incidents. Police forms vary from one agency to another, but all forms will contain some of the basic information included in the following ones. Write briefs for each one of these reports, attributing your information to police reports. You decide if the physical description of the victims and offenders is necessary. These reports are based on forms used by Kansas police departments. You may substitute your city for the cities in the reports. Use delayed identification leads for each of your stories.

23-1a. Motor vehicle accident

Motor Vehicle Accident Report

(Check one) ___ Fatal √ Injury ___ Hit/run	√ Property Damage under $500 ___ Property Damage over $500

Milepost	County Hwy/Road/Street & Speed limit 13th St. and Missouri Ave. 35 mph	City/town Lawrence	Local case no. 1395693

Distance ft/mi.& Dir.from/at hwy/road/street 10 ft. from 13th St. at Missouri St. intersection	Investigating Dept. Lawrence P.D.	Investigating Officer Ron Williams	Reviewed by Lt. J. Mullens

Collision diagram (Show unit movements, roads, north N)

```
                     Veh. 2
                       I ▼
13th ------------------------------- I------
W            ➡  ➡  ➡➡ ✕
          Vehicle I      I
                         I
                         I  Missouri N ▲
```

Describe pre-crash movement or action and direction of vehicles and pedestrians/cyclists.

Operator of Veh. #1 was driving east on 13th when Veh. 2 going south on Missouri failed to yield right of way and collided with it.

Date of accident
02/01/93

Time
0800

Time arrived/& Day
0904 02/01/93

Object damaged & nature of damage Veh. 1. left front door dented, windshield cracked Veh. 2, fender dented	Name and address of object owner Doolittle, Brenda, 1225 Pennsylvania Ave. Lawrence

Unit 1	Driver/Pedes Name, last, first & initial Doolittle , Brenda M.	Phone 555-1442	Color Year & make of vehicle Blue 1989 Ford	Model & body style Escort sedan hatchback

Driver/pedes. address (Number, street, city, state, zip code) Same 1225 Pennsylvania Ave., Lawrence, Ks. 66045	State License Plate # KS COI-123	Year 1993	Removed by: Owner

Driver's license state and number 1315121212	Date of birth 1/30/63	Sex F	Vehicle Identification no. 1223456666	Odometer 55.678

Registered owner full name ("Same" if driver) Same	Phone	Total no. of vehicle occupants including driver 1	Fire? no	InsuranceCo./policy Allstate- 12345678

Owner Address ("Same" if driver)   Same

Special conditions (if any) for unit above none   1.hit/run 2. Non-contact 3. Stolen 4. Parked 5 Police pursuit 6 Driverless

Unit 2	Driver/Pedes. Name, last, first & initial Collier, Scott D.	Phone 555-5432	Color Year & make of vehicle White 1992 Honda	Model & body style Civic sedan

Driver/ped address (Number, street, city, state, zip code) 1234 Green Street, Lawrence, Ks. 66045	State License Plate # KS FOI-999	Year 1993	Removed by: owner

Driver's license state and number 9876543212	Date of birth 1/10/73	Sex M	Vehicle Identification no. 9876543777	Odometer 22,000

Registered owner full name ("Same" if driver) Same	Phone	Total no. of vehicle occupants including driver 1	Fire?	Insurance Co./policy Midwestern 7654321

Owner Address ("Same" if driver)   same

Special conditions (if any) for unit above   1.hit/run 2. Non-contact 3. Stolen 4. Parked 5 Police pursuit 6 Driverless

Record all injured and uninjured occupants and pedestrians. (Use supplemental page if necessary.)

Unit	Last name	First	Initial	Address	Sex	Age	S.Blt	Eject	Trap	Injury	EMS unit
1	Doolittle	Brenda	M.	1225 Pennsylvania Ave.	F	30	N.	N.	N.	bruises	N

EMS unit none	Injured taken by: herself	Injured taken to: Lawrence Memorial Hospital

Dr./pd # Violation charged   Citation No. Operator 1- Cit. No. 33393 Failure to wear seatbelt. Op. 2, Cit. 44493 Failure to yield right of way

Motor Vehicle Accident Report

(Check one) √ Fatal ___Injury √ Hit/run ___Property Damage under $500 ___Property Damage over $500

Milepost	County Hwy/Road/Street & Speed limit NE 23st St. and Main Ave.	City/town Lawrence, Ks.	Local case no. 34567893
Distance ft/mi.& Dir.from/at hwy/road/street 00 ft. from 23rd St. on Main St.	Investigating Dept. Investigating Officer Lawrence P.D. John S. Weary		Reviewed by Lt. J. Macho

Collision diagram (Show unit movements, roads, north N)

```
   N   ➡  ➡  ➡  ➡  ➡  ➡
       |=======================X========
       |           Main
       |
       |
     23rd
```

Describe pre-crash movement or action and direction of vehicles and pedestrians/cyclists

Car of unknown nature going east on Main hit victim and threw him to side of road. Hit/run driver. Victim's girlfriend, Michelle Glauber, says she and victim left Benchwarmers bar and had a fight. He got out of her car and was walking home east on Main St. when struck by unidentified black sedan.

Date of accident: 01/30/93
Time: 0230
Time arrived & Day: 0240 1/30/93

Object damaged & nature of damage
Pedestrian death

Name and address of object owner
see under unit

Unit	Driver/Ped Name, last, first & initial	Phone	Color Year & make of vehicle	Model & body style
Ped	Hale Donald U. ,	555-4455		

Driver/ped address (Number, street, city, state, zip code) 3131 Johnson St. , Lawrence 66046	State License Plate # Year	Removed by:

Driver's license state and number N/A	Date of birth 01/-9/65	Sex Vehicle Identification no.	Odometer

Registered owner full name ("Same" if driver) Phone	Total no. of vehicle occupants Fire? including driver	Insurance Co./policy

Owner Address ("Same" if driver)

Special conditions (if any) for unit above   1   1.hit/run   2. Non-contact 3. Stolen 4. Parked 5 Police pursuit 6 Driverless

Unit	Driver Ped Name, last, first & initial	Phone	Color Year & make of vehicle	Model & body style
	Glauber, Michele F.	555-6789	White 1992 Ford	Taurus Sedan

Driver/ped address (Number, street, city, state, zip code) 3131 Johnson St. , Lawrence, Ks. 66046	State License Plate # Year KS MFG-023 1992	Removed by: owner

Driver's license state and number same	Date of birth 1/2/70	Sex Vehicle Identification no. F 1235667890	Odometer 12,000

Registered owner full name ("Same" if driver) Phone same	Total no. of vehicle occupants 0	Fire? no	Insurance Co./policy no. Allstate 987456

Owner Address ("Same" if driver)   Same

Special conditions (if any) for unit above (Code no.)   1.hit/run   2. Non-contact 3. Stolen 4. Parked 5 Police pursuit 6 Driverless

Record all injured and uninjured occupants and pedestrians. (Use supplemental page if necessary)

Unit	Last name	First	Initial	Address	Sex	Age	S.Blt	Eject	Trap	Injury	EMS
Pedest.	Hale	Donald	U.	3131 Johnson St. , Lawrence, Ks. 66046	M	28	n			Y	Y

EMS unit Lawrence Lifesavers	Injured taken by Ambulance	Injured taken to Lawrence Memorial DOA

Dr./pd #   Violation charged   Citation No. - Case under investigation.

Standard Offense Report

1. Dispatched 1	Name of agency	Case No.	Date of Offense	Time	Date of Report
2. Citizen					
3. On view	Topeka P.D.	1395893	1/25/93	0100	01/25/93

Location of offense	Time Reported	Time arrived	Time Cleared
515 SE Mission St.	0100	0110	0330

Offense -	4
Offense-List most serious first	Type of premise: (List no.)
	1. Street 9. Restaurant
A. Attempted Burglary (felony)	2. Single residence 10. Storage/warehouse
	3. Multiple residence 11. Tavern/bar/liquor
B.Criminal damage to property (misdemeanor)	4. Commercial 12. Vehicle
	5. Gas station 13. Bank
C.	6. Convenience store 14. Open area (park, field, etc.)
	7. Pharmacy/doctor office 15. Other
	8. Public community bldg.

Codes: O	V=Victim	O=Offender	W=Witness	RP=reporting party

Type : (Use no.) 1

1. Individual	3.Society/public	5.Religious organization	7.Other
2.Business	4.Financial Institution	6. Government	8.Unknown

Name: Last	First	Middle	Code
Garcia	Jesus	---	O

Address: Street	City	State	Zip
Homeless			

Telephone No. (Home)	Race	Sex	Res/non. Res.	Age	Date of Birth	Height	Weight	Hair	Eyes
	H	M	R	22	1/10/61	6'2"	210	brown	brown

Codes: V=Victim	O=offender	W=witness	RP=reporting party

Type : (Use code.) V   2/5

1. Individual	3.Society/public	5.Religious organization	7.Other
2.Business	4.Financial Institution	6. Government	8.Unknown

Name: Last	First	Middle	Code V
Salvation Army			

Address: Street	City	State	Zip
515 SE Mission	Topeka	Kan.	66607

Telephone No. (Home)	Race	Sex	Res/non. Res.	Age	Date of birth	Height	Weight	Hair	Eyes
555-0987									

Describe briefly how offense was committed.

Officer Dean Williams and myself responded to an alarm at the Salvation Army building at 0100. When we arrived, we saw a man running from the building. Williams gave chase and caught perpetrator. Mr. Garcia informed us that he had broken into the building in search of food. He said, "I was trying to find some food and I had no place to stay." Mr. Garcia has no known address. He was taken to the Shawnee County Jail. Charged with attempted burglary, criminal damage to property.

Property Description 4

Type property loss 1=None 2=Burned 3=Counterfeited/forgery 4=Destroyed/damaged/vandalized 5=Recovered 6= Stolen 7= Unknown

Type loss	Description	Quantity	Value	Date Recovered	Property total
Window on east side of building broken. No indication of food or other items missing.					

Reporting Officer	Off. Ed Kellerman Badge/ID 03567	Date 01/25/93	Typed by: RCK

23-2. Burglary

Write this story in hourglass form. Be careful to attribute any accusatory statements to the police.

You call the local sheriff's department. A spokesman for the Pasco Sheriff's Department [or your county's department], Jon Powers, tells you that five boys, one 11, one 14 and three age 15, were arrested yesterday. He says he cannot release their names because they are juveniles. He said the boys have all been charged with burglary to a vehicle. He says they all admitted to the crime.

You ask for details and he tells you that they were charged with breaking into a food supply truck with a crowbar and stealing assorted boxes of candy, cookies and snacks. He says the goods were worth more than $500. Powers gives you this scenario: The stealing started late last night when two of the boys, who are brothers, saw the truck in the parking lot. The older brother, 15, took a crowbar from a neighbor's yard and pried the padlock off the truck's rear door. He and his brother, 11, then took a carton of candy from the truck. They later told the other boys what they had done.

Powers says the boys tried to carry the goodies home, but the boxes became too heavy for them. They left a 50-pound box of Milky Ways on a bench in front of a Winn Dixie supermarket (according to the police report). You ask what other kinds of candy and snacks they took. Powers says the stolen material included the case of Milky Way bars, boxes of cheese crackers and popcorn and a carton of chocolate creme-filled cookies. You ask what kind of truck it was. He says the truck was Lance Inc. food truck that was in a parking lot on Darlington Road. Lance supplies food for vending machines.

Based on a story from the *St. Petersburg* (Fla.) *Times.* Used with permission.

23-3. More burglary

Write this story in storytelling style with an anecdotal or narrative lead. Your information comes from an interview with Jim Beatty and police. You are writing this for Monday's newspaper.

Jim Beatty owns the J.B. Speed & Custom Shop, a motorcycle shop, at 1028 Watt St. On Saturday night, burglars broke into his store at took an estimated $20,000 worth of tools, engine parts, clothing, a valve cutter and two motorcycles belonging to customers, according to police. No arrests have been made. The van was found abandoned and empty in New Albany over the weekend.

This information comes from Beatty: He said he had a hunch the burglars would return. On Sunday night he armed himself with a loaded shotgun and crouched in the dark at his shop. At 9:25 two men broke into the store. Beatty said he aimed his shotgun toward the door. He planned to chase them away by firing a shot in their direction. The gun misfired. The next shot exploded into the air. The two retreated through the door. Beatty chased them down the street. He fired several more shots toward the fleeing men. The pair split up. Beatty followed one man behind the Quadrangle Shopping Center at 10th and Watt streets. He lost sight of him. Insurance does not cover his losses. He said he will reimburse his customers for their losses. The lost tools, which make up about half of the total losses, have brought his business to a halt.

Here are direct quotes from Beatty. (Place them where they fit best in the story. You do not have to use them in order or in one block.)

"I was underneath the desk because I knew they were coming back. I'm sitting here now thinking why didn't I shoot them. I shot over their heads. But why didn't I shoot them? Then we'd know who it was. But I don't want to go to jail. They're greedy. That's the worst kind of criminal. They should have been happy with what they got but, no, they had to come back. I've still got plenty of stuff in my shop to work on, but I don't even have a wrench to turn a bolt with. Everything was going so great. But I can't handle this. I'm a small businessman."

Based on a story from *The* (Louisville, Ky.) *Courier-Journal.* Used with permission.

23-4. Robbery roundup

Write this story in inverted pyramid style with a roundup lead, a lead that combines the two events. Information comes from Lt. Mack Innis of your police department.

A robbery occurred last night at 11 p.m. at Movies at Home, 2905 S.W. 29th St. Suspect described as a thin black man, about 5 feet 11 inches who wore his black hair in Geri curls. He was wearing stonewashed blue jeans, a blue sweatshirt and a blue baseball cap with the word "Sox." Suspect had been in the store earlier in the day. When he returned at night, he was in the story about 15 minutes when he picked up a compact disk, went to the counter, put the disk on the counter and cursed as he demanded money and pulled a handgun. The clerk gave him bills from the cash register and was going to give him coins, but the robber didn't want them. He threatened to return to the store if the clerk called police.

Another robbery occurred yesterday at 11:25 p.m. at the Kwik Shop at 801 S.W. Topeka Blvd. The robber was described as a black man in his middle 20s about 5 feet 10 inches and 140 pounds. He wore Chic women's jeans, gloves of an unspecified color, a white satin jacket and a maroon and blue beanie-style hat. He entered the store, picked up a package of gum and put it on the counter. When the clerk began to ring up the purchase, the man said, "I have a gun. Will you turn around, please?" He showed no weapon but reached into the drawer, took bills and left the store south on foot. No arrests have been made.

Based on a story from *The Topeka* (Kan.) *Capital-Journal.* Used with permission.

23-5. Shooting

You are a reporter for your local newspaper. This news occurred on a Saturday, and you are writing for Monday's paper. Use a creative lead or a hard-news lead. If you use the latter, update the story by using a second-day lead, giving the most current information first.

Background from a variety of neighbors:
Richard and Laurette Brunson were married yesterday on the front porch of the couple's home on N. 10th Street in your community. About 30 relatives and friends attended the 2 p.m. wedding. The bride had three children who were at the couple's home at the time of the incident. Brunson worked for a construction company and his wife had been working for a government housing program but quit recently. Neighbors said she wanted to open a day care center. The following incident happened on their wedding day.

From police:
Richard Brunson, 50, shot his wife, Laurette Kenny Brunson, 38, with a .22-caliber handgun. The shooting occurred at 5 p.m. It happened after she threw a plate of wedding-reception macaroni salad at him. The couple had been living together in the house for four or five months before they were married. A neighbor called police. By the time police arrived, the groom was gone. His whereabouts are still unknown. Laurette Brunson is in St. Joseph's Hospital.

From hospital officials:
Mrs. Brunson is in satisfactory condition. She has a bullet hole in her stomach.

From Laurette Brunson: No comment.

From Vicki Holmes, who lives across the street: "It looked like everything was going real good. Their wedding cake was gorgeous. I watched them carry it out of the house." She said the bride and groom were dressed in white. She wore a tea-length dress and he wore a tuxedo. She said a Baptist minister conducted the ceremony. A buffet-style meal including fried chicken was served. "The bride and the maid of honor chitchatted for quite a while during the reception. They were all laughing." Holmes said she left shortly before the shooting. She said the wedding reception had just about ended by then and most of the guests had left.

From neighbor Michael Martin: "I've never seen him violent, never heard them yelling. It blows me away."

From Walter Corse, another neighbor: He and several neighbors heard the sound of the shot from the couple's home. "Her son came out and says she's been shot and can't breathe."

From Marilyn Corse, mother of Walter Corse: "I just feel so bad for the kids having to see this. He left with no shirt and no shoes."

Based on a story from the *St. Petersburg* (Fla.) *Times.* Used with permission.

23-6. Homicide

You receive this information from police reports. Assume it happened the day you receive the reports. Write it for tomorrow's newspaper. You may attribute whatever you need to police reports and to Sgt. Mac Duff of your local police department.

Type of offense: Homicide

Arrests: Suspect #1: White male, named Mack Beth, age 30, address Inverness Avenue; Suspect #2: white female, 30, Ladeemack Beth, wife of suspect No. 1., same address.

Charges: Suspect #1: Three counts of first-degree murder; Suspect #2: Accomplice to murder.

Place of arrest: At suspects' home.

Time of arrest: 3 a.m.

Victims: Three white males: Victim #1: King Duncan, 70, Dunsinane Castle Road, Scotland City; Victim #2: white male, I.M. Guard, mid-30s, Dunsinane Castle Road, Scotland City; Victim #3: Mei Tuguard, mid-30s, Dunsinane Castle Road, Scotland City.

Weapons: Two 7-inch daggers

Arresting officer: Sgt. Mac Duff

Remarks: Police were called by a neighbor who saw Mrs. Beth wandering around the neighborhood and screaming about blood. Victims were visiting home of Suspect #1. All three suffered multiple fatal stab wounds. Victim #1 found in bed of Beth home; victims 2 and 3 also found in another bedroom of Beth home.   Suspect #1 taken into custody. Suspect was mumbling about witches. Appeared incoherent. Suspect claimed he went out for a walk about midnight to search for witches. Suspect said he found three witches brewing something in a cauldron and chanting "Double, double, toil and trouble; fire burn and cauldron bubble." Suspect said witches were old hags who gave him three warnings, including one to beware of Mac Duff. Suspect said he returned to his home and found King Duncan (Victim #1) dead with multiple stab wounds. Suspect #1 then confessed that he had killed Duncan's friends because he thought they had killed Duncan. He said daggers covered with blood were found on pillows of Victims 2 and 3. We checked for fingerprints and found daggers with Suspect #1's prints.

Suspect #2 in state of hysteria when taken into custody. Suspect was rubbing hands vigorously as though she were trying to wash them. Suspect #2 kept muttering about blood on her hands. Suspect #2 refused to answer questions. She responded only with these comments: "Out, damned spot! Out, I say. One, two. Why then, 'tis time to do't. Hell is murky. Who would have thought the old man to have had so much blood in him?"

Disposition: Suspect #1 was taken to county jail and charged with three counts of first-degree murder. Suspect #2 was charged with accomplice to murder and was taken to county mental hospital for observation.

23-7. Fire – apartment

You are calling the fire department at about 9 a.m. today to check about any fires that occurred overnight. Fire Battalion Chief Stephen McInerny gives you this information:

There was a fire in ground-floor apartment in 2700 block of Northeast 30th Place. Four fire engines and 16 firefighters responded at 1:15 a.m. this morning. Apartment is rented by Mark Alan Leszcynski.

Cause of fire: Stove was turned on and some cookbooks and towels on the stove ignited. When firefighters arrived, they found a 2 1/2-year-old cocker spaniel at the front door.

Estimated damage: $9,000 smoke damage to apartment. Other units not affected. Four gray finches in apartment died. Apartment uninhabitable for the time being.

The fire chief said that apparently the dog started the fire by jumping on the stove, using one of the knobs for a foothold. The setting on the burner was on medium high. He apparently was looking for food.

When firefighters arrived, the dog had crawled to the front door and he appeared to be dead. "The dog was clinically dead; it had no pulse and no respiration." He said firefighter Bill Mock took the dog outside and administered cardiopulmonary resuscitation and oxygen and the dog came back to life. He was taken to the animal hospital. He said it is not unusual for dogs to be caught in house fires but it is unusual for them to be revived from the dead.

"That's twice in a little more than a year we've revived dogs that have been clinically dead as a result of a fire. We're getting pretty good at it."

From owner Mark Alan Leszcynski: He said that he and a house guest went to a bar just before midnight and left the dog alone.

"The dog is a little mischievous. I've caught him doing this before. He has a never-ending appetite. I had just reprimanded him for going into my house guest's suitcase and getting some candy."

From Dorian Colorado, the veterinarian at your local animal hospital: "When they brought him to me, he was absolutely in shock and very disoriented. He and I spent a long night. He was treated for smoke inhalation."

Based on a story from the *Sun-Sentinel,* (Fort Lauderdale, Fla.). Used with permission.

23-8. Fire – fatality

You are making routine calls to the fire department and you receive this report from the dispatcher. Attribute information to fire department officials. This story has more details than the previous one and is more serious because of a fatality. Write the story in inverted pyramid order or hourglass form.

Information comes from Neil Heesacker, a spokesman for the fire department in your community. Firefighters responded to a fire at an apartment in a 32-unit apartment complex, Anderson Villa apartments, at 15758 S.E. Division St. at 6:39 a.m. The fire was brought under control at 7:05 a.m. The blaze caused an estimated $50,000 to the apartment building and $10,000 damage to the contents of the apartment. The value of the apartment building is estimated at $480,000. The family's belongings in the apartment that burned were valued at $80,000. The apartment was rented by Linda Lee Fuson. Her two sons, Kenneth A. J. Fuson, 10, and Michael Fuson, 14, were in the apartment at the time of the fire. Linda Fuson was not. She arrived some time after 6:40 a.m. Her whereabouts before then are unknown. The fire burned through the floor and blistered the gypsum walls and melted the family's television set. Three pet birds died. The fire also caused smoke damage to the apartment of Pat and Lisa Hampton, who live across the stairs from the Fuson family. The cause of the fire is under investigation. A neighbor, Darren Nitz, 31, is credited with saving Michael Fuson's life. He lives on the first floor, just below the Fusons' apartment. Michael Fuson suffered burns over a third of his body. He is in critical condition at Emanuel Hospital and Health Center's burn unit. He has second- and third-degree burns on his hands, arms, face, neck, back, buttocks and thighs. Kenneth Fuson was trapped in his bedroom. He died in the fire. Fire in an enclosed area such as an apartment can push temperatures to 1,700 degrees Fahrenheit near the ceiling and 1,000 degrees on the floor.

Information from Interview with Darren Nitz: "About 6:35 a.m. I heard neighbors pounding on my door and yelling about the fire. I didn't think much about it at first, until someone said two children were trapped in the apartment. Michael was about seven feet from his bedroom door. He was saying 'I can't, I can't,' and rolling over and over. I said, 'We've got to get out of here.' I tried to grab hold of his arm but couldn't because he was so badly burned. I put him over my shoulder and carried him outside. He told me that Kenneth was still upstairs. I went back to the top of the stairs but the flames reached the front door. Another neighbor, Brad Lindsey, grabbed a fire extinguisher and followed me."

From Brad Lindsey, 24. "It was fully going when we got up there. Just after we got up them, it just vacuumed and shot right across the stairway. Nitz and I went back down the stairs. There was no way either of us could do anything about it."

Based on a story from *The Oregonian.* Used with permission.

23-9. Criminal case

You are checking court records and you find this case, which strikes you as unusual. You check with the district attorney, Janet E. Justice, (named in the court record). She tells you that it is a "very bizarre case." She tells you that the woman who is charged with the crime kept her husband's body in her home for 10 years. You may attribute all this background to Justice: The woman's husband, Charles N. Truelove, was 40 at the time of his death, believed to be from a heart attack. The body was found in a mummified state. It was a skeleton covered with a thin layer of dehydrated skin. The body was lying in a bed in a rear bedroom. It was bare to the waist but had on pajama bottoms, underwear and socks. The district attorney says she was told by investigators that the woman changed her husband's clothes daily and that she talked to her husband daily as though he were still alive. She says no foul play was suspected. The husband was last seen by outsiders 10 years ago. She says investigators had checked on Charles Truelove's disappearance, but the wife told them he was just ill, and they had no probable cause to investigate further. Police finally entered the house when a relative of the Truelove family told them Charles Truelove was dead, and his wife was tending his corpse as though he were still alive. This information is based on an actual court case but the names have been changed. You may use your state for the location. The case number 93CR indicates the year and a criminal case. You may change the year to be current. Write a story using this information and the three court records to explain how the case was resolved. You may assume the woman was arrested the date of the first complaint. She entered her plea and was sentenced on the date of the second court record. You may use yesterday as your time frame for the sentencing.

The State of (your state),   Plaintiff
vs.
Carol J. Truelove,   Defendant
DOB: 2/3/43; W/F;5'5"; 120#
Rural Rte 3, Box 20
Your county, your state

| COMPLAINT | No._____93CR-123

_____Janet E. Justice_____
of lawful age, being first duly sworn on oath, for complaint against the above shown defendant, alleges
and states:

COUNT 1
That on or about the 30th day of January_____,1993, the above named defendant, within the above
named County in the State of (your state), then and there being, did then and there contrary to the

statutes of the State of _____ unlawfully and willfully and intentionally fail to give notice promptly to a coroner of a death. (Class A Misdemeanor)

Sections violated and class: State statute 21-1234-A Misd.,   Witnesses: Jeffrey Truelove
Penalty sections: SS (Your state statute) 21-1298

Summons issued for defendant's appearance on
2____ day of February _____, 1993, at __11:00 A.M.   (signature of Janet E. Justice) _____
                                                                                                  Complainant
Subscribed and sworn to before me this 30th day of January , 1993. (Signature of notary public)

* * *

The court record also contained a summons which repeated the charge. This is the record of the arraignment and disposition of the case:

State of (Your state),   Plaintiff   Case No._____ 93CR 123 _____
    vs.   Division No._____ II _____
Carol J. Truelove, Defendant

JOURNAL ENTRY

Now on this 2nd_____ day of ____February_____, 1993, the above captioned action comes on for hearing. The Court finds that all interested parties were legally notified and said matter is properly before this Court.
    A written complaint has been filed charging the defendant with

_____ I. Failure to provide prompt notification to a coroner of a death _____

Parties appearing before this Court:
    _____Janet E. Justice_____District Attorney's Office
    _____Sherri Savior_____Attorney for Defendant
    _____Carol J. Truelove_____Defendant in person.

    The matter then was heard, the witnesses testified and evidence received; the Court being fully advised in the premises finds as follows:

( ) The defendant is FOUND NOT GUILTY of Counts_____of the complaint.
( ) The defendant is FOUND GUILTY of Counts_____of the complaint.
(√) The defendant enters a PLEA OF GUILTY to Counts_____I_____of the complaint.
( ) The defendant enters a PLEA OF NOLO CONTENDERE_____of the complaint.

IT IS THEREFORE BY THE COURT ADJUDGED AND DECREED THAT
_____30 days in jail_____

(√) Defendant is granted probation from the sentence of confinement upon the terms and conditions set out in the Order of Probation.
Costs are assessed to defendant in the amount of $_____92.00_____
                                (Signature of judge) James W. Padlock _____
                                        Judge of the District Court

This is the third court record:

State of (Your state),   Plaintiff

Case No._____93cr 123_____

vs.

Division No._____II_____

<u>Carol J. Truelove, Defendant</u>

ORDER OF PROBATION

On this 2nd day of February 1993, the defendant is before the Court and represented by her attorney, Sherri Savior; the State appears by Janet Justice. The Court, after due consideration of all information given, finds that the best interest of the defendant and society would be served by placing the defendant on probation.

IT IS THEREFORE BY THE COURT ORDERED that the defendant be given probation as to the remainder of the sentence of 30 days, defendant having served 0 days; subject to the following conditions:

(1) Obey the laws of the United States, the State of ...., or any other jurisdictions to whose laws said defendant may be subject.

(2) Remand to the custody of the State the corpse of husband, Charles N. Truelove, for burial in the city cemetery.

(3) Agree to leave corpse undisturbed after burial. Defendant is prohibited from returning corpse to the sanctity of defendant's home.

(4) Discontinue discussions with son Jeffrey, 12, about defendant's beliefs that corpse of husband is alive. Inform son that husband died of heart failure.

(5) Attend counseling sessions with court-appointed therapist for such time until therapist deems defendant no longer requires counseling.

It is further ordered by the Court that this probation is to be in effect for a period of 2 years from this date and shall be supervised.

_____*James W. Padlock*_____
Judge of the District Court

I have received a copy of this Order and have read and understand the conditions of probation, and I will comply with all conditions. I understand that if I do not comply with the conditions, the Court may issue a warrant for my arrest, or the Court Services Officer may arrest me without a warrant, and my probation may be revoked, changed or extended as provided by law.

_____*Carol J. Truelove*_____
Address: Rural Rte 3, Box 20
Your county, your state

Using the following court record in which the name of the plaintiff has been changed, write a brief story as though this suit were filed yesterday in your county.

IN THE DISTRICT COURT OF YOUR COUNTY, YOUR STATE

RUTH LOUISE CLUTZ, Plaintiff

Case no. __93-150__

vs

Div. No. ____ II ____

KROGER COMPANY, Defendant

PETITION

COMES NOW the Plaintiff, Ruth Louise Clutz, and for her cause of action states and alleges that:

1. Plaintiff, Ruth Louise Clutz, is a resident of your city, your county, your state.

2. Defendant, Kroger Company, is an Ohio Corporation with its principal office at 1014 Vine Street, Cincinnati, Ohio, 45201. Kroger is registered as a foreign corporation doing business in the State of Kansas. Its registered agent is the Corporation Company, Incorporated, 534 South Kansas Avenue, Topeka, Kansas 66603.

3. At all times mentioned, Defendant was, and still is, the owner of, and in possession and control of a building located at 23th and Naismith Drive, in the City of........., County of............, State of ....

4. Said building is used and occupied by Defendant for the purpose of conducting business by the sale of groceries, meats, vegetables and other food products.

5. On July 27, 1992, at about 11 o'clock a.m., the Plaintiff was lawfully in Defendant's store as a customer of Defendant for the purpose of purchasing goods. As the Plaintiff walked into the store toward the grocery carts, while walking along one of the aisles, the Plaintiff slipped on one or more grapes that had collected on the floor of the store, and the Plaintiff fell heavily on the floor, sustaining the injuries set forth below.

6. The accident and resulting injuries to the Plaintiff were caused solely by the negligence of Defendant without any contributory negligence on the part of the Plaintiff.

7. The negligence of Defendant at the above time and place, among other things, consisted of the following:

a. In careless and negligently permitting the allowing of grapes to collect on the floor of the aisle of the store through which the Plaintiff was walking.

b. In carelessly and negligently permitting grapes to remain on the floor of the aisle through which the Plaintiff was walking, all of which rendered the floor slippery and unsafe.

c. In careless and negligently failing to remove the grapes from the floor.

d. In failing to properly maintain the floors of the store and, particularly, the floor in the are of the accident, in a clean and safe condition for the customers using the facilities of the store.

e. In failing properly and adequately to supervise and oversee the store so as to prevent the collection of grapes and other dangerous substances on its floors.

8. Defendant had actual knowledge of the fact that grapes had collected on the floor of the aisle for a long period of time, and of the fact that the floor was thereby rendered dangerous to

persons passing over it. Or, if Defendant lacked the actual knowledge, the conditions existed for so long a time prior to the happening of the accident to Plaintiff, that Defendant, in the exercise of due care, could and should have had such knowledge and notice.

9. As a proximate result of the accident and of the Defendant's negligence, Plaintiff was disabled and sustained the following injuries: a fracture of the right hip, severe permanent injury to the muscles of the right hip and right thigh. Plaintiff has suffered and will continue to suffer in the future severe pain in the entire right hip and thigh and is unable to stand for any length of time sufficient to do housework or to participate in any other normal activity of home life without experiencing great pain.

10. As a result of the above and foregoing, Plaintiff has been damaged in an amount in excess of Ten Thousand Dollars ($10,000.00).

WHEREFORE, Plaintiff prays for judgment against the Defendant for a settlement for a sum representing the damages she has sustained as a result of the negligence of the Defendant, which said damages, exceed the sum of Ten Thousand Dollars ($10,000.00) and for her cost.

Lawrence L. Seaman, Jr.
Lawrence L. Seaman, Jr.
Attorney No. 10832
2619 West 6th St.
Your city, your state, zip code
555-1442
ATTORNEY FOR PLAINTIFF

CERTIFICATE OF SERVICE

I hereby certify that a true and correct copy of the foregoing Petition was sent Certified Mail, postage-prepaid, to the Corporation Company, Inc., registered agency of Kroger Company, 534 South Kansas Ave., Topeka, Kansas 66603.

Lawrence L. Seaman, Jr.
Lawrence L. Seaman, Jr.

You are checking through cases in the civil section of your county court and you find these petitions for name changes. The petitions were filed at various time during the year. You think there might be an interesting story based on these court records. All these petitions have been approved by a judge. You will call the petitioners and get comments (which follow these records). These records are based on actual court records and a news story. Although one of the names might be considered insensitive to homosexuals, it is taken from a real court record and is the reason why the man wanted his name changed. Be aware of sensitivity when you write the story.

IN THE CIRCUIT COURT OF (YOUR COUNTY, YOUR STATE)

Joseph Wierdo, Petitioner

Case No. <u>93 C638</u>

Division_____<u>IV</u>_____

PETITION

COMES NOW the petitioner, Joseph Wierdo, and prays for his cause of action and states as follows:

1. That he resides at 700 Louisiana Your city, your state.
2. That the petitioner request a change of name from Joseph Wierdo to Joseph Wier.
3. That the current name of petitioner has caused him great embarrassment and suffering.
4. That petitioner is a citizen in good standing and the request for the name change is not to avoid any legal actions against said petitioner.
5. That petitioner is not seeking for redress as a means of avoiding any debts owed to any parties.
6. Wherefore, petitioner prays for favorable judgment from the Court.

> Joseph Wierdo
> City, state, zip code
> 555-8765
> On behalf of himself
>
> By _____ *Joseph Wierdo* ____
> Joseph Wierdo

IN THE CIRCUIT COURT OF (YOUR COUNTY, YOUR STATE)

Richard Goon, Petitioner

Case No. <u>93 C520</u>

Division <u>IV</u>

PETITION

COMES NOW the petitioner, Richard Goon, and prays for his cause of action and states as follows:

1. That he resides at 200 Bayside Drive, Your city, your state.

2. That the petitioner request a change of name from Richard Goon to Richard Lee.

3. That the current name of petitioner has caused him great embarrassment and suffering.

4. That petitioner is a citizen in good standing and the request for the name change is not to avoid any legal actions against said petitioner.

5. That petitioner is not seeking for redress as a means of avoiding any debts owed to any parties.

6. Wherefore, petitioner prays for favorable judgment from the Court.

> Richard Goon
> City, state, zip code
> 555-8765
> On behalf of himself
>
> By _____ *Richard Goon*
> Richard Goon

You call Joseph Wierdo but you cannot reach him. You check the directory and find another Wierdo, Sharon Ray Wierdo. She tells you that she is Joseph's ex-wife. When you tell her about the petition her ex-husband has filed, she is upset that he didn't include her in it. "Did you think I want to be left a Wierdo?" she says. She says she only uses the full name on official documents but otherwise goes by the name Sharon Ray. "I guess I'll have to pay to do it myself," she says, referring to an official name change.

You check with the court clerk and find that more than 300 people filed to have their names legally changed this year. It costs $200 to file the papers, but it is a simple form and you don't need a lawyer to do it, the court clerk tells you.

Circuit Court Judge Jack Musselman says some judges hold hearings for name changers and others merely sign a form if it's filled out properly. "It's perfunctory, more or less," he says. But in the petition, he says, they must swear that they are not running from the law or don't owe anybody money. However, the court does not do background checks.

"You know that a lot of times people are trying to avoid creditors," the judge says. "There's no real way of checking that out."

Circuit Court Judge Mel Grossman tells you that most of the name change petitions are from divorced women, foster children who come of age and want the name of the family they've stayed with or people with "an extremely ethnic name" who want something more mainstream. "I can't recall anyone looking to play games," he says.

You call Richard Goon. He says he got tired of the name and the grief that it has brought him since he was a child. "It wasn't as bad as it used to be in school and everything, but still, it bothered me," he said. He is 36 years old now.

He said he chose the name because he is a fan of Bruce Lee and "I kind of wanted to try to keep something that was Chinese."

Based on a story from the *Sun-Sentinel*, (Fort Lauderdale, Fla.). Used with permission.

23-11. Court terms quiz

Circle the correct answer:

1. At an arraignment a person is:
   a. Sentenced
   b. Formally charged with the crime and given a chance to enter a plea
   c. Given a chance to choose an attorney
2. Change of venue is:
   a. A change in the plea
   b. A change in the location of the trial
   c. A change in the charge
3. A deposition is:
   a. A decision to discontinue the case
   b. Deposing the judge in the case
   c. A written statement of testimony
4. A grand jury is:
   a. A larger jury than is usually called
   b. A group of citizens empowered by the court to investigate a possible crime
   c. A jury that hears civil cases
5. An injunction is:
   a. An order by the court to cease an action
   b. A point in the case when two motions are joined
   c. A judgment by the court to discontinue the case
6. A plaintiff is:
   a. A person who is charged with the crime
   b. A person who files a civil lawsuit
   c. A person who is being sued in a civil lawsuit
7. Nolo contendere means:
   a. Not guilty
   b. Guilty as charged
   c. Not fighting the charge
8. A tort is:
   a. A criminal case involving political charges
   b. A civil case involving allegations of wrongdoing
   c. A case involving a grand jury
9. A true bill is:
   a. A truthful finding by a judge
   b. A finding of truth by a jury, resulting in a not-guilty verdict
   c. An indictment issued by a grand jury
10. A brief is:
    a. An abbreviated summary of the case
    b. A legal document filed with the court by the lawyer
    c. A brief summary the lawyer makes to the jury
11. A docket is:
    a. The room containing all the court files
    b. A list of cases pending court action
    c. A list of verdicts issued by the judge for the week

12. A suspended sentence is:
   a. An order to delay the sentencing until further information is available
   b. An order to cancel punishment if the defendant meets certain conditions
   c. An order to drop all charges

13. A plea bargain is:
   a. An agreement between the prosecutor and defense attorney to accept a lesser charge and lesser sentence in exchange for a guilty or no-contest plea.
   b. An agreement between the plaintiff and defendant to bargain on the charges
   c. An agreement between the plaintiff and the defendant to bargain for a settlement of a suit

14. Extradition is:
   a. A decision by the prosecutor to submit additional charges to the court
   b. A procedure to move a person accused of a crime to a state where he or she currently is to the state where the crime occurred
   c. A procedure to authorize extra police personnel to hunt for a criminal

15. An affidavit is:
   a. A written list of charges
   b. A confession
   c. A sworn statement of facts

Using the following words, write a coherent story about this court case. You will be judged only on whether the words are used in proper context. You may use your imagination to make up the facts in the case that follows these terms:

Change of venue
Affidavit
Felony
Misdemeanor
Subpoena
Mistrial
Bond
Arraignment
Suspended sentence
Plea bargain

Here is the basic scenario for the case: A woman, 18, named Gold E. Locks has been charged with a felony, breaking and entering, to the home of the Pa Pa Bear and his wife, Mama Bear and their child, Bay B. Bear. Write a story about her trial.

23-12. Style quiz

Correct the style errors and poor or inappropriate wording in the following sentences.

1. John Powers, a spokesman for the Pasco Sheriff's department, said the boys left a 50 pound box of milky ways on a bench.

2. The robber was described as a black man in his middle 20's about five ft., 10 in and 140 lbs.

3. The fire in the apartment at the 2,700 block of Northeast 30th Pl. caused an estimated 9000 dollars worth of damage.

4. The boy suffered second and third degree burns over 1/3 of his body.

5. The weapon was a 22-caliber handgun.

6. Firemen arrived on the scene about six thirty in the morning.

7. Fire in an apartment can reach 1,700 $^{\circ}$ near the ceiling.

8. Judge Padlock ordered the woman to attending counseling sessions.

9. The mummified body was found on January 30.

10. The plaintiff prays for judgement in excess of ten thousand dollars.

Disasters and Tragedy 24

This chapter will give you practice writing another kind of disaster story and a sidebar. You also should evaluate some of the material for ethical concerns.

24-1. Explosion mainbar

You are a reporter for *The Sun,* a daily newspaper in San Bernardino, Calif. It is shortly after 8 a.m. You are listening to the police radio and you hear a report that there has been an explosion. You call the police dispatcher and learn that a gasoline pipeline exploded in the same neighborhood in which a 69-car runaway freight train derailed about two weeks ago, either an ironic or relevant coincidence. When the freight train derailed, it crashed into a string of homes and killed two crew members in the train and two boys in one home. Police spokesman Gary Fahnestrock tells you: "There has been an explosion. We haven't sorted anything out yet."

Your editor tells you to get to the scene and if it is serious, involving any injuries or death, the newspaper will put out a special edition in two hours – a new front and back page for the morning newspaper that has already been published. You have very little time, so you get to the scene where confusion reigns. You gather as much information as you can and return to the newspaper to write this story on deadline. You have about 45 minutes until deadline. You have gathered the information that follows for a location map. Here are your notes for the story:

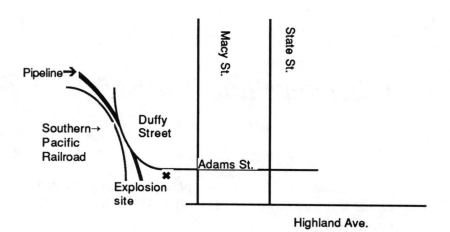

The explosion occurred at 8:11 a.m. in the neighborhood bounded by Duffy Street and Highland Ave., exactly the same area where the freight train derailed two weeks ago. When you arrive at Duffy Street, you see flames shooting about 100 feet into the air and seven homes on fire.

You try to talk to as many people as possible. Here are your sources:

David Andries, an official of the Calnev gas company: He says the explosion was caused by a 14-inch gasoline pipeline that ruptured. The pipeline, which is buried six feet underground, carries unleaded fuel from Colton (a neighboring community) to Nevada. He says it sprayed fuel on the houses when it ruptured. "We don't know the cause of the break. It could have been the train, obviously," he says.

Gregory Garcia, a spokesman for the mayor of San Bernardino: About 700 people have been evacuated to the Red Cross evacuation center. The center has been set up at the Job Corps Center, 3753 Kerry St.

Theresa Schorder, a Red Cross worker: By 10 a.m. 30 residents from Duffy and Donald streets neighborhoods arrived at the center. Two vans and a bus are being used for the evacuation.

Paul Allaire, San Bernardino Fire Department spokesman: Two people have died in a home on Duffy Street. One body was burned beyond recognition. The other victim is believed to be a man. Firefighters are looking for a third victim in the home.

San Bernardino Councilwoman Valerie Pope-Ludlam who was at the scene: "A woman ran out of her house, she left behind her sister and her cousin and a 6-month-old baby inside, and she looked back and the house blew up behind her."

176

Phil Arviso, a council aide: He said he talked to the woman whom Pope-Ludlam mentioned. He said she was Robbie Brown of 2327 Duffy St. He said Brown said her relatives, Keesha Jefferson, Charlene Jefferson and Charlene's baby were in the house. "She actually said her house blew up behind her as she came out. The house is gone. If anybody was in there, they went with it."

Bill Stewart, an insurance agent who was visiting a client, Martha Franklin in a house in the 2300 block of Donald Street which borders Adams Street (about a block away from the explosion): "We were sitting at the table and we heard this loud noise, and it just started getting bigger. I ran to the window and looked out and could see nothing but smoke; then we both hit the floor. We waited for it to blow over, but it didn't go away. Then we started to head for the door and when she opened the door, the smoke just started rolling in. We looked outside. The grass was burning – green grass burning. Everything was burning, even the concrete."

Calnev pipeline General Manager Jed Robinson: He said the pipeline can carry more than 3.3 million gallons of fuel jet fuel, gasoline and diesel – which flows through the 14-inch pipeline daily. The pipeline was carrying unleaded gasoline. He said valves along the pipe fall into place whenever anything in the pipe starts to flow backwards, toward Colton where the pipeline starts. He said a valve near the fire may not be completely closed, and that could influence the time it takes to put out the fire. "With that kind of a volatile fuel, you have to use some sort of foam. Normally where there is not an awful lot of fuel, you just contain it and try and let it burn out." He said he didn't know how much fuel is in the pipe.

Miretta Brumlow, a resident of 2351 Adams St. near the site. She was at the first aid center set up at Macy Street. She was still wearing a nightgown. "I felt my whole house shake. I thought it was an earthquake. Then I looked out and I saw the fire and I just started crying. I ran to the bedroom and got my daughter and grandson out, then I started looking for my pets, and then I just had to get out. I think my cats are still in there. Everything I own was in that house." She said she is a student at San Bernardino Valley College, but she hasn't attended school since the railroad disaster because she's been afraid to leave her children at home. "Thank God I didn't go to my class at eight o'clock this morning."

San Bernardino City Attorney Jim Penman, who toured the area this morning from a helicopter: "We were assured by the pipeline people it was safe (after the railroad accident) and the experts who examined it said there was no danger."

From hospital officials: Seven burn victims were admitted to the San Bernardino County Medical Center. Their conditions were not available. Other people admitted and treated were: Tina Blackburn – in serious condition with second- and third-degree burns over 15 percent of her body; Michael Howard with burns on his hands; his wife, Janet Howard, with third-degree burns and their two children, Shirley, 1, and LaKedra, 2, who were being treated for smoke inhalation. Diane Tucker was treated for minor cuts.

Observations and general Information you receive from various sources: Southern California Gas Co. workers were in the neighborhood to shut off gas lines to avoid any possibility of natural gas explosion, they said. A thick cloud of gray-black smoke from the explosion was reported visible as far away as Riverside and Ontario (neighboring communities). Highland Avenue at Macy was closed to motorists.

You are out of time. You must return to the newspaper and write the story. Use today as your time frame. This story will be in print in about 90 minutes.

Based on a story from *The* (San Bernardino, Calif.,) *Sun,* Used with permission.

24-2. Explosion sidebar

You have written your mainbar on deadline and you are now reporting a human-interest story for a sidebar for the next day's newspaper. You go to the Red Cross shelter set up at the Job Corps Center on Kerry Street to interview residents of the area who are there because they have been evacuated from their homes. The general reaction you get is that the residents are very angry. They are upset because the freight train derailment two weeks ago traumatized them, and they thought their homes were safe after that disaster. Here are the comments from your sources:

Georgia Mitchell of 2337 Duffy St.: Her house was destroyed and her daughter, a son-in-law and two grandchildren were injured. Two weeks ago she watched the train derail in front of her home. "If it wasn't safe for us to live, why'd they tell us it's OK to move back there?"

Maxie Charles of 2441 San Benito Court: He said the federal government should step in and provide emergency relief. "This should be declared a disaster area. And if they want to keep these pipelines, they should pay us off and we will be happy to move out."

Bonita Campbell, of San Carlo Avenue: She was walking around the Job Corps ground in the gown, robe and slippers she wore when the explosion occurred. Her family got out of their home safely; her two dogs were waiting in her car. "Right now I don't know what to think. I don't know what to do. I know I can't continue to live like this not knowing what's going to happen."

Vincent Hemphill, 25, who grew up in the house at 2604 Duffy St.: He said even if his home survived, he won't go back. No one should return to those unlucky streets, he said. "They had no damn business trying to patch no pipe up anyway. They should have discontinued that until they fixed it.   (Referring to the neighborhood): It's messed up. I think they should just, like, take the whole neighborhood and move us out of there. It's a disaster for all of us now. "

Patrick Thomas of 2313 Adams St.: He was holding his daughter, Lisa, 15 months old. His home that he rents was unscathed by the train wreck. But yesterday when he last saw his home, flames were crawling up one side. The home was situated five houses away from another house that blew up on Adams Street. "I am mad. I am mad as hell – at the railroad, at whoever put that fuel line in, at whoever built those houses over a fuel line, at the city for not doing something."

Mark Kingston, area resident: "It makes me sick that this fire happened, especially if somebody knew it needed to be repaired. Somebody ought to be hung out to dry."

Clemmie Williams, 51, of San Benito Court: He says the right side of his face still stings where a medic smeared white salve over a burn. He said two days ago he whiffed something in the air near his home that smelled like a mixture of fuel and ammonia. He said the odor lasted about 10 minutes, so he let it pass without concern. "They (Calnev officials) said there was no leakage so we assumed it was OK."

Based on a story from *The* (San Bernardino, Calif.,) *Sun,* Used with permission.

Profiles

25

This chapter combines many of the feature techniques you have studied, such as storytelling, use of anecdotes and descriptive writing. Although exercises are presented in this chapter, the best way to learn how to write profiles is to interview people. Even if you think a person is interesting, you still need a newsworthy focus so you can write a nut graph explaining why you are writing about this person.

25-1. Profile analysis

This is a profile about a professor who was featured during African-American History month. If you were coaching this writer, what suggestions would you make to improve this profile? What questions would you have asked the profile subject? Discuss techniques that you would have used.

Sadye Logan sits in her incense-scented office.

She speaks quickly, and her eyes dance with excitement as she discusses her favorite subject — family.

Logan, associate professor of social welfare, has been an instructor at the University of Kansas for nine years and has spent those years studying the family unit.

Logan said that the family was the most important factor in shaping an individual and that this was why she decided to study the subject.

"For me, everything begins with the family," Logan said. "It is a major institution. It is still the seed of hope for future generations, for the country, for the world."

Logan holds a particular interest in African-American families.

She said that all types of families had problems but that some more strongly affected African-American families, such as the rise in single-parent families, increasing poverty and unemployment, inequality of income and substance abuse.

Logan said that despite these problems, African-American families had an amazing vitality and resilience.

"They have a hopefulness that's born out of an inner strength," she said.

Students in Logan's Social Work Practice II course praise their instructor and her teaching style.

"I don't really feel like she is a lecturer," said Christy Shunn, a Lawrence graduate student. "Her agenda is our agenda. It's student-based and conforms to what we need."

Marsha Page, a Lawrence graduate student, agreed that Logan primarily was interested in student needs and described her style as interactive.

"She attempts to create a very easygoing atmosphere," Page said. "That's really a great approach for this course."

Logan spent her early years in Charleston, S.C. before moving to New York City, where she said she matured and grew up. She received an undergraduate degree in psychology and speech therapy from South Carolina State College. She later received a master's degree form Hunter College in New York City and a doctorate from Columbia University.

After finishing her education, Logan taught at the University of Texas at Austin and Fordham University at Lincoln Center.

"I look at what I had done prior to teaching as preparation for what I'm doing now," Logan said. "I do this because I enjoy it."

You are interviewing a professor on your campus. He has an unusual style of teaching, and he won a prestigious award for his outstanding teaching in 1989. This year he has been nominated again for this award. You go to his classroom so you can see him in action, and you later interview him in his office. You also get comments from his students. Using the notes, write a profile of this professor; substitute the name of your college for the one in this story, if your instructor prefers.

The professor is Dr. Daryl Evans. He teaches Sociology 104. His classes are huge – more than 1,000 students. In 1989 he won the HOPE Award, (Honor for Outstanding Progressive Educator) at The University of Kansas [or use your college or university.] In 1991 he was one of three winners of the Burlington Northern Foundation Achievement Award, which honors outstanding university teaching and rewards scholarly excellence.

Background: He received his bachelor's degree from Colorado State University and his doctorate from the University of Colorado, Boulder in 1979. He taught for a year at the University of Colorado. He had large classes of 500 students. In 1981 he came to the University of Kansas, where he has been ever since.

He teaches sociology, but his research is in the area of disabilities. He has also done several studies on life support decisions concerning elderly people and on parental decision making in the treatment of newborns with disabilities. He has also written a book, *The Lives of Mentally Retarded People*.

You are interviewing him in his office on the seventh floor of Fraser Hall. Every time you stopped by, a line of students was outside the door waiting to talk to him. You observe his office. Two bookcases filled with books, two grey tables – one serving as a desk piled high with papers, books and soda cans – line the walls of his long narrow office. Photographs cover the walls. Some are of wolves, eagles and different landscapes. Other are American Indian artwork, postcards and advertisements. The floor of his office is crowded, too. Five chairs, including a rocking chair, sit in a circle on top of a faded dark green and mauve swirled rug. A small round table sits next to his rocking chair so he can rest his white, coffee-stained mug there as he settles into the chair, crosses his legs, and devotes his attention to you. He looks a bit like Gene Wilder. He has curly, almost frizzy, brown hair touched with grey and almost long enough to put into a small ponytail. He wears an earring in his left ear and a silver bracelet with a large green stone on his wrist. He is wearing a great suit and shiny brown penny loafers.

You ask him about his interest in disabled people. He tells you that his interest stems from his own disability. He has epilepsy. He says he tells his class that if he has a grand mal seizure, not to get up and help because his teaching assistants (he has several for his class of more than 1,000 students) know what to do. He tells his students to sit back and watch and they will discuss it when it is over. He says it is important for students to observe something like that in an unhorrifying atmosphere because it frightens so many people. In all the years he has been teaching at the University of Kansas (more than 11 at this point) he has never had a major seizure in front of a class, but he says he thinks it is important for students to know it is a possibility. He says if he experiences a petit mal seizure, a mild seizure where he blanks out for only a few seconds, he can just start reading from his notes and not be completely lost when he recovers. He says that happened to him once in front of a class, but no one even noticed.

You check his background and discuss his awards, and you ask him how he manages to do his research and devote so much time to his students. He says he balances research and teaching "by not sleeping very much." But he says his main love is teaching. "I don't tend to distinguish between work and pleasure," he says. He says even when he is listening to music or watching a movie, he is on the lookout for things to use in class. He always looks for a way to apply everything he loves to teaching.

For example when you visited his class, he used a clip from Woody Allen's "Annie Hall" to show the different interpretations of the meaning of words and the duality of language. He says by using movie clips, he hopes to utilize students' own methods of learning.

"I knew I wanted to be a professor when I was 8 years old," he says. But he says he just didn't know what he wanted to teach. He studied in a seminary for a while, but he realized that wasn't for him. He says he thought about economics, but finally ended up in sociology.

He says his philosophy of teaching is what he tells the students: "Dare to fail." The other part is giving the students tools to guide their lives and to hone their ability to think critically. He says he hopes to seduce the students into reading and writing and thinking with a sophisticated sense of thought.

You observe him in class. His class meets every Tuesday and Thursday mornings at 11. As students pile into Crafton-Preyer auditorium, music blares from the big black speakers above the stage. Sometimes it's country, sometimes it's hard rock, sometimes it's gospel, and sometimes it's hard to tell. The music is to get the students' attention. When the music stops, everyone knows class is ready to begin and Evans says he doesn't have to waste time getting them to be quiet.

182

Before class starts, he is down on stage talking with some of his teaching assistants He is setting up the white three-tiered cart he uses in class for writing on the overhead projector. The overhead shines on a large movie screen framed by the backdrop of the dark maroon theater curtain. All at once, the music stops, the lights go out and the auditorium is silent as an image is projected on the screen. The 1,000 students watch as a scene from "Annie Hall" by Woody Allen appears.

His teaching assistants help by providing concrete examples of what Evans is trying to teach. The examples range from skits to poetry readings and stories to tales of personal experience.

Once class begins, Evans darts around the stage, gesturing with his hands, kneeling and jumping, but doing these actions with a purpose. He always comes back to the large black notebook that rests on top of his cart.

After the class, you have a brief interview with him, and ask him about the difficulty of keeping 1,000 students' attention. He says: "It doesn't feel any different teaching to 150 student than it does to 1,000 students. I'll say the same kinds of things."

You ask about his entertaining way of teaching. He says the class isn't just fun and games. It's not "infotainment." He says: "We're very serious educators. If we wanted to entertain, hell, we could have that place rockin'!"

But he does admit that he entertains students at the end of the year in the final class. "I hate that I teach so many students, so we want to compensate the students for choosing to be so patient," he says. He does that by organizing a skit with his TAs, a final performance. He says the best skit was in 1989 when the performance was about racism. "We weren't too pleased with last year; it was too oblique," he says. Last year's performance was live music, a student-written and produced documentary film, a slide show and literature of tales of personal experience to encourage students to think about their ability and power in society. His TAs had brushed stripes of neon paints across his face and torso while Evans had said, "If you raise your voices, it will take time and energy and you will be marked forever." This year, he says, the topic is stigmatized persons, and he says it should be good. He says everyone is welcome to attend, even if students are not in his class.

25-3. Vignette

Your newspaper is publishing a series of stories called "Generations," featuring local people of different ages, backgrounds, races, and cultures. The point is to show the reader how these people feel about a number of issues in the '90s. *The Wichita Eagle,* which produced this series, did it in a form of question and answer. Rather than run the full dialogue as the *Eagle* did, view the reporters' questions as your own and the sources' answers as your notes. Then write a vignette with the generational focus. Although a good vignette should contain more details about the person and preferably some show-in-action techniques which these sessions lack, these exercises will give you practice in selectivity. Choose only the quotes and information that you think will be relevant to a vignette of less than 500 words.

John January's story

Editor's note: "Generations" is a series of articles that describe life in the '90s through interviews with Kansans of all ages, all backgrounds. Eagle reporter Martha Sevetson interviewed John January for this installment. This is an edited transcript of their conversation. (The story was accompanied by the following highlights box.)

John January
Age: 25
Marital Status: Married to Ann Marie January
Children: None
Occupation: Advertising copywriter at Sullivan, Higdon & Sink.
Education: Bachelor's degree in communications, Wichita State University
Family background: Born in western Kansas, spent much of childhood in Dighton. Moved to Clearwater when he was a teenager. Father was a teacher.
Residence: Rents an apartment in midtown Wichita

Reporter: *At 25, you are a college graduate working for an advertising agency and living in a midtown apartment. You are married but have no children and few financial obligations. In a snapshot, this is your life today. How did you get here? By choice? By coincidence? How would you describe the path you followed from childhood to now?*

January: I think more by choice than by coincidence. I had a very planned way of getting here. I worked very hard and focused by efforts very intently on getting here, almost to a fault. Because things are so competitive in the advertising field, I knew I was going to have to work very hard to get a job, even. I was terrified that I wouldn't. Petrified that I'd graduate and there'd be nothing there. . . .

When I came into college, I hadn't even really thought about what I'd like to do. But about my second year I stumbled onto the interest in communications and found out it was real competitive, and put my nose to the grindstone. . . . I did as many internships as possible, and I utilized those. I networked with those people – I hate that term. But it's really what I did. And I think because of that, those connections and the attitude that I showed through doing that, helped get me the interview at Sullivan, Higdon and Sink.

When I was in high school, I did a couple of things extracurricularly well. I was pretty good at theater and had done a bunch of it, high school plays. And everybody had always said, "Oh, you're so good at that." So my drama teacher said, "There's a scholarship you can apply for in the theater department," so I did that. And I got the scholarship and helped pay for school.

But because I wanted what I have, because I wanted a stable sort of white-bread, all-American existence, I ruled theater out really quick. It just didn't match the life I wanted to lead. It's a very gypsy-like existence. Plus, I mean, I'm not Robert Redford or Robert DeNiro or anybody like that, either.

Reporter: *It sounds like you thought a lot about what you were going to do, especially during college. You really planned your life out; you set priorities. Do you think that approach to life has served you well? Do you have any regrets about being so focused and not just sort of following whatever whim you had at the moment?*

January: I certainly think it served me well. And I don't have any regrets really, from my standpoint. But I say that, all the while knowing that I'm really a chicken. The reason that I was so focused in college and so one-minded about things is that I'm really terrified of doing something that requires uncertainty. Uncertainty's not a real pleasant thing for me to deal with. . . .I would have been a basket case if I didn't try to manage the uncertainty in my life. That's really what that whole thing was about. I found something that I really dug, that I really thought would be good and I really wanted to do. And found what it was going to take to make it the most possible for me to do that. And I did that.

And I have a friend — this is the perfect example — I have a friend who just went to Chicago to be an actor. And he, what he did was, he waited until after he got married. So he got married, then he and his new wife packed all their stuff and went to Chicago. They didn't have a job lined up. They didn't have any money in the bank. They had credit-card bills to pay. But they took that leap of faith and they went up there, and now he's working at a Chicago theater. A little one, he's not making any money yet. He's working in the daytime at a telemarketing place. But he's doing what he wants, and he made it.

And he said to me, when he first told me he was going to do that, he said, "John," he goes, "It's really hard for me to tell you this, because I know you think I'm stupid." And I said, "Troy, I don't think you're stupid. I think you have a lot more guts than I ever would."

Reporter: *When you were a child, or when you were a teen-ager, what expectations did you have for life?*

January: My dad, as an educator, moved a lot. We moved quite a bit when I was a kid, so we didn't buy houses. We rented them. And we always rented them out in the country. They were generally these old, sort of run-down farmhouses. They were great homes, which I would love today. But they weren't like what my city-kid friends had — what I call city kids, they lived in the town, OK? It was way out in western Kansas.

And my sister, one of my sisters lived in a really nice house, so I always viewed myself as moving to the city and living there. And I did view myself as being successful and having money. . . . And I think the reason was that for a lot of years when I was growing up, my parents really didn't have a lot of money. We weren't poor, but we didn't have a lot extra. I sensed that. I could

see that in my parents and the way that they approached everything. . . . I was certainly aware of the fact that if my dad wanted a new car, he wasn't going to get it. We always drove older, used cars. In fact, my new car that I bought when I got my job was the first new car that anybody in my family ever purchased. My mom and dad to this day have not purchased a new car, their whole life.

Reporter: *How do you feel right now about the choices you have made up to now? Especially the balance between career and family, or career and personal life, something most people seem to struggle with. Do you feel like you are, or you are on track to, devote too much of yourself to your job? Have you sacrificed any part of your job for your marriage? Or have you found that balance? And how do you think you will balance things in the future?*

January: As far as, personally, balancing between my job and home life, that mix is very good because I'm in an excellent position. The place that I work for really values that. They expect you to work extra when it's needed, but that's not all the time. We have flexibility in that.

The hard part about balance as I see it is balancing a two-career family, and we really struggle. I think everybody in our position really struggles about how do you balance your own goals and your own desires with this other person that you committed to spend the rest of your life with, their goals and their desires. Balancing what I want and what I need and what I think I need to accomplish with what Ann Marie believes she wants and what she needs and what she needs to accomplish, is really hard to do.

We're both on an equal plane; her career is not more important than mine, but my career is certainly not more important than hers. I really believe that, and so does she. Because of that,

185

because of the opportunities that either one of us might have throughout our lives, there may be periods of separation, where we're not in the same city. And that is really a radical concept for people like my parents, who, we've had conversations with them, they just shake their heads at things like that. But it's a reality. It is something that people, that I really think families in the '50s didn't have to deal with. It's an added stress on families today that wasn't there before.

Reporter: *You grew and entered adulthood after a period of immense social change. How do you think your times affected your life? How do you think it would have been different if you had grown up in the '50s and entered adulthood in the '50s?*

January: I think that my generation is, if not the first, then one of the first where it's not even considered that there won't be two careers in a marriage. That's not even given a second thought. And so I think that's a huge change. That's not to say that the traditional nuclear family that is still sort of portrayed in many cases doesn't still have its influence on us. I think everybody in my generation really goes round and round with that. People in my generation are still pioneering what this new family's going to end up being. There's no model for us out there. We're our own models, and we're watching very carefully what the boomers are doing. If there's any model, it comes from them.

Reporter: *How do you think your life would have been different if you were a baby boomer? Would it have been easier then?*

January: Yes. The baby boomers, I think there's a lot of resentment in my generation with the baby boomers. It was easier for them. They had Depression-era parents who enjoyed a new prosperity in this country and were able to get, were the very definition of the American Dream, the old American Dream, and were able to give them educations. Were able to provide them with all kinds of opportunities.

The opportunities were a lot more plentiful. But it wasn't as easy for them as it was for their parents. But I think they had it a lot easier than we do. There just aren't a whole heck of a lot of great opportunities out there.

Reporter: *We talked earlier about your life now, and basically you're just starting out, both in your career and your marriage. Where do you see yourself heading? What is the toughest decision facing you?*

January: I think what's next for us is getting ourselves in a position where we can think about what's next for us. Ann's in school right now, and there are certain expenses associated with that. There were certain expenses associated with my schooling that I'm still paying for. I think we'll both feel really good when we see that suddenly we have the flexibility to think about what's next. Even though we don't own a home and we don't have kids, we do feel a certain bit of inflexibility right now because of the economy and because of paying off things like school and cars.

Reporter: *How do you define success, or the American Dream? Do you define it the same way you did when you were younger?*

January: When I was a kid, the American Dream was your cliched American Dream: a house, two cars and two golden retrievers and a white picket fence. Although I had kind of the revisionist classic American Dream in that I was the father that also did the grocery-shopping, folded the clothes and helped my busy wife and supported her in her career, and we took turns going to the PTA meetings because we were both too busy to individually handle it. So that's how I viewed it as a kid. I don't see it at all that way now. Now, just personally, the way I define success is happiness, is finding that balance between a healthy, happy home life. If we can achieve that, I would then consider myself successful. If Ann and I can both come home from work, look each other in the eye and say, "Gosh I sure like what I do and I sure like what we've got going." Success to me is that. And that's a big change.

The Wichita (Kan.) *Eagle.* Reprinted with permission.

186

Features
and Specialty Stories

26

This chapter will give you practice writing general features, medical, business and sports stories. Although some of the subject matter is specialized, the writing techniques for these stories are the same ones you have been taught to use throughout the book. For most of the stories in this chapter, assume you are working for the *Sun-Sentinel,* a metropolitan newspaper in Fort Lauderdale with a circulation of about 300,000.

26-1. Feature – Barefoot U.

Your editor assigns you to write a feature about New College in Sarasota, Fla., a very non-traditional type of college that was named the best U.S. public education buy in 1990 through 1992 by *Money* magazine. Your editor wants a feature that explains what makes this college so unusual. You start with the public relations department of the college, which gives you this information for facts boxes that will accompany your story. After that you interview a range of people, from the president of the college to students. Here are the facts boxes followed by your notes, which include your observations. Using information from the facts boxes and your notes, write a feature story.

<table>
<tr><td valign="top">

History

1960 – Chartered as a private liberal-arts college
1962 - Located on the former Ringling family estate
1967 - First class graduates
1973 - Joins the University of South Florida and becomes public.
1992 - Gordon Michalson Jr. is named dean and warden.

</td><td valign="top">

Facts
Location 116-acre campus on Sarasota Bay
Enrollment 510 students
Tuition $1,855 for in-state and $7,567 for out-of-state students
Student-teacher ratio 10-to-1.
Applicant accepted ratio: 8-to-1.
Average SAT for incoming freshmen: 3.62 (on 4.0 scale)
No grades – students negotiate contracts with professors
Bachelor degrees - 29 majors
Honors college of Florida state university system
Faculty: 90 percent have doctorates
Named best U.S. public education buy in 1990-92 by *Money* magazine.
Source: University of South Florida at New College

</td></tr>
</table>

Your observations:

Most of the students walk around without shoes. In fact, you find out that New College is nicknamed "Barefoot U." The majority of men wear earrings and women don't shave their legs or armpits. Cars sport bumper stickers with political messages such as "Zappa for President" or "Draft Quayle" (held over from 1992 when the vice president was Dan Quayle). The administration is housed on grounds overlooking Sarasota Bay. The grounds were once owned by the Ringling family of Ringling Bros. Circus fame. The dormitories, built by internationally acclaimed architect I.M. Pei, are on the opposite side of the campus, within sight and earshot of Sarasota-Bradenton Airport. U.S. 41 (Tamiami Trail), slices through the heart of the 116-acre campus. You find out that there are no fraternities or sororities, and the college does not have a football team.

Background from the Office of Information:

The college was founded in 1960 by Sarasota business leaders determined to create an innovative private college in their community. They picked the name, New College, to mirror the top academic philosophy from New College, Oxford. The spirit has been maintained since, even after New College avoided bankruptcy by becoming part of the University of South Florida establishment in 1975. There are no grades. Instead, students negotiate a contract with individual professors. They must also pass oral baccalaureate exams to graduate.

From the Office of Admissions and David Anderson, director of the office:

Admission records show 1,110 people applied and 158 were enrolled as entering freshmen or transfer students in August. Of the school's 510 students, 431 are white, 23 are Asian, 10 are black, 26 are Hispanic and 20 are from other minority groups. Anderson says the campus has three black male students. Admissions Director David Anderson says 47 percent of the students stay and graduate. He is working hard to improve that percentage. He says he is being more selective about the freshmen he admits. "Beyond grades, we are not looking for the traditional extra-curricular types, the cheerleader, prom queen, three-sport varsity athlete," Anderson says. "We look for students in non-traditional activities such as Greenpeace, animal rights or community service. Students here need to be independent sorts who do not shy away from challenges or tend to go with the crowd." He says that seven of every 10 New College students go on to graduate school. New College is the honors school of Florida's state university system.

You interview New College President Gordon Michalson Jr.: He became president in August of 1992. He previously taught religion for 15 years at Oberlin College in Ohio. His formal title is dean and warden of the college, but students call him Warden Gordon. He is 43. He says: "New College's academic tradition is very well-known across the country. I came here as a guest lecturer in 1983. It has a barefoot, green-hair atmosphere where students can be active in individualized learning."

One drawback Michalson sees is the small-town aspect of the campus. "Our size does create some student life problems. Everybody knows everybody's business. Except for swimming in the pools and weekly dances, there is not much to do."

You interview David Schneck, a dean at New College: His office is a few door up the hall from Michalson's. Schneck is also in charge of the USF (University of South Florida – the state system to which New College belongs) program for commuting students. He says: "Freshmen within two weeks shed their shoes, other parts of clothing, let their hair grow, sport earrings, tie-dyed T-shirts, torn jeans and nose rings. This campus is almost a photograph of the '60s, a real time warp."

But he tells you that the campus is shared by a more conservative group of working professionals who are taking night classes. At dusk, angry words are sometimes exchanged over turf rights or political differences.

"I guess you can say there is a rivalry here, a generation gap," says Schneck. "Yes, there is some real tension here. I won't deny that."

You interview Professor Arthur McA. Miller, better known as Professor Mac: He is considered a maverick. The doorway to his office sports a sign: "Welcome to the Mac Zone." In his smoke-filled office is an oversized Mickey Mouse watch sharing space on the wall with an African mask. He was among the first group of professors hired in 1964 and has never left. He is a tenured professor of poetry and chairman of the humanities department. You notice an electric typewriter, but no computer. He says he only abandoned his manual typewriter a few years ago, but he refuses to use a computer. He tells you: "I strongly believe in hands-on education. If you don't do it, you don't learn it. To appreciate poetry, you have to write it and see how damn hard it is."

You interview the following students:

Mtetwa Ramdoo, born in Trinidad and raised in Brooklyn: She says she keeps coming back each fall with one hope: "I look to see if there are any black males. We have so few here. I guess black males just don't qualify. This school is not racist, but I am bombarded by one culture and no other."

Mitch Silverman of Sunrise (Fla.): He is 27 and is majoring in political science. He says he knew he wasn't cut out for traditional college life, so he picked New College. "I'm more conservative in terms of my exterior appearance. I do own a blazer and tie," Silverman says. "New College is a place where you can march to a different drummer and that's OK. You can really be yourself here." Silverman says New College's no-grade policy can be deceivingly difficult. "I blew my first contract." (He's referring to the contracts students must negotiate with professors.) "I learned quickly that you have to be self-disciplined and self-motivated to make it here."

Silverman is editor of a campus publication called "The Nerve" and is active in student plays. "In theater productions at New College, you are either very good or very bad. There seems to be no middle ground," he says.

Forest Turbiville of Tampa (Fla.): He says he is one of the few conservative students on campus. He is easy to spot. He wears a baseball cap, socks and shoes, and tucks in his shirt. "People accept you for who you are," he says. "There are not prejudices here that I can see. This place is friendly and challenging. I know it sounds strange, but after one year here, I can actually feel myself getting smarter."

Based on a story by Arden Moore, *Sun-Sentinel* (Fort Lauderdale, Fla.). Used with permission.

26-2. Medical story

You are working for a newspaper in Charlotte, N.C., where an experimental program to help children with autism is being conducted. Your editor assigns you to write a feature about this controversial program, auditory training. You will need to explain what autism is and make sure you include pros and cons about this program. You also need to make sure you define any medical jargon. Some of the paragraphs, taken from a story in *The Charlotte Observer,* may be used as they are written. You will have to decide how to organize this story. Here are your notes:

Background from medical articles, books and various authorities:

Autism is a brain disorder that is considered baffling by medical experts. Autism remains a painful mystery that strikes about one in 1,000 people. Its cause is unknown and there is no medical test to show that a person has it. Instead, symptoms of a severe communication and behavior disorder lead to a diagnosis of autism.

People with autism appear to be living in their own world. Many are silent; some repeat meaningless phrases. Their emotions and behavior seem inappropriate; they may show no affection for family members, flap their hands, fixate on an object while ignoring everything else.

Because autism is a communication disorder, few can say what is it like from the inside. But Temple Grandin, in her 1986 book, *Emergence: Labeled Autistic* (Arena Press, $10) described a characteristic of autism as speech sounding like an oncoming freight train.

And in 1990 *Reader's Digest* published the story of Georgie Thomas, who took auditory therapy from French physician Guy Berard in 1977 when she was 11 and autistic. It sparked a dramatic turnaround that led to her graduating from college with honors, marrying and leading a normal life. She, too, told of feeling battered by overwhelming noise. Her story created hope for families of people with autism.

Auditory training is an experimental technique that arrived in the United States less than two years ago. Auditory training works on the premise that some of these problems stem from distorted or abnormally sensitive hearing. Everyday sounds, including the human voice, may be painful, frightening or incomprehensible. The training attempts to eliminate or reduce abnormalities. It also has been used to treat people with learning disabilities, attention deficit disorders and some hearing problems.

Even experts in auditory training can't say how it works or predict who will benefit from it. A family may spend about $1,000, put a child through the 10-day training and see no results.

Advocates acknowledge that auditory therapy is still experimental and doesn't work for everyone. Specialists with the Center for the Study of Autism in Newberg, Ore., are studying U.S. children who have received the training; they plan to release

190

the results this summer.

In October (this past October) an auditory training specialist came to Charlotte to administer auditory training to 15 children with autism. The results were mixed.

The training takes 10 days. First, children are tested to see if they show abnormal sensitivity to particular pitches of sound. Next, they spend two half-hour sessions per day for 10 days listening to music, in which various pitches are emphasized at random. If a child is overly sensitive to a certain pitch, that pitch will be blocked out.

Afterward, many parents report seeing improvements in their children's attention span, communication or ability to interact with others. However, many also report temporary flare-ups in behavior problems.

The key question is why these changes happen. The Center for the Study of Autism offers the following theories:

• The varying pitches, coming at random, may teach people to shift attention more easily. That may help them follow speech and hand gestures.

• Autistic people may be tuning out sounds; the training may help them tune back in.

• The tuning may help them better understand and cope with speech and other sounds.

You interview the parents of two children who have had this auditory training in Charlotte. One parent is Debbie Heath, whose son, Michael, 7, improved after the training he had for 10 days during the fall. She lives in the Mint Hill suburb. She says Michael has started answering the phone, understanding instructions and helping around the house. "He is so different now; he is not even the same child," she says.

Michael started making more eye contact and showing a longer attention span after about five days of training, she says. However, about two weeks after the training he also began having tantrums and seeming unhappy. That ended after a couple of weeks. Now Michael does things he's never done before: helping clean up the kitchen, getting himself ready for bed, showing affection.

Heath says she can't say for sure that the training is responsible, but "if it isn't , I've never seen such a coincidence. I've never seen such progress as fast."

Debra Fisher of Stanley County is the mother of Bo, a 5-year-old who also had the auditory training. With Michael Heath, Bo slipped on headphones and listened to distorted pop music during the auditory training. Mrs. Fisher says she saw the first progress when she brought Bo to their home after an auditory training session. Normally a loner, Bo saw some children playing across the street and ran to join them. Since the training, he's been speaking more, making eye contact more often and doing better in speech classes, she says. Now Bo speaks better, plays more with other children and looks at people when they talk to him.

Connie King is the mother of Chris, 7, who also had the auditory training. She is president of the Charlotte-Mecklenburg chapter of the N.C. Autism Society. But Chris showed no dramatic improvement. However, she encourages other parents to try the training – as long as they understand there are unanswered questions and no guarantees. "This is not a cure," King says. "This doesn't work for everyone. Parents who go into this have got to understand that." Mrs. King says the tape sounded like "a lot of strange sounds," even though she could detect the underlying music. Her son said, "This music is crazy; why do I have to listen to it?"

The only change King has seen is that Chris started sleeping through the night after the training. Perhaps that's because he's less bothered by night noises, she said.

Bo, Michael and Chris all show sings of having overly sensitive hearing. Bo covers his ears or sticks Play-Doh in them, especially when watching television or hearing a hum from fluorescent lights. Michael runs in screaming when someone used a chain saw outside. Chris has complained that the bubbling filter in his fish tank keeps him awake at night.

The parents agree that if a family can afford the auditory training – Woodward charges $925, and not all insurance policies will pay – it's worth a try.

"To me, what you have got to lose?" Heath says.

You interview Jack Wall, director of North Carolina's TEACCH (Treatment and Education of Autistic and related Communication handicapped Children) clinic in Charlotte. He says advocates of auditory training offer little hard data and some claims that are almost impossible to prove, such as taking credit for improvements that occur months after the training. "I hope it's true, but I feel like people who are doing this need to be cautious," he says. "Parents tend to have high hopes. This group, probably more than any group I've worked with in 20 years in human services, is sort of primed for any sort of fad."

You interview Deborah Woodward of McLeansville, the audiologist and nurse who did the training in Charlotte this fall. She says: "I wish I knew more about exactly how it works." She and Melanie Highfill of Winston-Salem are apparently the only audiologists in the Carolinas doing the training for autistic children. Woodward says she was initially skeptical about the training, but saw enough good results that she started offering it last year.

Based on a story by Ann Doss Helms, *The Charlotte* (N.C.) *Observer*. Used with permission.

26-3. Business story

You are working for the *Sun-Sentinel,* a newspaper in Fort Lauderdale. The city and surrounding South Florida communities have a high percentage of retirees, who have moved there from the Northeast and other parts of the United States. You are scanning the obituaries and you notice that many of the funerals are scheduled in the home states of these residents. You start to wonder about how the bodies are shipped back to these states, and you check into it. You find out from a number of airline and funeral experts that more bodies are flown out of Fort Lauderdale-Hollywood International Airport than any other place in the world! At least 10 to 15 bodies are flown aboard carriers from Fort Lauderdale every day. Many of the dead from Dade and Palm Beach counties are flown out of Fort Lauderdale because of its central location on the Gold Coast, funeral directors say. You tell the business editor, who says it sounds like a good business story and asks you to write it.

Stop here and write a list of sources. Whom would you call for information about the number of people who died in the state? What other sources would you use to find out how many bodies are flown aboard air carriers nationally? How would you get anecdotal material from people whose relatives will be buried out of your state? Make a list of questions, as well.

On the next page you will find notes from various sources so you can write your story.

Here are your notes:

You have called many funeral directors and culled the following information, which you plan to attribute generally to funeral directors:

Dozens of funeral homes in South Florida are in the business of shipping human remains. Here's how it works: Funeral homes, which generally make all the arrangements to ship remains, carefully package whole coffins or just a body in a special shipping crate. Then, the crate is dropped off at an airline's freight center in a van – never a hearse – and discreetly stowed in a plane's cargo compartment. If you're a passenger, you won't know the dead are on board your plane. The decision to fly a loved one home for burial can be costly to a person's estate or for a grieving family, as much as $2,000 above the normal costs of a funeral. Funeral homes charge about $200 for a special particle-board crate, or what is called an air tray. If the body is not embalmed, it must be placed in a metal crate and packed with ice; this method is used by Orthodox Jews, whose beliefs forbid embalming.

From various airline companies (More information about the process):

In most ways, the airlines treat the dead exactly like any other cargo. However, because of bulk – the coffin, remains and crate weigh about 400 pounds – generally only two bodies are allowed on a plane at once. Delta Air Lines, for one, ships about 3,500 bodies per month around the country, with Fort Lauderdale being its busiest city.

Although it is rare, human remains have been temporarily lost in transit, just as baggage has been lost.

Airlines charge a flat price to ship human remains, generally $250 to $300 for a domestic flight and between $1,500 to $2,500 to Europe. Also, family members who fly on the same plane with the deceased have to buy tickets. For example, several airlines have discounted fares of about $375 per person for a round trip from Fort Lauderdale to New York City. If those fares dry up, most airlines will charge full fare, or up to $680 one-way under current rates. But most families say cost is less important than fulfilling a loved one's wishes.

From a spokesperson for the Florida Health Department:

About 4,000 dead people from Broward County (Fort Lauderdale is a city in this county) are shipped out of state each year. The vast majority are flown; less than 1 percent are removed by car, bus or train. That is by far the most of any area in Florida. In 1991, for instance, 2,700 human remains from Dade County (the county for Miami) and 2,360 human remains from Palm Beach County were shipped to other states. Overall, about 25,500 people , or 19 percent of Florida's total deaths, leave the state for burial each year.

From Tim Neale, spokesman for the Airline Transport Association in Washington, D.C.:

He says: "It's very big business and especially big for South Florida because you have so many people who retire down there and want to be buried where they came from."

From a spokesperson for Fred Hunter's funeral home in Broward County:

The funeral home ships about 350 bodies per year, with the majority of those from Broward County.

From the U.S. Department of Transportation's Office of Consumer Affairs:

In one instance a year ago, a body was placed on a United Airlines flight from Ontario, Calif., to Springfield, Ill., via Denver. The flight out of Denver was canceled, and the dead person was late for the funeral.

From Eugenie Wikberg of Fort Lauderdale, listed under survivors as the daughter in an obituary about Madeline J. Krauss of Boca Raton: The obituary said interment for Mrs. Krauss would be in Newark, N.J.

Wikberg says her mother made her own burial arrangements far in advance of her death. She was 87 and was born near the New Jersey shore. She wanted to be buried there because she had family, friends and memories there. She had retired to Boca Raton, Fla. But on Aug. 21, two days after she died, her body was shipped to Newark, N.J. (the closest airport to the New Jersey shore). She was entombed in the family mausoleum in New Jersey on Aug. 22. "This had been planned long before she came to Florida," said Wikberg. "It was a simple as that." After flying home with her mother to oversee all the arrangements, Wikberg said, "It wasn't too pleasant. But I felt good about it."

Based on a story by Ken Kaye, *Sun-Sentinel* (Fort Lauderdale, Fla.). Used with permission.

26-4. Sports story

You are a sports reporter for the *Sun-Sentinel* in Fort Lauderdale, Fla., and you are covering a men's college basketball game between the Miami Hurricanes (considered your home team) and the Providence College Friars in Rhode Island. This is a Big East conference game. The focus and emphasis of your story will be on the Hurricanes. Here are some facts, statistics and quotes from the coaches of each team. Find a theme and weave in game highlights and statistics and stress analysis of why Miami lost.

Background:

Miami (8-13, 5-8) which means 8 wins, 13 losses so far this season in total games played; 5 wins (all at home), 8 losses in Big East conference games. 0-7 in Big East road games (meaning they have lost all conference games played on the road)

Overall and including this game, Miami has lost 32 consecutive games on the road; last game won on the road was on Feb. 20, 1990 at Davidson (72-64 score) under previous coach Bill Foster. That was three years ago from this game against Providence. Under current coach Leonard Hamilton, the record is 0-30 on the road.

Hurricanes last season were 0-11 and 0-11 in 1990-91 on the road. Altogether since 1985, Miami is 9-56 on the road.

Next game - Saturday at home against conference leader St. Johns (14-6, 9-3).

Providence (12-9,5-8) 12 wins, 9 losses so far this season in total games played; 5 wins, 8 losses in Big East conference games. This win gives the Friars a back-to-back Big East wins. The Friars upset Georgetown Saturday night 68-50. Providence is 4-3 (4 wins, 3 losses at home). The last time Providence played the Hurricanes in the Miami Arena (a month ago), Providence lost 75-66 after building a 16-point lead.

Game highlights and pertinent information:

Score: 75-60, Providence wins; ties for conference standing (5-8) with Miami at seventh place

Location: Civic Center, Providence

Attendance: 9,579 (Less than capacity, which is 13,471)

Miami shot a season-low 35 percent, 21 of 60 (its third lowest scoring rate this season).

Center Constantin Popa (7- feet, 3-inches) was held to seven points and took only six shots. He scored three straight 20-point conference games but was contained for most of this one. Point guard Michael Gardner scored 1 of 12 shots. Guard Trevor Burton was scoreless.

Miami trailed by 17 at the half (35-18). The first half featured poor shooting. In the second half, Popa was held to two points. Miami had 11 turnovers, mostly on errant passing and had three out-of-bound missteps.

Post-game comments from Miami coach, Leonard Hamilton:
(You don't need to use them in one block.)

"For some reason, this team took on a different personality tonight than what I'm accustomed to. I do feel that maybe there is a little more to it going on the road and winning in the Big East than I actually realized. We are a better team than we showed tonight. . . . We became very, very tentative offensively for the first time this year. Tonight was a game where the other team shot the ball well and put us totally out of tempo. This is the type of game you forget about. We just have to continue playing well at home and then figure out how to win on the road. They (Providence) did a good job of pushing him (Popa) out and being physical with him. People are doing that a lot more now that he has become more of an offensive threat. This is the first time he's not been as involved in our offense in 11 games."

Post-game comments from Providence coach Rick Barnes:
"We shot better, did a better job on their big guy (Popa) and moved the ball around more." (For Barnes, this is his 100th winning game in five years as coach at Providence College.) "We played Popa like we used to play Alonzo Mourning in past years. He's a big part of their team."

Post-game comments from Miami guard Trevor Burton, (Miami's third leading scorer at 12.0 points per game):
"We took good shots early but they didn't fall. Providence wasn't hitting great shots, but theirs were falling. We started missing, put pressure on ourselves and before we knew it, it was total chaos."

Based on a story by Sharon Robb, *Sun-Sentinel* (Fort Lauderale, Fla.). Used with permission.

Media Jobs and Internships 27

This chapter will provide information to supplement the textbook material on how to seek internships and jobs. An optional form for resumes is included.

27-1. Research the organization

Before you decide where to apply for a job or internship, you should conduct research about the kinds of opportunities that are available and about the particular organization to which you wish to apply. Check directories for organizations related to your field. Remember that even though these directories may list key personnel such as editors, those people may no longer be in the positions listed; you should always call to find out the person (and spelling of his or her name and title) to whom you should send your application.

Using the directories that apply to your field, list at least three organizations in which you would be interested for an internship or a job. Include the address of the organization and name of the person to whom you should apply. Here are a few directories, most of which give circulation, key managers, addresses and telephone numbers:

Newspaper Directories
❑ *Media Encyclopedia – Working Press of the Nation – Newspaper Directory.*
❑ *Editor & Publisher Yearbook.* Lists newspapers by daily and weekly publications.
❑ *Gale's Directory of Publications.* Lists magazines, journalis and newspapers.

Broadcast Media Directories
❑ *Media Encyclopedia –Working Press of the Nation – Television and Radio Directory.*
❑ *Broadcasting Yearbook.*
❑ *Television/Cable Factbook.*

Magazines and Public Relations Directories
❑ *Gale's Directory of Publications.* Lists magazines, journalis and newspapers.
❑ *Media Encyclopedia –Working Press of the Nation – Magazine Directory.*
❑ *Gebbie House Magazine Directory.* A guide to company internal magazines.
❑ *Bowkers.* Publications by trade organizations.

Advertising
❑ *Standard Directory of Advertising Agencies*

27-2. Design a resume

The following resume is a different format from the one in your textbook. Decide which form you prefer or design your own. This resume was designed by University of Kansas student Elizabeth Jurkowski.

Elizabeth Jurkowski

School Address
Street addres
Town, State Zip code
Telephone number

Home Address
Street address
Town, State Zip code
Telephone number

Education

University of Kansas
Bachelor of Science, Journalism
Majors in Magazine and Business Communications
Degree expected, May 1994

Work Experience

Center for Continuing Education, Lawrence, Kansas
Public Relations Intern (September 1992 to December 1992)
  • Designed a media kit for the Center of Environmental Training
  • Wrote press releases and news articles

Owswego County School Library System, Mexico, N.Y.
Promotions Intern (February 1991 to May 1991)
  • Wrote promotional brochures
  • Wrote a public relations strategy for the Oswego County Board of Cooperative Education Services

Congressman James T. Walsh, Syracuse, New York
Congressional intern (October 1991 to December 1991)
  • Assisted congressional staff with casework and requests for federal information
  • Assisted staff members with legislative research

Honors

Dean's List, University of Kansas

References

Congressman James T. Walsh
Address
Telephone number

Jane Doe, Professor
School of Journalism
University address
Telephone number